*The Cautious Jealous Virtue*

# The Cautious Jealous Virtue

*Hume on Justice*

Annette C. Baier

HARVARD UNIVERSITY PRESS

Cambridge, Massachusetts

London, England

2010

*Library of Congress Cataloging-in-Publication Data*

Baier, Annette.
  The cautious jealous virtue : Hume on justice / Annette C. Baier.
  p.    cm.
  Includes bibliographical references and index.
  ISBN 978-0-674-04976-5 (alk. paper)
  1. Hume, David, 1711–1776.   2. Justice (Philosophy)
3. Hume, David, 1711–1776. Treatise of human nature. I. Title.

  B1499.J86B35 2010
  179'.9092—dc22          2009028101

# Contents

# Preface

This book looks at Hume's famous account of justice in his *Treatise,* at its relation to other virtues, at changes to what he says about it and its fellow virtues in his *Enquiry Concerning the Principles of Morals (EPM),* and on to some of his remarks about justice in his *Essays,* and in his *History of England.* The Part I chapters look at justice and equity, those in Part II at related virtues, and at related matters of Hume interpretation. The chapters in Part II are all republished essays; the Introduction, chapters in Part I, and Conclusion are new.

Hume's account of what justice is, and how it relates to the rest of morality, has been much discussed. Morality for Hume is a matter of approbation for a set of character traits, rather than obedience to a set of action-guiding rules, but the virtues he calls artificial do consist in willingness to keep rules directing us how to act, so they form the deontological element in Hume's ethics. The rules we are to keep depend on the established customs in our own society, customs that enable us to trust each other in some important matters. Rules allocating property vary a lot from society to society, and they, along with promise-keeping, constitute the core of what Hume in the *Treatise* terms "justice." What counts as a binding promise varies less from society to society, but there are some variations, in matters such as the need for witnesses. I look at the differences between these two parts of what Hume first takes justice to comprise in Chapter 5, and find promise-keeping to be more natural than he allows.

My title is taken from Hume's characterization of justice in *EPM,* and some of my attention is given to the sense in which it is cautious and jealous. It is cautious, since it constrains our freedom to do as we please, and we are rightly cautious about accepting such restraints. It is jealous, since it decrees each person's due, and we are jealous of our due, resent being denied it, and are apt to compare it with what others are getting. We resent unfairness and injustice, to ourselves and to others, and Hume regards the capacity for resentment as an innate one. I look at his account of it in Chapter 7. Since I draw on Hume's *History* in many of the chapters in Part I, I look in the Introduction at general changes to be found there in Hume's moral outlook. In Chapter 1, I look at what Hume says about loan repayment, since this is the first act required by justice that he considers in the *Treatise,* and he uses it to pose his famous puzzle about the motive to just acts. Unlike the many others who have discussed this topic, I raid Hume's *History of England* to shed light on the matter. In Chapter 2, I consider the relation of justice to self-interest, and in this and other chapters I allude to several recent interpretations of Hume on this topic, including those of Sophie Botros, Jiwei Ci, Rachel Cohon, Don Garrett, Russell Hardin, James Harris, Eugenio Lecaldano, Tito Magri, David Norton, and Howard Sobel. In Chapter 3 and to some extent in Chapter 5, I look at the place of equity in Hume's thought. In Chapter 4, I look at how Hume's conception of justice grows, from the property-limited focus of the *Treatise,* to considerable concern, in his *History of England,* for what we today call retributive justice, and even to some concern for distributive justice. In a late essay, "Of the origin of government," he says that the whole point of government is the maintenance of "twelve judges," judges of the high court who deal with appeals from the lower courts. This comes as a surprise to readers of his *Treatise,* where "justice" is simply respecting customary property and promissory rights. The twelve judges have more on their agenda than the protection of property and promissory rights. In Chapter 5 and the Conclusion I come back to the original *Treatise* account, and suggest that there promise was assimilated too closely to property, partly because both were involved in loan repayment, Hume's first example of an act of justice. I look again in Chapter 5 at the place for equity, and find it more obviously present in keeping promises than in respecting property rules, rules which may be "frivolous" and fanciful. The link between justice and equity is more evident in some taxation policies, and redistributions of property, than in the original artifice of property that Hume describes, though his second and third artifices, transfer by consent and promise, incorporate a more automatic element of fairness, unless of course the consent or the promise is coerced. I suggest that Hume may have overassimilated promise to property and its transfer.

Hume has recently been somewhat condescendingly praised by Russell Hardin, in *David Hume: Moral and Political Theorist* (2007), as a "proto-game-theorist." Hume's account of a "convention" has been long admired, and David Lewis used it, and hailed it, in his book on convention. What neither Lewis nor Hardin really explains is why some coordinating conventions, and not others, give rise to obligations and correlative rights. The ones Hume attended to do give rise to them, and I discuss why in Chapter 2. The answer, briefly, is "the circumstances of justice," that part of Hume's theory which John Rawls admired and took over, and that has recently been amended in Jiwei Ci's *Two Faces of Justice*. These circumstances also explain why justice must be "cautious," conditional on most others in a society observing the restraints that the just person does. Justice as Hume understands it is a "punctilious" and cooperative virtue, which could not be cultivated in the absence of fellow-cooperators, respecting the same rights that we respect. Unlike benevolence, it is an *essentially* social and cooperative virtue. There could in a group be only one generous or benevolent person, or only one forgiving person, but for any of them to be just and honest, most others must also have these virtues, if Hume is right that they depend on acceptance of conventions.

The chapters in Part II examine the relation of justice to the other "artificial" virtues it is linked with in the *Treatise,* namely, fidelity to promises, which is often included by Hume in justice, "allegiance to magistrates" or law-abidingness, and chastity, demanded of marriage-intending young women, and of married women. Among the conventions Hume sees as giving rise to rights are those constituting marriage. I am no game-theorist, but maybe a proto-one. William Charron tells me that replying to my "Good Men's Women: Hume on Chastity and Trust," in Banff, in 1978, was what got him into game theory, which he regularly teaches. So I include that essay here, as Chapter 9, along with Chapter 6, "Hume's Account of Social Artifice: Its Origins and Originality," in which I look at Hume's debt to the Natural Law tradition; Chapter 7, "Hume on Resentment," where I claim that *EPM* extends the "circumstances of justice" to include some approximation to the equality of power to "make resentment felt," and so comes closer than Jiwei Ci recognizes to granting P. F. Strawson's point, in his influential "Freedom and Resentment,"[1] that injustice is naturally resented; and Chapter 8, on promises, which is republished from my *Postures of the Mind.* Chapter 10 is about the changes Hume made in *EPM.*

It has been a while since there has been a book-length treatment of Hume's justice. Jonathan Harrison in 1981 devoted a book to Hume's *Treatise* account of justice, going carefully through it, section by section. In 1991 Frank Snare devoted the last part of his *Morals, Motivation and Convention: Hume's Influential Doctrines* to it. More recently it has been given some attention by Jiwei Ci, in *The Two Faces of Justice* (2006), by Russell Hardin, in *David Hume: Moral and Political Theorist* (2007), and by Jordan Howard Sobel in *Walls and Vaults: A Natural Science of Morals (Virtue Ethics According to David Hume)* (2009). None of these books make more than passing reference to Hume's *History,* and none see any great difference between Hume's *Treatise* views and those expressed in *EPM* and in his political essays. Since the fullest account of convention is found in the *Treatise,* it is natural to give it most attention, but I find significant changes in Hume's later versions of justice, and find his treatment of some episodes in English history to illuminate some of his points in the *Treatise.*

Early critics like Balfour found Hume's account of justice offensive and Hobbesian, because of its *Treatise* claim that justice was not a "natural" virtue, and later critics, like D. D. Raphael, found it strangely limited, because of its focus on property rights, its ignoring of claims of desert, and its apparent lack of any gesture toward egalitarianism. I agree with Raphael (who taught me), but I also admire Hume's insights, and think he did, in the end, enlarge his views of justice to include more of what Raphael rightly thinks should be included in the concept. (Flavio Baroncelli in his "Dialogue of the Dead" between Hume and John Rawls has Hume conceding as much to Rawls.) Hume's early treatment of justice had, as its focus, the need to appeal to local custom and "convention" to see what the rules of justice are, allocating each her due, to understand what honesty taken as respect for property rights is, and to see how recognition of what counts as a promise or a contract is needed to understand the virtue of "fidelity." Hume never claimed that his *Treatise* list of artifices was complete, and in his *History* he extends the coverage of the virtue of justice.

His first thesis, that justice depends on a community understanding, agreement, or "convention," is never given up, but Hume comes to see that there are also, implicit in these origins of justice, standards of fairness or "equity" which can be invoked to criticize and reform some local customs, such as those that James I reformed in Ireland, where property had been divided at the death of an owner between all his children, and redivided at the death of any of them, so no one could count on secure possession of anything, and therefore people had no incentive to improve their land, or even build on it. They were denied the fruits of their labor, and James changed this. James also changed what punishment murderers could expect, abolishing the "eric" or fine for a killing, which had varied with the gender and status of the victim. Murder in Ireland became a capital offense, as in England and Scotland. I look at this enlargement of Hume's view of justice in Chapter 4, and throughout Part I consider the place Hume gives to the natural virtue of equity.

I am indebted to several people who have read some of the chapters in draft form and offered helpful comments. These include Sophie Botros, Rachel Cohon, Richard Dees, Aaron Garrett, James Harris, Elizabeth Radcliffe, Rob Shaver, Jacqueline Taylor, and Anik Waldow. I am also indebted to Liz Duvall and Susan Zorn for help in compiling and editing this book.

Chapter 6, "Hume's Account of Social Artifice: Its Origins and Originality," originally appeared in *Ethics* 98, 4 (July 1988): 757–778. © 1998 by Annette C. Baier. Chapter 7, "Hume on Resentment," originally appeared in *Hume Studies* 6, 2 (November 1980): 133–149. Chapter 8, "Promises, Promises, Promises," originally appeared in *Postures of the Mind* (University of Minnesota Press, 1985), 174–207. Chapter 9, "Good Men's Women: Hume on Chastity and Trust," originally appeared in *Hume Studies* 5, 1 (April 1979): 1–19. Chapter 10, "Incomparably the Best?" originally appeared in *A Companion to Hume,* edited by Elizabeth S. Radcliffe (Wiley-Blackwell, 2000), 293–320.

My father was a clerk in New Zealand's Justice Department, working in its magistrates' courts, so I found out quite early in life what magistrates were, and what link with justice they had. As a small child in Oamaru I played in the empty courtroom of its splendid courthouse, on whose grounds a plaque in memory of my father stands, by a tree he planted. I would pretend to be, in turn, the accused, in the dock, and the magistrate, on the bench, when allowed into those grave precincts for short times, on the occasions when I was deposited with my father while my mother shopped on Thames Street. Both my parents were later very proud of my academic successes, though they had expected me to be-

come a lawyer, to exploit what they saw as my talent for being argumen-
tative. Philosophy too gives scope for that, but my parents would have
been especially pleased had they known I would write a book about justice, and my mother would have been pleased had she known it was to
be about a Scot's account of justice. Her mother, Jane Brown Bremner
(née Bryce), and her father, David Bremner, came to New Zealand from
Scotland, as children, on sailing ships. I dedicate this book to the memory of my parents: Annie Fife Stoop (née Bremner), my mother, and
Frederick Stoop, my father, who worked for justice.

# Abbreviations

T    David Hume, *A Treatise of Human Nature,* edited by L. A. Selby-Bigge and P. H. Nidditch (Oxford, 1978), giving page number.

D    David Hume, *Dialogues Concerning Natural Religion,* edited by Norman Kemp Smith (T. Nelson, 1947), giving page number.

E    David Hume, *Enquiries Concerning Human Understanding and Concerning the Principles of Morals,* edited by L. A. Selby-Bigge and P. H. Nidditch (Clarendon, 1975), giving page number.

Es   David Hume, *Essays, Moral, Political, and Literary,* edited by Eugene F. Miller (Liberty Classics, 1985), giving page number.

H    David Hume, *The History of England, from the Invasion of Julius Caesar to the Revolution in 1688,* 6 vols. (Liberty Classics, 1983), giving volume number, chapter number, and page number. For appendices (App), volume number, appendix number, and page number are given.

L    *The Letters of David Hume,* edited by J. Y. T. Greig, 2nd ed., 2 vols. (Oxford, 1969), giving volume number and page number.

*The Cautious Jealous Virtue*

# Introduction:
# What the Historian Taught
# the Moralist

Hume, in his early essay "Of the study of history," wrote, "I think it is a remark worthy of the attention of the speculative, that the historians have been, almost without exception, the true friends of virtue" (Es 567). He contrasts how Machiavelli writes about such matters as assassination in his "general reasoning" in *The Prince* with how he writes when dealing as a historian with assassinations of actual Florentine princes. When Hume himself turns from speculation about virtue, and in particular about justice, to history, is there any similar change to be remarked? Does he become a truer friend to virtue, or a friend to different virtues, than he appears to be in his *Treatise* and *Enquiry Concerning the Principles of Morals (EPM)?* In Chapter 4, I shall consider how Hume enlarges his view of justice when he considers the history of English jurisprudence, when such things as the invention of the jury system get added to the social artifices, and justice for him comes to include criminal justice.

Alasdair MacIntyre, who calls Hume's *History of England* "a history of moral character," says that in it Hume simply applied, in his character appraisals of monarchs and others, the standard of moral merit he had worked out in the *Treatise* and *EPM*.[1] I find this an oversimplification. For one thing, the *History* is also a history of the English constitution, and of the rather minor role that wise legislative decision played in its development into a "plan of liberty." It is a history of English custom

1. Alasdair MacIntyre, "Artifice, Desire, and Their Relationship," in *Persons and Passions: Essays in Honor of Annette Baier,* edited by Joyce Jenkins, Jennifer Whiting, and Christopher Williams (Notre Dame, 2005).

and law. The development of England into a limited monarchy was one that made the character of the monarch of less and less importance to the good government of the country, so that, by Hume's own time, even a monarch's madness need not be fatal. Hume's *History* is also a graphic account of the role played by the Christian religion in Britain: at first mind-numbing superstition, then, from the Reformation on into the seventeenth century, a socially divisive force inspiring terrible persecutions. And insofar as the *History* is concerned with moral character, it does not simply use the earlier-compiled catalogue of virtues in its praise of those judged to deserve praise. Richard Dees is nearer the truth when he says that the character sketches in the *History* recognize what few moral theories recognize, that there can be conflicts between the virtues, and that real people have complicated, even convoluted and contradictory characters.[2] In the *History* there is a frequent contrast between a monarch's showing on the domestic front and his or her public performance. Mary Tudor and James II did unexceptionally as spouses, very poorly as monarchs, while some of the great monarchs and wise legislators, such as Henry II, did not do so well with wife and children. Henry's son John was more consistent, spectacularly bad on all fronts. Henry VII sacrificed marital happiness for Lancastrian loyalty (he married a York princess, then treated her as an enemy in his camp). Elizabeth Tudor avoided the contrast between domestic and public performance by the desperate measure of avoiding domesticity altogether.

Monarchs need special skills, and, apart from justice, they are ones that Hume had not in his general ethics especially attended to. That in itself is not surprising—general ethics are for the generality of subjects, not for sovereigns—but a contrast between professional and private virtue is found quite generally. And all monarchs begin as children in families. In the Stuart dynasty, the first that Hume wrote about, three out of four of the kings (James I, Charles II, and James II) had lost a royal parent by beheading, and the fourth lost his own head, so royal childhood was not the securest place for moral training. In his essay "Of the middle station in life," Hume lists eight (out of twenty-eight) competent royal rulers of England. None of the Stuart kings make this list, and that is not surprising. In the *Treatise* he had spoken of parents "rubbing off rough

2. Richard Dees, "Hume on the Characters of Virtue," *Journal of the History of Philosophy* 35 (1997): 45–64, reprinted in Rachel Cohon, *Hume: Moral and Political Philosophy* (Ashgate, 2001), 463–482.

corners" in their young children's characters, but of course childhood forms as well as reforms character. There is a silence about moral education, formative or reformative, in *EPM*, but a little is said in the *History*, for example, about the upbringing of Henry VIII's three children, who all became monarchs. Henry had written a book called *The Erudition of a Christian Man*, and took pains to see that his son and immediate successor, Edward, was properly educated. Edward shared his classes with his cousin and brief unfortunate successor, the Lady Jane Grey, who was the more apt pupil. But Edward inherited his father's taste for theology, and was upset at the Catholic religion of his older sister Mary, who as a child was left in the care of her divorced Catholic mother, and was no scholar. (She boasted of never having read a Protestant book, not even her father's.) Henry had both his daughters at times declared illegitimate, so theirs was a strange upbringing. Elizabeth, who was made a motherless child by the beheading of her mother, and a multiply-step-mothered child by her father's four subsequent remarriages, was brought up as an Anglican, with Roger Ascham as her tutor, and seemed to emerge well prepared for her long reign. Hume says she valued her independence above all, and ruled herself as well as she ruled her subjects. But it was scarcely parental influence or example that gave her this on the whole admirable character. There is little in the way of a recipe for moral merit to be gleaned from Tudor family history, any more than there is from the Stuarts'. The catalogue of vices is well exemplified by Henry VIII and his elder daughter, Mary, and the catalogue of virtues is exemplified in Edward, Jane, and Elizabeth, but just why each turned out as he or she did is left a mystery. All knew insecurity, all lived in a time of religious dispute and persecution, and Mary famously increased the latter. For all of them, even the Plato-loving Jane, who sent Mary her Greek New Testament as she went to the scaffold, moral merit went hand in hand with piety. Piety is a significant absentee from Hume's list of virtues in *EPM*. It is when he becomes a historian, after having been a natural historian of religion, recognizing the near-ineradicability of religion, that he seriously considers the status of piety, and that of attitude to religion more generally, when these are looked at from the moral point of view, that is, one that is impartially concerned with the human good. He still finds it responsible for much evil, but also sees how piety often strengthens good personal character.

In *EPM* Hume sets out to describe and take up this viewpoint, and from it to compile a "catalogue of virtues," to analyze out, and list, the various strands that go into "that complication of personal qualities which form what, in common life we call PERSONAL MERIT." He says that language will guide us, since every tongue has one set of words for praising, another for criticizing. He turns mainly to historians, the experts on virtue, for the language of praise,[3] and he leaves his account of the virtues as a mere catalogue, without any attempt to say how, in a given person—say, the imaginary Cleanthes—the various virtues combine, or how they came to be present in him. No synthesis or genesis of the good personal qualities in a meritorious person follows the analysis. The catalogue has two cross-cutting subdivisions, agreeable or useful to self or to others, but these do little to tell us anything about how a person's virtues or vices hang together, or how he or she came to possess them. Cleanthes is said to have one virtue, his serenity, that "runs through the whole tenor of his life," but it seems insufficient to tie together his assiduous application to study, his quick penetration of men and business, his wit and good manners, his gallantry without affectation, and his greatness of mind. What makes Cleanthes tick? Who brought him up? What, if any, are his ruling passions? What friendships does he have? What causes is he true to? What religion, if any, does he love? Is his justice cautious and jealous? We are not told.

It is one thing to have a list of good character traits, such as that which *EPM* compiles. It is another to understand how some subset of such virtues are to be combined, in given social conditions, to make an admirable person, and one who does well and justly in all the roles, public and domestic, that he or she fills. The *History* attends to some of these matters, neglected in *EPM*. It attends to parental influence, to education, to youthful friendships like those of Henry II and of Henry V, and to choice of advisors. It looks at tradeoffs between domestic and public virtues, at psychologically realized combinations of agreeable and useful virtues, at sacrifices, such as that of Lady Jane Grey, of what is agreeable to self with what was seen as duty to others. It discloses no recipes for turning out a good character: none of the eight monarchs Hume judged to have ruled well left a successor who also ruled well, and some of them, such as Henry II and VII, left children who were more notable for vice than for virtue. The monarchs of good character seem like miracles, given the in-

---

3. See Chapter 10, "Incomparably the Best?"

security and the tradition of violent overthrow that they were born to. But to expect recipes for good character from either the historian or the moralist is to expect too much. At least the history gives us stories of the youth and maturity and death of real people with their real ruling passions and their besetting vices.

Like Machiavelli, Hume writes one way about virtue and vice "in his general reasonings" (Es 567), another way in his historical findings about the characters of real people. There is, in the *History,* not only the attention to the psychological and social realities that shape individual character, but also some revision of what does and does not count as moral merit. As I noted earlier, piety is not on *EPM*'s list of virtues. Indeed, the book is famous for its transferal of the "monkish virtues" into the column of the vices, and it was not merely monks, among Hume's readers, who were offended. No religious virtues get a place in his catalogue. It seems a wholly secular version of morality. The closest virtues to piety, in its catalogue, are "decency" and "discretion." Now few monks in Hume's *History* come in for much praise, except for their assiduity in copying books before the invention of the printing press, for their charity to the needy, and for their hospitality to travelers. The *History* does, as one would expect, document the bad moral effects of superstition, of "bigotted zeal," of persecution and religious strife. It is a "book of martyrs," indicting both Catholic and Protestant persecutors, but there are some surprises. An argument, of a sardonic sort, is offered for having an established religion. Love of the established religion of one's country turns out to be a virtue, or, more accurately, the showing of it is an important virtue in a monarch. Judging James II, Hume writes that he lacked due love of the religion and constitution of his country, essential in a sovereign. "Had he been possessed of this essential quality, even his middling talents, aided by so many virtues, would have rendered his reign honourable and happy. When it was wanting, every excellency, which he possessed, became dangerous and pernicious to his kingdoms" (H 6.71.520). *EPM* does not tell us that excellencies of character could become pernicious, or that some virtues are key ones, let alone that love of any religion, or at least willingness to make a decent display of it, could be such a key virtue.

James II failed to show love of the faith whose defender he was supposed to be. His offensive display of his Catholic faith came too soon after the scare of the gunpowder plot during his grandfather's reign, too soon after the great rebellion against monarchy itself, which brought his father's beheading, and much too soon after the paranoia over another imagined "popish plot" during his brother's reign. His brother, Charles II, had been willing to pretend to be a good Anglican, while really, Hume says, he was a deist when well, a Catholic when poorly. (A priest attended his deathbed.) He went along with demands from Parliament for severe punishment on the popish supposed plotters. Hume does not admire his performance as king, but it is not his hypocrisy that damns him. It is more his inaction over the succession, his passivity in allowing his Catholic brother to succeed him, even though he had plenty of evidence that the English public was not ready for that degree of religious toleration. James was willing to tolerate all forms of Christianity, including the Quaker variant, in return for having his Catholicism tolerated, but that attitude showed insufficient understanding of what the establishment of religion involves, for a head of state. Charles understood that better, so pretended to be an Anglican, and Hume seems to find that pretense preferable to James's refusal to pretend. Hume praises the Huguenot Henry of Navarre for his prudent conversion to Catholicism once he became Henry IV of France. (He even arranged for a theological debate in which the Huguenot participants, his former religious advisors, diplomatically let themselves be worsted by the Catholics, to ease his change of religion.) Henry saw that, to be a good ruler of France, he must accept the established religion of the French.

It is when Hume, in the course of his account of Henry VIII's attitude to Luther and the German Protestants, "takes matters a little higher," that he gives us his reason for approving of having an established religion, and for respecting the one that we find in place. (In his essay "Of a perfect commonwealth," parishes form the electoral districts, and ministers of religion are appointed by a civilly appointed council of religion. There the established religion is Presbyterian, but that may be because the essay was published in Edinburgh, not London, so it was the default religion, so to speak.) It will usually be the religion of the majority that is established, but in times of religious strife, such as those following Henry VIII's reign, it will take a ruling from the state to determine which is to be the officially sanctioned religion. Hume speaks admiringly of Bishop Tunstal, who retained his Catholic faith when Henry broke with Rome, but went along with Henry's rulings, then with the more extreme

Protestantism of Edward VI, before being allowed to return to Catholic ceremonies when Mary assumed the throne.[4] For Hume, the point of establishing any religion is to "bribe clerics to indolence" by having them depend on the state, rather than on their followers, for their stipend. An established religion is a necessary evil, a way of palliating what cannot be cured, namely, the human impulse toward religion, and our tendency to disagree about the details of our religious faith, when there is a free market for such faiths. The worst outcome is religious persecution and wars of religion. The best is mutual toleration, most likely, Hume seems to think, if the clerics of the majority religion are bribed into indolence with state salaries. It is a recipe for minimizing religious zeal. For someone who accepts this way of thinking, going along with the established religion of one's country will be much like observing the highway code. The details are arbitrary, but none the less functional for that. Even when, as in Tudor times, the religious rules change fairly frequently, the good citizen, like Bishop Tunstal, values peace and order above indulgence of theological preference.

This is a fairly cynical attitude to religion, and to religious disagreement, but it is the view that Hume's study of the history of his country led him to adopt. It represents a change from both the scathing attitude to popular religion in his earlier works, and the famous condemnation of all clerics as professional hypocrites in a note to his 1748 essay "Of national prejudices." It is a change of attitude to hypocrisy as well as to religion. Both, he came to see, are inevitable, given human nature and the demands of social living. Once people come to think about the content of their religious faith, as they were encouraged to do by the reformers, it can no longer function as an indolent, fairly harmless, and more or less mindless superstition, perhaps consoling in times of trouble, and something that unites them with fellow-believers, thus reinforcing social and personal morality, but becomes a source of perplexity and disagreement, an occasion for hypocrisy, as well as for faction and intolerant zeal. Hume writes, "The profound ignorance in which both clergy and laity formerly lived, and their freedom from theological altercations, had produced a sincere but indolent acquiescence in received opinions. . . .

---

4. See my chapter "Hume and the Conformity of Bishop Tunstal," in *Death and Character: Further Reflections on Hume* (Harvard, 2008).

As soon as a new opinion was advanced . . . they felt their capacity to-
tally unfitted for such disquisitions, and they perpetually fluctuated between the contending parties" (H 3.31.211). The result was a vehe-
mence proportionate to their real perplexity, a zeal proportionate to their
pretense of certainty, and a willingness to persecute those who went a
different way.

It is in the Tudor volumes that Hume gives us his considered conclusion about the place of religion in human society, and about the dangers
of encouraging people to be self-conscious about their faith. But earlier,
in the Stuart volumes, he had detailed the most graphic story of what
can happen when there is organized resistance to the established religion: the story of the gunpowder plot. One thing he stresses there is the
good character of the plotters, their admirable self-discipline, fidelity to
their cause, their courage, and even their vision. They saw that there was
no point in assassinating one Protestant monarch if he would simply be
replaced by another, just as Protestant. A more radical approach was
needed—to get rid of all the adult members of the royal family, and all
their aristocratic and parliamentary supporters, in one explosion. Hume
calls their plot "a nobler and more extensive plan of treason" (H 5.6.26)
than merely planning an assassination. He stresses their courage, their
previous good character (one of them, Digby, had been honored by Elizabeth, whom Hume thinks showed wisdom in her choice of advisors).
The "steady attachment to religious prejudices" of the noble and vision-
ary plotters shows, he writes, both "the strength and the weakness of the
human mind" (H 5.46.250). It also shows the entanglement of religious
faith with moral courage. The "true religion," for Hume—what really
ties and reties us to one another—is dedication to a shared morality. But
popular religions also strengthen some parts of that shared morality. The
plotters' religious zeal gave them courage, as well as ruthlessness in their
willingness to sacrifice the lives of the Catholic members of Parliament,
such as Mounteagle, along with those of the Protestants (this was approved by Bishop Garnet, their Jesuit advisor), and gave them the patience and care needed for the plot to get almost carried out. There was
courage and dedication, commensurate with their "widest departure
from morals." This extraordinary episode, as much as any Hume wrote
about, including the beheading of Charles I by self-righteous Puritans,
shows that great virtue can coexist with dangerous destructive and self-
destructive zeal, zeal in a cause to which the conspirators were bound by

mutual promises.⁵ Hume the historian would not have been surprised at the religiously inspired suicide-bombers of our times. The gunpowder plotters were their Christian forerunners. And much of Hume's history is a story of a succession of religious martyrs, Catholic and Protestant, who suffered and died for their faith. His attitude toward them, toward all those who refused to follow the official faith of the day, but insisted on their version of the true faith, is a mixture of admiration and horror, horror both at those who lit the fires and at those who went into them, sometimes even "embracing the faggots." He dwells on these feats of religious heroism, and rightly, for a historian who wants to be a true friend to virtue. As moralist, he wants to understand what inspired the persecuted as well as what drove the persecutors. He wants to do justice to both.

Another thing Hume emphasizes about the gunpowder plotters is their ties of friendship and fidelity to one another. In their case friendship cemented criminal conspiracy, but usually friendship works for, not against, virtue. Capacity for friendship is an important moral quality, and one that Hume regularly looks for when summing up a monarch's character. Monarchs face special obstacles in forming friendships, which require some degree of equality. Henry V is praised for maintaining a friendship with the Earl of Marche, who had been his competitor for the throne. Charles II is found incapable of trust and friendship, although generous to his mistresses and civil to his long-suffering wife. Of course, the desirable capacity for friendship has to be distinguished, not just from loyalty to fellow-conspirators, and promise-keeping, but also from the connected but deplorable "weakness for favourites," a peculiarly royal weakness, which presupposed inequality and royal patronage. Poor Edward II suffered from this weakness, and died for it, with a red hot poker up what Hume delicately calls his "fundament." Charles II had mistresses, not male favorites, while his grandfather, James I, did allow himself some suspect pleasures in his male friendships, but not, Hume judges, "criminal or flagitious." He "laid aside the scepter and took the birch into his royal hand" (H 5.47.53) to teach the handsome young Scot Robert Carre some Latin grammar. He never showed "any tendency, not even the smallest, towards a passion for any mistress"

---

5. I discuss the potential of promise for such socially disruptive acts in Chapter 5, "The Janus Face of Hume's 'Justice.'"

(H 5.49.122). Kings are not expected to confine their affections to their queens, but mistresses are preferable to "favorites." Hume has harsh words for queens who fail in marital fidelity, even when, like Isabella, wife to the unfortunate Edward II, they have had to put up with their royal husbands' weakness for good-looking male favorites. That is because a royal spouse's first duty is not to mess up the clarity of the perceived succession. Some of Hume's favorite kings, like Henry II, had many mistresses and several illegitimate children. (Henry I, whom Hume says was "addicted to women," had thirteen, but no legitimate male heir, so there was dispute about the succession.) Mistresses are taken in stride, as long as the succession is seen to, with legitimate children in place, ready to take over. But it was not easy, even for the best of monarchs, and even when they left male heirs, to pass on the capacity to rule England. Edward I, the "lawgiver," gave his successor, Edward II, a "bad education," and Henry II did little better with John, his youngest and favorite son, whom Hume calls a "complication of vices" (H 1.11.452). Given the generally poor showing that English monarchs had made in leaving a suitable successor, it seems a bit harsh on Hume's part to criticize Charles II for leaving the throne for his Catholic brother to take over.

Hume's withdrawn essay "Of the middle station in life" (1742) claims that ruling England is not a very demanding task. "There are more natural Parts, and a stronger Genius requisite to make a good Lawyer or Physician, than to make a great Monarch . . . the governing of mankind well, requires a great deal of Virtue, Justice, and Humanity, but not a surprising capacity" (Es 548–549). Rulers need to show justice. Does Hume think that upholding their country's constitution and established religion is included in "justice"? Justice of the sort he expects monarchs to show includes respect for the traditional rights and liberties of subjects, and fairness in the administration of criminal justice. James I is praised for introducing justice to Ulster, when he gave its inhabitants "a fixed habitation," by reforming the law of "gavelkinde," which had land divided between all a dead owner's children, then redivided when any of them died, and gave them some security of person, by changing the law on murder, earlier punished by a fine which varied with the rank and sex of the victim. "Laudable acts of justice," by James, come to include insisting on the "full severity of the law" to punish murderers. This is a very different act of justice from that which Hume begins with in the *Treatise*, that of restoring a loan, and I discuss this enlargement of his concept of justice in Chapter 4. That spectacularly bad king, John, lacked both justice and the essential virtue of piety to his country's religion—indeed, was supposedly willing to become a Muslim, to get the help of the sultan of Morocco against France. The scope of Hume's "artificial" virtues, of those that consist in conformity to established customs that are beneficial to the group, does not seem, in the *Treatise*, to include conformity with religious customs, unless these are made obligatory by a magistrate's orders. Respect for established religions could, however, plausibly be seen to come under this category of obedience to magistrates, and Hume seems, in the *History*, to be treating religious nonconformity as an offense against established convention, with the benefit of doubt as to whether such conventions are generally beneficial being given to the established religion, however frequent the changes in what is established. We have seen how he approves of Tunstal. He is praised for seeing that public peace and tranquillity, the rationale for all artificial virtues, was more important than truth to "the old religion." His integrity was such that his repeated compliance was not seen as time-serving, but as true love of his country.

Monarchs need a great deal of virtue, including the virtue of justice, but not great capacity, in order to govern well. One thing this claim, which Hume may have revised after he became a historian, and appreciated how much more capacity is needed in an absolute than in a limited monarch (he withdrew "Of the middle station in life"), makes clear is that Hume is willing to speak with the vulgar in distinguishing virtues from abilities, and the *History* regularly makes this distinction. Hume boasted that he never replied to his critics, but this does not mean he did not correct his views when a critic had made a sound point. Alexander Gerard's claim that Hume's 1748 charge against the clergy, in a footnote to his essay "Of national characters" accusing them all of hypocrisy, lacked empirical support may have led Hume to soften his anticlerical stance, especially in the *History*, where he seems to go out of his way to deny that professional churchmen, such as Becket, or, later, Latimer, Cranmer, or Tunstal, were religious hypocrites.[6] And the thesis that some virtues are key ones, either in a professional role or in ordinary life, and that other putative virtues depend on these for their value, is

---

6. I discuss this in "Hume's Excellent Hypocrites," in *Death and Character.*

precisely what was objected by Balfour against Hume, after the appearance of *EPM*. Balfour did not like Hume's views about the mere utility of chastity, but his most serious charge against Hume was that almost all the entries on Hume's list of virtues will become satanic if accompanied by an ill will. Balfour's master stroke is his invocation of the Duc de Sully's characterization of the young Servin, a member of Sully's entourage. After learning of all his shining abilities and accomplishments, we are told of his monstrous vices (among others, he was "an abandoned debauchee, a blasphemer, and an Atheist").[7] Servin was, in Sully's judgment, both miracle and monster. Balfour believes that the one essential virtue is the will to do good to others, and that qualities like intelligence, wit, and charm can be found in the worst of people, there intensifying rather than mitigating their vice. Hume's judgment about James II, that because he lacked the one thing needful, his other excellencies became "pernicious," seems almost to imitate Balfour's about the charming monster Servin. But he is not granting Balfour that it is only qualities of will that matter, that intellect's value needs unlocking by a will to use it to do good. There was not much wrong with James's will to love his God and his fellow-Catholics, or even his fellow-men, more generally. Hume says he was "honourable in his dealings with all men" (H 6.71.520). What he lacked was the sense to see that, to love his fellow-Englishmen, he must at least pretend to love their established religion.

Charles II was willing to pretend to the Anglican faith. But his deficiency in respect of capacity for friendship extended to bad relations with his advisors, and bad judgment in appointing them. He went through advisors fairly fast, and after the dismissal of the first Earl of Shaftesbury, he appointed as his successor a man, the Earl of Radnor, whom Hume judges to have possessed "whimsical talents and splenetic virtues" (H 6.58.379). By contrast, Elizabeth appointed good advisors, in particular William Cecil, Lord Burleigh, who had become her trusted friend before she assumed the throne, and remained her friend until his death. Of course, Charles II had a tough childhood; his grandmother and his father were beheaded, and he was brought up in France in the Catholic faith of his widowed mother, then launched into the hands of rigid Covenanters when he first returned to Britain, before being re-

---

7. James Balfour, *A Delineation of the Nature and Obligation of Morality* (Hamilton, Balfour, and Neill, 1753; reprint Thoemmes Antiquarian, 1989), 116.

stored as defender of the Anglican faith. His "careless and dissolute temper" (H 6.63.185) and his distrust of his courtiers may have been a protective shell against the sort of treatment his father had received from his subjects. He reacted by becoming the merry monarch, while his brother James reacted by taking the religious upbringing they had shared more seriously. James loved his Catholic religion more than the established religion of his country. He lacked what Hume deems an essential virtue in a monarch.

Hume may have converted to the Balfour thesis, may have come to believe that some character traits, such as self-command, even the self-command needed to pretend to a religious faith other than one's own, are more essential than others, whose value depends on the presence of the key ones. But he is not conceding that stupidity cannot, in a person with power over others, be as fatal as ill will. James II, unlike his brother, was in his domestic life "irreproachable." But his talents were only "middling," and he was not bright enough to see, as his brother did, that pretending to the established religion was the better part of wisdom. Stupidity in a monarch can be fatal. Hume finds it in Mary Tudor and finds it to have poisoned her seeming virtues, her piety, sincerity, and marital fidelity. He is scathing about her devotion to her haughty husband, Philip of Spain, eleven years younger than she was, and planning all along to make marriage proposals to her younger sister Elizabeth, once Mary was dead, in order to secure dominion over Britain. Hume relates how she became besotted with Philip's picture before she had even met him, how she moped and languished in his absence. Elizabeth may have been just as besotted with Essex (twenty-five years younger than she was, the son-in-law of her first favorite, Leicester), but she did not, until the very end, let that interfere with her wise ruling of her subjects. Essential virtues there may be, at least for heads of state, key virtues that unlock the potential goodness of other personal qualities, and fatal vices, which poison them, but such key virtues and vices are not the ones that Balfour named. The fatal vices, for Hume, are stupidity, cruelty, and bigotry, not atheism and sexual license.

We might regret that Hume did not, late in life, return to *EPM*'s question of what constitutes a meritorious character, developing the *History*'s hints about more and less essential virtues, and about how to combine the virtues. When Hume praises Alfred, the *History*'s man of apparently perfect virtue, he speaks of his many virtues being "happily tempered together," their being "justly blended," each preventing the other "from exceeding its proper bounds": "He knew how to conciliate the most enterprizing spirit with the coolest moderation; the most obstinate perseverance with the easiest flexibility; the most severe justice with the gentlest lenity; the greatest vigour in command with the greatest affability of deportment; the highest capacity and inclination for science with the most shining talents for action" (H 1.2.75). These are more suggestive metaphors than sketches of a theory, but they do indicate that Hume may have seen the need, not just for concessions to the Aristotelian doctrine of the mean, but also for something like Plato's account of how different virtues are to cooperate in a well-constituted soul, the need for some hypothesis about which virtues can serve as foundation for others, which virtues can protect others from possible loss or corruption.[8] But even the near-perfect Alfred failed to pass on to his sons the capacity he had shown: the elder, Edward, had his military prowess, but not his wisdom, and another son, Ethelward, had his "passion for letters," but no leadership skills. (He lived privately, not called on to rule.)

Hume tells us that Alfred himself was "sensible that the people at all times . . . are not much susceptible to speculative instruction," so "endeavoured to convey his morality by apologues, parables, stories" (H 1.2.80). Hume left the revised version of his conclusions about the complication of personal qualities that makes for moral merit in the form of the more or less true stories, and the apologues, that are to be found in his History. Those of us who want more than just a catalogue of virtues, or even a revised catalogue, who want to develop a theory of how the different Humean virtues relate to one another in action, how the artificial virtues combine with the natural ones, and how they all combine in the admirable person, as well as how they can be nurtured, would do well to look there for hints of what such a theory could be.

Had Hume worked out just what goes into that capacity for friendship which he treats, in the History, almost as an acid test of character, we might have the beginnings of an account of what binds the various aspects of personal merit together, what "constitution" it takes to make an admirable person, and one who makes a good and lasting friend. The one who sees all others as possible betrayers, or as competitors for scarce goods or scarce affection, may make an advantageous marriage, or bribe

8. I explore such a thesis in "Demoralization, Trust, and the Virtues," in *Setting the Moral Compass*, edited by Cheshire Calhoun (Oxford, 2004), 176–188, reprinted in my *Reflections on How We Live: Essays on Ethic* (Oxford, 2010), 173–188.

the attentions of a lover, but is unlikely to make a good friend, or recognize a suitable advisor. How a person sees any potential friend, any possible "second self," in relation to herself (her first self) is an important indicator of her chances of combining virtues agreeable or useful to self with those agreeable or useful to others, just as her attitude to the relation of the useful to the agreeable will affect her chances of combining useful with agreeable virtues. Those who see themselves as alone against a hostile world will be as unlikely to make friends as to nurture any qualities agreeable or useful to others. They are unlikely to show fidelity to promises, or even common honesty. As the expectation that the agreeable is always the enemy of the useful is a regular spoiler of innocent pleasures, so an air of suspicion, and the expectation that all life is a zero-sum game, can poison all relations with others, and rule fidelity and friendship out. Friendship can interfere with justice, when it leads to corruption in judges, to their favors to their friends, but within the friendship itself, both equity and altruism on a small scale are cultivated, and so friendship can encourage a sense of justice and the virtues of equity and humanity. Really wicked people have no friends, at most only co-conspirators. Henry II and Becket were good friends, and although that friendship soured, while they were king and chancellor justice was well served in England. Once they became enemies, there were injustices, Hume thinks, in Henry's measures against the proud and ungrateful Becket, even before his murder. At first the murderers received only excommunication for killing Becket, since that was what canon law prescribed, but later Henry insisted that they receive the civil penalty of banishment and dispossession. Henry's "care in the administration of justice had gained him so great a reputation that even foreign and distant princes made him arbiter, and submitted their differences to his judgment" (H 1.9.373). His "violent and unjust persecution of Becket" (H 1.8.322) was a passing blip on the otherwise good record of Henry as magistrate, supreme declarer and enforcer of justice in his extensive dominions.

Adam Smith, lecturing his Glasgow students on how to write about a person's character, speaks of the "air of the man," as the first thing that strikes us when we meet someone for the first time. It is impossible, he believes, to convey this air in words.[9] This ineffable "air," when it is at-

9. Adam Smith, *Lectures on Rhetoric and Belles Letters,* edited by J. C. Bryce (Liberty Classics, 1985), 80 (lecture 15).

tractive, may be the same as Hume's "a MANNER, a grace, and ease, a genteelness, an I-know-not-what, which some men possess above others, which is very different from external beauty and comeliness, and which, however, catches our affection almost as suddenly and powerfully" (E 267). Smith thinks that this "air" proceeds not from any one character trait, but from the whole mix in the person's character. Henry II clearly had this winning air. Hume calls him "affable and entertaining," and he obviously was a good woman's man, charming and seducing woman after woman, even his son's royal fiancée, as well as inspiring great loyalty in his knights. Must we leave this "grace and air" as an "I know-not-what"? It certainly usually lets us know if a newly encountered person could become a friend, and it is part of what makes the friends we have into welcome company. (Voices can also matter here.) Hume in *EPM* writes that this personal "manner" "must be considered as part of ethics left by nature to baffle the pride of philosophy" (E 267). Did it continue to baffle the pride of the historian-philosopher? Hume writes of Henry II's character as if its mix was quite clear to him, and judges him "the greatest prince of his times for wisdom, virtues, and abilities" (H 1.89.370). Here wisdom is singled out, as if neither quite an "ability," nor any ordinary virtue. It is clearly not the same as Henry's charm, but may, like that, have involved a mix of good traits, not just intelligence, but foresight and a sense of what is fair and just. Henry had legislative virtues, and they are rare and precious. Hume's original account of law, and of the magistrate's task, was that customary law has authority, and all that magistrates need do is declare it and enforce it. Henry changed the English law in important ways, advancing its protection against crimes against the person as well as against property, and increasing its equity. He was also aware that some wrongs are against the public: he made arson and counterfeiting crimes with severe penalties. In English history Edward I is the one usually called the lawgiver, but Henry II has almost as good a title. Henry did not plunder and banish the Jews, rightly seeing the contribution they were making to the nation's economy, and giving them the law's protection. As Hume points out, Edward, "the English Justinian," "took care that his subjects should do justice to each other, but desired always to have his own hands free in all his transactions" (H 2.13.143).

One important thing that Hume the historian has taught Hume the moralist is that doing justice to each other comprises a lot more than respecting each other's property rights. When we add this to the new emphasis on mixes of virtues, and on "tempering," the concern for education, and the recognition of love of one's country's religion as a needed virtue in a head of state, and a capacity for friendship as a virtue in anyone, we really cannot help regretting that Hume did not, after finishing his *History*, rewrite *EPM*, the book he, perhaps mistakenly, called incomparably the best of his writings. He allowed that he was not the person to judge that, and in my judgment the moral wisdom of his *History* exceeds that of *EPM*, where wisdom, indeed, is not especially stressed. There is an occasional reference to the sage in his temple of wisdom, and to the infinite wisdom that made the world, but these are more ironic than serious claims. Only when Hume in *EPM* comes to prefer Cicero's four cardinal virtues over those of the "divines in disguise" who overstress benevolence, and understress that sagacity that leads us to cooperate in the conventions of justice, does he recognize that, without wisdom, the potential of many other virtues may have to lie dormant. There is not much that is useful to say about wisdom, but a comparison of, say, Henry II and Edward I, or Henry VII and Elizabeth, would instruct us in the different dimensions of that key virtue, especially as a virtue of leaders and legislators. It takes some degree of wisdom to discern it when it is there to be found, and Hume shows himself as a wise historian. He *is* a historian of moral character, as well as of social customs and plans of liberty, and in his *History* we find his "farther reflections" both on justice, which comes to encompass everything that jurisprudence encompasses, and on its fellow-virtues. In the following chapters the virtues of justice and equity will be my main concern. In Chapters 3 and 5 I look at their relation to each other, in Chapter 2 I look at their relation to prudence, and in Chapter 4 I look at how Hume enlarged his views of justice, once he became a historian. For not only does justice have a history, in any nation, but a person's understanding of it can also show development, as I believe that Hume's did. His purposes in the *Treatise* were well served by his first example of what justice requires of us, that we repay any loan we have taken out, if those purposes were to show the vital role of "conventions" in determining what justice demands of us. He went on to look at more conventions than property conventions, but does not claim in the *Treatise* that he has exhausted the list of those that had come to exist in his own society, let alone those that might come to be adopted later. He did in an essay look at liberty of the press, and what constraints we recognize in that, if it is not to become licentiousness, and in the *History* he looks at such once new customs as trial by jury. So his account of justice, in his moral philosophy, was all along open to continuation by the historian. His conjectural history, in the *Treatise,* was both revised and continued once he looked at the real history of his own society.

# I

JUSTICE AND EQUITY

1

# A Solemn Bonfire?
# Hume on Loan Repayment

Wherein consists this honesty and justice, which you find in restoring a loan, and abstaining from the property of others?
—Hume, *A Treatise of Human Nature*, 480

The many Hume scholars who have disagreed about what Hume is saying about the approved motive for repaying a loan,[1] in the first section of Part 2 of Book 3 of the *Treatise*, have given little if any attention to his choice of an example. He sets up a puzzle about justice as a virtue, by first seeming to agree with Cicero and others that no action can be obligatory unless there is some approvable natural motive to perform it. Then he looks in vain for any such motive, one which is always there when a person repays a loan. He says it would be arguing in a circle to say the approved motive is the wish to do one's duty, to do what will be approved, unless one can also say what natural approvable motive there is to perform such an act. Don Garrett, in what he calls his squaring of Hume's circle argument in the *Treatise* Book 3, Part 2, Section 1, begins by taking Hume's thesis that justice is an artificial virtue as the claim that it takes artifice or contrivance to produce "the moral approbation that

1. Some of these are Marcia Baron, "Hume's Noble Lie: An Account of His Artificial Virtues," *Canadian Journal of Philosophy* 12 (1982): 539–555; David Gauthier, "Artificial Virtues and the Sensible Knave," *Hume Studies* 18 (1992): 401–427; Annette C. Baier, "Artificial Virtues and the Equally Sensible Non-Knaves: A Response to Gauthier," *Hume Studies* 18 (1992): 429–439; Stephen Darwall, *The British Moralists and the Internal "Ought": 1640–1740* (Cambridge, 1995), ch. 10; J. L. Mackie, *Hume's Moral Theory* (Routledge and Kegan Paul, 1980), 79–81; Rachel Cohon, "Hume's Difficulty with the Virtue of Honesty," *Hume Studies* 23 (1997): 91–112; and Frank Snare, *Morals, Motivation and Convention: Hume's Influential Doctrines* (Cambridge, 1991), chs. 7–10.

constitutes it as a virtue," as if the artifice goes into the approbation of justice, not into what is approved.[2] This sounds more like Mandeville than Hume. James Harris thinks that the implication of Hume's first negative discussion of the motive for justice may be "that justice is not, for Hume, a state of character," so not a personal virtue at all.[3] This sounds more like Rawls than Hume, since today justice is thought of more as a virtue of institutions and societies than of persons. In drawing his conclusion, Harris is influenced by Knud Haakonssen, who thinks justice for Hume is mainly a matter of abstaining, that "just acts" are "pieces of inactivity."[4] This inactivity, however, would still be one of persons, not institutions. And restoring a loan is a real act, sometimes a difficult one, yet also a case of refraining from keeping what belongs to another. Acting to improve the justice of an unjust society also requires real action by reformers and legislators, and Hume mentions several such acts in his *History*, especially when criminal justice is the topic. But such legislative or reforming acts of justice and injustice were not what Hume began with, as a typical act of justice. He began with loan repayment. It is a case where several artifices operate—property conventions, conventions about transfer of property by consent, and contract—since the borrower agrees to repay by a certain future date. The fault of many who discuss this puzzle of Hume's is to suppose that it is intended to create a question about the motive for conformity to Hume's first artifice, which turned possession into stable property, and so created property rights, whereas in fact it is talking about a situation which could arise only after three artifices are in place, property, its transfer by consent, and binding agreement. Had he wanted to raise a problem about motivation to conform only to the first, abstaining from theft would be what he would have considered. The nearest thing to loan repayment in what follows, in Hume's account of the artifices, is the case of horse hire, in Section 6,

2. Don Garrett, "The First Motive to Justice: Hume's Circle Argument Squared," *Hume Studies* 33, 2 (2007): 257–288.

3. James Harris, "Hume on the Obligation to Justice: The Argument of T 3.2.1," talk to Hume Society, 2008. In a later paper, "Hume's Peculiar Definition of Justice," forthcoming in a volume about the *Treatise* edited by Peter Kail and Marina Frasca Spada (Oxford), Harris slightly modifies this claim, saying only that there is nothing virtuous in the sense of praiseworthy about not stealing, or paying one's debts. But did Hume think that care of one's children was praiseworthy? Virtues are what we approve; we only praise exceptional degrees of them, or displays of them in difficult conditions.

4. Knud Haakonssen, *The Science of a Legislator: The Natural Jurisprudence of David Hume and Adam Smith* (Cambridge, 1981), 18.

when he looks back at all the conventions of justice. It is a pity he did not then allude again to loan repayment, to help his future commentators avoid becoming too bogged down in Sections 1 and 2, and treating Section 1 as if it is only conformity to the first artifice that its puzzle question applies to.

Rachel Cohon wonders if artificial virtues are virtues only in the sense that artificial limbs are limbs, despite Hume's many claims about the importance of justice, as a virtue. This is only an interim doubt on her part—she ends by seeing the initially interested motive to justice as transformed, over time, by its having been approved, so the "undoubted maxim," that approved motives have to be natural ones, does turn out to be doubted, when what ends by being approved as the motive to justice, for people in a "civiliz'd state," is a moralized motive, duty for its own sake. Sophie Botros finds "smoke and mirrors"[5] in Hume's presentation of the puzzle about the motive to justice, since she, like Cohon, doubts the sincerity of Hume's apparent acceptance of the "undoubted maxim" needed to generate the puzzle. For her, Hume is a conjuror.

Sometimes there was more than smoke, when debts were due. Those who owed money in York in 1189 to the Jewish moneylenders (since usury was a sin, no Christian could be in this business) hated the thought of repayment so intensely that they burned the Jews to death in the castle, then, at the cathedral, made a bonfire before the altar of all their bonds of debt. Hume in Chapter 10 of his *History of England* relates the background to this atrocity with his typical irony: "The prejudices of the age had made the lending of money on interest pass by the invidious name of usury: Yet the necessity of the practice had still continued it, and the greater part of that kind of dealing fell every where into the hands of the Jews, who being already infamous on account of their religion, had no honour to lose, and were apt to exercise a profession, odious in itself, by every kind of rigour, sometimes by rapine and extortion" (H 1.10.378).

Hume then tells how Henry II, in his wisdom, had protected "this infidel race" from all injury and insult, and in return got some special taxes from them, so they had the confidence to come to his son Richard, at his coronation, with large gifts. They were repulsed. Then there was a

5. Sophie Botros, "Hume, Conjurer of Justice: Smoke and Mirrors in the *Treatise*," talk to the Institute of Philosophy, London, April 2008.

massacre in London, which spread to York, where five hundred perished in the castle. "The gentry of the neighbourhood, who were all indebted to the Jews, ran to the cathedral, where their bonds of debt were kept, and made a solemn bonfire of the papers before the altar. The compiler of the annals of Waverley, in relating these events, blesses the Almighty for thus delivering over this impious race to destruction!" (H 1.10.379). Hume allows himself a rare exclamation point here. When he sums up Richard's reign, he talks of his shining military talents, the love of the people for him, his troubadour poetry, and his crusader zeal, as well as his vengefulness, haughtiness, and cruelty. Since Hume believed that the crusades exhibited the height of human folly, he was unlikely to be dazzled by Richard the Lionheart's "shining" achievements. It is his father, Henry II, whom Hume admired, and part of what he admired was his understanding of finance, and of the need for moneylenders, as well as the need both to make sure they did not extort more interest than was equitable, and to give them, like anyone else, the protection of the law. Hume's own essay on interest is a careful look at what determines the rate of interest, and shows full awareness for the need for lenders as well as borrowers, the proportion between whom, by the law of supply and demand, determines the interest rate. Expelling most of the lenders, as Edward I did when he expelled the Jews, merely put up the rate. Hume speaks in Appendix 2 of his *History* of the "barefaced acts of tyranny and oppression" by the Norman kings of England against the Jews, of the "bigotry" of the people, and of the "immeasurable rapacity" of most of the monarchs (H 1.App 2. 483). Only Henry II appreciated the vital role the Jewish moneylenders were playing in the economy of England.

Why did Hume, to present his *Treatise* puzzle, choose loan repayment, rather than a simpler case of honesty, a real "piece of inactivity" such as refraining from an easy theft, resisting any temptation one might feel to shoplift a small item that takes one's eye in a local shop, or to steal apples from a neighbor's tree, whose branches overhang the street? (When I was about eight, a wicked little boy dared me to take a packet of chewing gum from a small shop, thinking I was too goody-goody to do so. I very nervously proved him wrong, but was consumed by guilt afterwards, and certainly was not tempted into a life of shoplifting. Indeed, I developed a real phobia of shops thereafter, cured only by taking a vacation job as a shop assistant.) Why did Hume choose loan repayment? Even rent payment would have been a slightly less loaded case, with almost the same complexity, if he wanted something combining property with contract, but without the anti-owner overtones. His readers would know about Shylock, who was treated a lot better by the Venetian authorities than Jewish moneylenders in York were treated. Some of Hume's first readers would know of the massacres under Richard I, even if few readers today know of them. They would know that sometimes the borrower resented the wealth of the lender, and resented the rate of interest charged. This common attitude of borrowers would not make repayment voluntary, which is the kind of case Hume really needs, if it is to be at all like conformity to property conventions after their first invention, before magistrates are there to punish theft (and to insist on carrying out the letter of any bond of debt, and to put bad debtors into debtors' prisons). The York gentry treated their loan repayments as not obligatory, and praised God for the destruction of those to whom they were owed. Did Hume want all these resonances of "the interested affection," equity of rate of interest included, to come in as we consider what reason a person has to repay a loan to a lender who may be a loan shark? "What if he be a vicious man, and deserves the hatred of all humankind? What if he be a miser, and can make no use of what I wou'd deprive him of?" (T 482). What reason did the York debtors have to repay their loans? Why did Hume not take a less loaded case? Even the return of the horse hired for a day, at the end of that day, or returning a borrowed book, would have raised the same issues, without the anti-Semitic overtones brought in by reference to vicious moneylenders. No particular opprobrium attaches to the hiring out of horses, and none at all to the loaning of books.

Hume was no anti-Semite; in his *History* he goes out of his way to detail crimes against Jews in England. So why choose loan repayment to a possibly vicious moneylender? I think Hume did want a fairly complex case, a case where several artifices are involved, transfer by consent as well as ownership conventions, and a case where private as well as public benevolence would be ruled out as a motive. Contract too comes in, whenever there are bonds of debt, at an agreed interest rate, for an agreed time, with an agreed forfeit for failure to repay. Loan, with an agreed forfeit for nonrepayment on time, is on the way to promise, where there is an agreed standard "forfeit" for failure to deliver, namely, one's good name, and others' trust. Horse hire may have been too simple, for Hume's purposes, if they were to really puzzle us. I think Hume

wanted Section 1 to make clear the need to understand conventions, and
their intricate intermingling, if we are to understand any obligation of
justice, when justice is seen as honesty in property dealings, and keeping agreements. In particular, we are to be helped to understand the "interested obligation" to justice, and how the interested passion can transform itself into acceptance of property and promissory rights. Section 1
is the lead-in to Section 2, where we are told exactly what a convention
is, and told the terms of the supposed first convention, instituting ownership, on the basis of present possession, and told how the interested
passion becomes "oblique," and regulates itself, when such a convention
is adopted. We are not expected instantly to understand what the approved motive for repaying a loan would be—that has to wait several
sections—and it only becomes clear in the "Farther reflections" of Section 6. By then we have learned about several different related conventions, the first creating ownership, and decreeing the different grounds
for it (prescription, accession, succession, as well as present possession or occupation), and later conventions enabling barter, gift, sale,
hire, rent, loan, and promise. To get a case that applies immediately, after property is invented, but before ways of transferring title to it are
adopted, we would need to take robbery or theft as the case. Hume in
*EHU* speaks of the shock he would get if his opulent and hitherto honest
friend stole his silver standish (writing set). Suppose we put Hume's
puzzle about the motive to honesty in this case: why not just take one's
friend's silver? It seems very easy to find a reason not to steal, in such a
case. The opulent friend could easily buy a silver standish, if he admired
Hume's. Stealing it would destroy the friendship. And the thief might
end in prison, or be transported to Australia. Of course, some of these
reasons for remaining honest are special to the relationship between
thief and victim, so let us change that to some temporary servant, who
cannot afford to buy what he covets, and is not Hume's friend. One answer, correct for every case of theft, would be that the thief might end in
prison, or Australia. Is the wish to avoid prison or Australia an approvable motive?

Hume's whole project in ethics is to give a secular basis for what earlier had been seen to have, at least in part, a religious foundation. What
corrupts morality, he agrees with Shaftesbury, is using the fear of God to
get people to behave well. To stress that theft is forbidden, and pun-

ished, is the secular equivalent of hellfire as a threat to keep us honest, and Hume surely does not want to rely on that, however splendid an artifice he thinks magistrates are, and however necessary, as a backup, the motives that they provide for honesty.[6] There must be a good reason *why* theft is forbidden, and punished by magistrates, and it is that reason Hume wants us to see to be the good reason not to steal: that the owner has a *right* to what he owns, and that that right can be transferred to another, permanently or for a fixed time, only with the owner's consent. He wants us to see that the mysterious notions of a right and a due have to come in, and that only convention and artifice can demystify them. It *is* almost a matter of conjuring, as he explains in the underdiscussed section on transfer by consent. In Scotland there was the custom of literally handing over a stone, or sod of earth, when right to land was transferred, or keys to a granary, when grain was handed over. This "sensible delivery" deceives the mind, "and makes it fancy, that it conceives of the mysterious transition of the property" (T 515). Hume likens such symbolic practices to Roman Catholic ceremonies using tapers and special costumes. Smoke and mirrors indeed. We deceive ourselves that transfer of a right is at all like transfer of a key, or that rights themselves are like ordinary things. Rights are insensible mysterious things, what Pufendorf called "moral entities," "imposed" and created by (divine or) human say-so, and this is the bottom line of Hume's puzzle about the motive to honesty. *The approved motive is respect for rights, and for the authority of the customary rules which confer such rights.* But since we do not easily understand what a right is, or what authority is, nor how they can be created by human conventions, including the convention that gives right-transferring force to the words signifying consent to transfer, and then to the words "I promise," which attach penalty, or what we could call a standard forfeit, to failure to deliver what one has agreed to deliver, Hume has to first make us realize what a complicated artificial thing a right or a due is, and what the authority of common law is, before we

---

6. It is only in larger societies that Hume sees this backup motivation as needed, to prevent the honest from becoming "cullies of their integrity." Contrary to what Russell Hardin says in *David Hume: Moral and Political Theorist* (Oxford, 2007), criminal justice is not an integral part of what Hume terms "justice." Hardin, 136, writes, "Implicit in all his discussion [of property] is the problem of criminal law, which is necessary for protecting property." It is only in Section 7, "Of the origin of government," that Hume links property to enforced law.

will appreciate how respect for customary property rights can be the approved motive to honesty. The reason we do not take others' silver
should be simply that it is theirs, not ours, by the rules we live by. Jonathan Harrison thinks that it is the lack of a sense-perceivable mark telling us which things are ours (a sort of name tag?) which makes the idea
of property and its transfer by consent not easily conceivable to us.[7] And
indeed the ideas of ownership and its transfer do pose problems for an
empiricist who thinks all ideas must derive from impressions. Harrison
points out that sensible symbols for the mysterious transfer will not
help, if the idea of the property transfer is really inconceivable. But
Hume has defined property or ownership in terms of secure possession,
and we can easily have sense impressions of possession. The symbolic
clod of earth is first in the old landowner's possession, then in the new
owner's, just like the land which changes hands. Of course possession itself, when it is of anything insensible like good nature or an intrepid
spirit, is not an idea Hume can give any clear derivation for. Possessed
character traits are "inner" supposed determinants of outward behavior,
directly known, if at all, only to the consciousness of their possessors.
Hume knew the idea of possession was complex. "We are said to be in
possession of any thing, not only when we immediately touch it, but
also when we are so situated with respect to it to have it in our power to
use it, and may move, alter, or destroy it, according to our present pleasure or advantage. This relation, then, is a species of cause and effect;
and as property is nothing but stable possession, deriv'd from the rules
of justice, or the conventions of men, 'tis to be considered as the same
species of relation" (T 506). He has a clear analysis of both possession
and property as causal powers, but he thinks the man in the street less
able to grasp the convention-dependent power of ownership, and of
property right, than to grasp the more sensible power of holding something in one's hand, with power to move it. Possession is fact, while
property is rule-protected fact about who has the right to possess. The
one who took out the loan may possess the funds, once the loan is due,
but the right to them lies with the lender. The concepts of a right and of
justice are mutually entailing, and Hume takes this to be typical when
there is social artifice and convention. The concepts of a promise and of

7. Jonathan Harrison, *Hume's Theory of Justice* (Oxford, 1981), 113.

its obligatory performance, and of a governor and of rightful allegiance to him or her, are also mutually entailing, both created by the same social inventions.

The motive for returning a loan should be that the repayment is due, that the lender has a right to the repayment, or else to the agreed forfeit. "Sympathy with the public interest"[8] or at any rate sympathy with typical right-holders, makes us approve of such a motive. In this case, however, given that moneylenders did not have a great reputation, and that Jewish ones were denied protection by the law in Britain, one might in fact get away with nonrepayment, even after magistrates have come in to punish thieves and other bad debtors. The rights of moneylenders were less well protected in England than in Venice (in Scotland they were slightly better protected, so some lenders had token offices in Scotland, so that they could, after "summary diligence," call in a loan or the agreed forfeit). Even today, in cases like student loans in New Zealand, where the government is the lender, some graduates just leave the country with large loans unpaid, and are not hounded by Interpol to secure repayment. We do not approve of such nonrepaying conduct, but neither do we call such people dishonest thieves. There is some room for argument over whether a loan from a "vicious" wealthy lender, or from an impersonal government, must be repaid by a young person with many other demands on her limited resources. When I received my tertiary education in New Zealand, there were no fees, so no loan was involved. Then I received a government scholarship to Oxford, and some of my respected mentors there were surprised that I was not bonded to return to New Zealand, to give my country the benefits of what it had invested in me. In fact I did return, as soon as a suitable job came up, and did feel grateful for what I had received, but no return was formally "owed." Fee-paying students today, who do get a large loan, then abscond to better-paying jobs abroad, may have a vague sense of guilt, but perhaps no greater than mine was, when after only three years teaching in New Zealand, I married and took off for greener pastures. What exactly who owes whom can be a tricky moral matter, and Hume wanted us to worry

---

8. I discuss some problems with this concept in Chapter 2, "The Interested Affection and Its Variants."

about why the secret loan from a wealthy lender should be repaid. He chose his example advisedly, even if he did decide not to repeat it in his *Enquiry Concerning the Principles of Morals (EPM)*.

Repayment of loan to a vicious lender has the wanted complexity and moral uncertainty. It forces the reader to worry about the concept of "owing" "debt" and "his right." It is designed to rule out Hutcheson's answer, benevolence,[9] as well as straightforward self-interest, as the answer to the question of what the approved motive can be. But it also has some ugly associations, of resentment of moneylenders. Hume could have included Jews with the women and slaves he mentions in *EPM* as those left out of cooperative conventions in Britain. He does not, but neither does he repeat his puzzle about the approved motive to loan repayment. No such puzzle is raised in *EPM*,[10] and transferring goods to vicious misers is mentioned there only in passing, in Appendix 3, to show how it is the inflexible rule, not each individual case, that has public utility, and that we feel approbation for. The case here is not loan repayment, but appropriation of a beneficent man's goods, to which he lacks title, and their transferal to a wealthy miser. Loans, and the motive to their repayment, are not mentioned. Another thing missing in *EPM* is sympathy with the public interest, as the reason that honesty is approved. By the time Hume returns to loans and debts, in his essays on the national debt, and on interest, and in his later history of the treatment, in Britain, of Jewish moneylenders, he seems to have regarded his choice of example, in the *Treatise* discussion of justice, as one of the several regrettable features of that "unfortunate" work. This could have been in part because of its anti-Semitic overtones, but mainly because the motive for that complex example had been to lead up to the invocation of "convention" to explain the rights and dues involved in it, and in *EPM* he first talks of a sense of common interest, mutually expressed, rather than of a "convention," whose usual sense, he says there, is mutual promise. Then he refers to the "common convention" by which the rowers coordinate their strokes, gold and silver become measures of exchange, and a common

9. Hutcheson had suggested that benevolence was the approved motive for justice, as for any other approved act, and that we have a special moral sense which tells us that we should be benevolent.

10. Another thing missing in *EPM* is sympathy with the public interest as the reason that honesty is approved. I discuss this change in Chapter 2, "The Interested Affection and Its Variants."

language grows up. The contrast between natural and artificial is muted, and the supposed need for there to be natural motives, for the moral sentiment to approve, is replaced by the "complicated sources" of honesty and truth. A lot has changed, by *EPM,* including what gets included in the rules of justice. He says that a common criminal has the rules he has broken suspended against him, so may suffer in his "goods and person, that is, the ordinary rules of justice are, with regard to him, suspended for a moment, and it becomes *equitable* to inflict on him, for the good of society, what otherwise he could not suffer, without wrong or injury" (E 187). Wrong or injury here includes bodily assault, and maybe the rules of justice the criminal has broken, when he himself is forcibly arrested, are rules forbidding assault of persons, as well as rules telling us which goods are ours. The scope of justice has been broadened.

In twentieth-century Oxbridge, the case of the obligation to return a borrowed book to its owner became a laughably trivial example of the sort of moral duty that was subjected to close analysis. Hume's error of judgment, in T 3.2.1, was the reverse; he took too charged an example, even for the purposes he then had in mind, to bring home to readers how convention and artifice have to come in, to understand the reason for paying anything that is due, be it rent, bills, loan repayment, or a borrowed book. But maybe he did not misjudge, for has anyone else, in the dozens who have written on this puzzle, connected Hume's puzzle case of loan repayment with his later treatment of Britain's moneylenders? He may have counted on abstruse thinkers wearing historical blinkers, and not been wrong about that. As Nietzsche charged, a lack of historical sense is a congenital defect of most philosophers. But not of Hume himself, and he did not want to encourage such an abstract approach to ethics—he wanted us to be realistic, to know a bit about the interested affection, and the desire for interest, and about the history of rapacity, of the profit motive, and of changes in property law in Britain, to know about equitable interest rates, and due and summary diligence, before we reach conclusions about what is and is not approvable, as an attitude to loan repayment. I do not agree with James Harris that Hume thought there was no such thing as justice or honesty as a personal virtue, that not even one just man can be found. There are plenty of people who pay their debts, even if they disapprove of the property conventions they were born into, and some who know that the reason they do is that the lender has a right to repayment, just as Hume had a right to keep his silver standish. Respect for rights is a perfectly genuine motive, even if rights themselves are "insensible." (Certainly the idea of them cannot be derived from any impression, other than the approbation we feel for those who respect them.) Garrett concludes that the approved motive for loan repayment is a disposition grounded in the desire to regulate self-interest by the conventional rules of justice, rules which have acquired authority by their acceptance in one's community (what Hume calls their "establishment," or becoming stable). This in a sense does square Hume's *Treatise* circle, but Garrett's "first motive" for justice uses the concept of justice, rather than explicates it. There is trivial sense in which, for Hume, there is always a desire to do what in fact one does do. The approved motive for benevolence is not the trivial desire to be benevolent, but the nontrivial desire to help particular others. Many people regulate their self-interest, as well as their benevolence, with direct debit contributions to selected charities, or serve their self-interest by ingrained habits of economy. Such individual self-adopted policies and habits do not give rise to rights. There are many good habits, but only some are of obedience to the rules of justice. The one who repays his loan, if he does so automatically, may not be so sure why he does, but if he reflects he will realize why, just as "a man who acknowledges himself to be bound to another for a certain sum, must certainly know whether it be by his own bond, or that of his father; whether it be of his mere good-will, or for money lent him, and under what condition, and for what purposes, he has bound himself" (T 547). Such a man will also know if he feels obligated, if he respects the authority of the local rules, and so respects the other's right, or just feels that he should avoid being sued. He is unlikely to be sued for not returning a borrowed book, but such a duty is included in the duty to return what one borrowed, by the time it was loaned for. The artifice of transfer by consent includes all cases of loaning and borrowing.

Hume himself produced a mini-treatise on loaning books in the postscript of a letter he wrote in 1754 to David Dalrymple, learned judge and historian, in which he asks for a loan of a biography of Oliver Cromwell, and in the postscript refers to Julian the Apostate's references to loans and Christian charity (L 1.188–189). Dalrymple kindly obliged, and said Hume had no need to invoke the Apostate (who had claimed that the Christians borrowed the virtue of charity from the ancient Homeric heroes), since he was once "'ἅπαξ φωτιζόμενος," which can mean "once baptized," in New Testament Greek,[11] a cruel barb on Dalrymple's part, as this was around the time Hume was in danger of being found guilty, by the church of Scotland, of infidelity and immorality. In this letter Hume toys with suggesting that there is a duty to lend what one does not at the moment need, as well as a duty to return what has been borrowed, and seems to see this as a natural duty, stemming from natural virtues, such as charity. Hume, in his long *Treatise,* chooses loan restoration as a case of the right kind of complication to make us aware just what an artificial and non-natural thing any right or due is, how much invention has to go into its creation. His thesis that all ideas derive their simple parts from prior impressions is repeated at the start of Book 3, but may seem in fact to play no major role in Hume's account of virtue. The especially reflective "impression of reflection," the moral sentiment, needs natural passions and motives to attend to, in order to do its work, or at least to begin its work, and, in the case of its approbation of justice, there was a special problem in finding what exactly it approves of, if, as I have claimed, that is respect for rights, and rights themselves lack impression-originals. Hume has a real intellectual problem on his hands here, and his solution has to be quite involved. He has to show us how artifice, in the form of a convention for common interest, can create insensible rights. He begins with loans, and comes back to them seven sections later in his treatment of allegiance. Rights and obligations arise within cooperative schemes from which all benefit, and to which all beneficiaries are expected to contribute. The right is to get what the rules say is one's due, and the obligation is to do what the rules require of one.

In *EPM* he has dropped the empiricist claim that ideas need impression-sources, dropped the maxim that approbation must be directed on natural motives, indeed dropped the sharp distinction between nature and artifice.[12] But the claim that cooperative schemes give rise to both obligations and rights is still there. Not all of us regard that *EPM* account of justice as "incomparably better" than the more intricate,

11. Liddell and Scott, in their *Greek-English Lexicon* (Oxford, 1888), give "to enlighten" as the first meaning for the verb "φωτίζω," but also add the meaning "to enlighten spiritually" and, from that, "to baptize," although the Greek also has the verb "βαπτίζω," to plunge into water, used originally of boats which sank, later for getting wet, then for being baptized.

12. For what is eventually dropped when Hume recast the *Treatise,* see "Hume's Post-Impressionism" and "Why Hume Asked Us Not to Read the *Treatise*," in Annette C. Baier, *Death and Character: Further Reflections on Hume* (Harvard, 2008), 257–264.

more intellectually challenging, and much longer story in the *Treatise*.[13] In the latter, the account of allegiance to magistrates is included under the title of Part 2, "Of justice and injustice," and I think it is only toward the end of Part 2 that we see how its initial puzzle is solved, since loan involves the first three artifices, and if the approved motive to repayment is to be distinguished from fear of magistrates, also the fourth. "The practice of the world goes farther in teaching us the degrees of our duty than the most subtle philosophy that was ever invented" (T 569). Hume knew about his society's practices in respect to loans and their repayment, but commentators on his *Treatise* account of justice have largely ignored them. Hume's own "most subtle philosophy" of justice is well informed about commercial and legal practices, and the mysterious rights and obligations they involve. We will not understand him, nor why he began Part 2 of Book 3 as he did, until we take the practices of his world into more account, in our attempts to understand what he is saying about the obligations of justice, or about the character of the just person. James Harris[14] notes that Hutcheson quotes Cicero on the *honestum* on the title page of his *Inquiry*. Harris sees part of Hume's point to be that we do not need Hutcheson's special god-given "moral sense" or Butler's conscience to know what is and is not honest or right. Hume too has the *exemplar honesti* on his title page to Book 3, and he knows, better than Hutcheson, just how difficult that virtue is, difficult to explain as well as to exemplify. In the case of loan, property conventions and promises both are involved, so it is in a way a good case to exemplify what Hume in the *Treatise* takes justice to comprise. In Chapter 5, I suggest that taking it as his initial example forged a closer link between property and promise than in fact obtains, but it certainly served his purpose, if that was to puzzle us about what it is that grounds rights.

13. See Chapter 10, "Incomparably the Best?" for a questionable judgment on this matter.
14. See note 2 for references to where he discusses this matter.

# 2

# The Interested Affection
# and Its Variants

There is no passion, therefore, capable of controlling the interested
affection but the very affection itself, by an alteration of its direction.
—Hume, *A Treatise of Human Nature*, 492

In the second of his *Treatise* sections about justice, Hume speaks of the
interested affection as what regulates itself when property rights are
invented, when a community sees a common interest in ending a hypothetical free-for-all scramble and tussle for scarce possessions, first
allowing each to keep what is then in his or her possession, thus stabilizing possession, and creating property rights, then accepting other
grounds of entitlement, discussed in Section 3, and inventing ways, discussed in Sections 4 and 5, by which property can be transferred in an
orderly manner with the owner's consent. Hume sometimes calls the interested affection "self-interest," sometimes "the love of gain," sometimes, more generally, "self-love," and he also has other less morally
neutral terms for versions of this passion; he speaks of "avidity" in this
*Treatise* context, as a passion that, unless it is regulated, would be destructive to society. In a money economy, avidity can take the form of avarice, the typical vice of the miser. In the *History* he refers to "plunder," to the "rapacity" of some of the Norman monarchs, as well as of
some moneylenders, who also were accused of "extortion." As A. O.
Hirschman[1] has taught us, "interest" means interest, as in interest on
loans or investments. If it is inequitably high, on a loan, we speak of ex-

1. Albert O. Hirschman, *The Passions and the Interests: Political Arguments for Capitalism before Its Triumph* (Princeton, 1977; reprinted 1997).

tortion. "Self-interest" is the love of gain, the desire to get more goods for oneself, for one's possessions to grow; and the interested passion, at both public and private levels, is the desire for gain, especially for fruitful investment of some capital. This desire, when it acts at its liberty, leads to social violence and insecurity. It is so strong a passion, Hume claims, that only if it turns on itself can it be restrained. Only because our ancestors expected that their gains would increase, if they adopted property rights, did they do so. "For whether the passion of self-interest be esteem'd vicious or virtuous, 'tis all of a case, since it itself restrains it: so that if it be virtuous men become social by their virtue; if vicious, their vice has the same effect" (T 492). Definite echoes of Mandeville are heard here. Hume believes that acting so as to recognize property rights, after seeing how much better off we are if we all do this, is the morally approved virtue of honesty, or of "justice" in his limited sense. Did he think it was the regulating or the regulated passion that was approved? Both, I think. The unregulated passion would be disapproved, since it leads to violence and rapine, but the passion that intelligently regulates itself, and lets itself be self-regulated, for the sake of the greater gains through orderly commerce than could have been expected through force and rapine, that canny passion merits approbation.

What also merits approbation, and has received it, is Hume's masterly account of the coordinating strategy by which this mythical agreement was introduced. Russell Hardin calls Hume a "proto-game-theorist," who, though lacking the advantages of modern thinkers who have had the categories of interaction listed and ordered for them by game-theorists, showed, in his social philosophy, "a sophistication and clear-headedness that is beyond most of us, and that has been beyond many commentators."[2] Hume understands coordination problems, as well as the prisoners' dilemma, and solves the coordination problem in his first convention, inventing property rights, by taking present possession as the salient solution. Here are Hume's famous words: "I observe that it will be in my interest to leave another in possession of his goods, *provided* he will act in the same manner with regard to me. He is sensible of a like interest in the regulation of his conduct. When this common sense of interest is mutually express'd, and is known to both, it produces

2. Russell Hardin, *David Hume: Moral and Political Theorist* (Oxford, 2007), 59.

a suitable resolution and behavior" (T 490). Thus is "the punctilious distinction between *mine* and *thine*" (E 189) invented. We should note the many references to interest, in particular to common interest, in Hume's *Treatise* formulation of the first convention. In its brilliant brevity, it describes the intelligent cooperative regulation of the interested passion by itself, when each agrees to let each keep, and thereafter own, what is then in his or her possession. We might also note that Hume presents it here as if only two people may be involved, perhaps two neighbors on one small island. Hardin thinks there is a difference between many-person and two-person strategies, but Hume seems to see a two-person strategy, for iterated cases, as spreading to larger groups. In his *Enquiry Concerning the Principles of Morals (EPM)* he supposes the first coordinative and cooperative conventions to start in extended families, perhaps in ones partitioning common possessions such as garments into private property, and then slowly to extend themselves to larger communities, by a "progress of human sentiments." It is because the force of disapproval for disrespect of rights will be strongest in small communities, where everyone is known to everyone, that Hardin thinks that in large communities we need the law, to punish rights violators, and in a sense Hume agrees, for it is when ownership and contract have enabled some to amass enviable riches that the temptation to break the customary rules becomes strong and troublesome, in Hume's *Treatise* story. That story is a conjectural history, in which conventions arise in a definite order: first property, then its transfer by consent, and by contract, and only after that magistrates, to declare and enforce justice. Each artifice remedies inconveniences the previous one had helped to create. Stabilizing possession needs correction by the authorizing of transfer by consent. "However useful, or even necessary, the stability of possession may be to human society, 'tis attended by considerable inconveniences . . . persons and possessions must often be very ill adjusted. This is a grand inconvenience, which calls for a remedy" (T 514). Transfer by owner's consent and by binding contract is this remedy. Contract and industry, over time, lead to large holdings, including large landholdings, creating opportunities for such thefts as sheep-rustling, and other "acts of injustice," especially when offenders can move to other areas, where their bad reputation does not follow them. It is small American tribes, where holdings are limited to huts and bows and arrows, and are fairly equal, so no one is tempted to take what is not his own, that Hume thinks may last longest, without the need for magistrates. (If they are attacked by other tribes, however, military leadership may arise.) Hardin ignores this sequential aspect of Hume's *Treatise* theory. Hume does not think "there is no property without law,"[3] since he sees it as quite possible for "men to preserve society for some time without having recourse to that invention" (government, magistrates) (T 539). Law in a sense there will indeed be, but only customary law, or common law, not what Hardin seems to mean by "the institutions of justice," such as police, courts, and prisons. Indeed, I think Hardin may not have taken in Hume's main point about what he calls "justice," which never in the *Treatise* includes criminal justice, that it is first a matter of an *informal* recognition of property and contractual rights, recognition that creates and establishes property, or ownership,[4] and only later gets into the hands of "magistrates," whose task is "the execution and decision of justice," "declaring" what the rules are, on particular matters, and enforcing them. Such enforcement aligns people's long-term interest in the rules being kept with their short-term interest, which, before magistrates, may have lain in breach of the rules, especially if they were becoming "cullies of their integrity" by keeping the rules "amidst the licentiousness of others" (T 535). Then, in the conditions in which magistrates have become necessary, it is quite true that "criminal law is necessary for protecting property."[5] Hume sees magistrates as protecting rights that pre-existed their own right to obedience, and sees them as in-

3. Ibid., 137.

4. Indeed, Hardin writes, "The conventions he discusses are not conventions that establish property but only that establish how we are likely to think about it in contexts of handling it" (89). This is an astonishing reading of Hume, whose question was "What *counts* as mine, my property, as distinct from what is merely in my possession?" It is hard enough to define "possession," but one's property is what one owns or *rightfully* possesses, what should not be taken from one without one's own consent. "Our property is nothing but those goods, whose constant possession is establish'd by the laws of society, that is the laws of justice. . . . 'Tis very preposterous, therefore, to imagine that we can have any idea of property without fully comprehending the nature of justice, and showing its origin in the artifice and contrivance of men" (T 491).

5. Hardin, 136. At this point in his exposition of Hume on "justice as order," Hardin quotes, out of context, Hume's claim, at T 497, about how dire the situation would be if rules of justice became generally disregarded, after a period of conformity to them, so that society "dissolves." Hardin says this is what would happen without "a system of law," but what Hume says is needed is "justice," by which he means conformity to the property conventions, not criminal justice, the preserve of the later artifice he calls "allegiance to magistrates."

vented to align people's long-term with their short-term interest. What Hume ironically calls "Laws of Nature" pre-exist legislatures and judges, but these are not, I think, what Hardin means by "law." Of course, these pre-existent rights to property are "artificial," not "natural" in the way Locke and Nozick thought they were. They depend on community custom or convention, just as the modes of greeting do. (Greetings are another example of coordinative behavior. In Austria hikers say "Gruss Gott" to total strangers met on narrow mountain tracks, to signify minimal goodwill, absence of aggression. In Manhattan, where the crowds are such that one could not possibly greet everyone, one shows this minimal goodwill by avoiding eye-contact, which can be interpreted as a challenge.) Hume thought there would have been many conventions in effect before magistrates were invented: sods of earth handed over to signify consent to transfer of land ownership, promises, perhaps also greetings, handshakes, hat-doffings, and, in the tropics, other equivalents of the "I come in peace" signal. (In New Guinea males in hill tribes grasp each other by the penis, but Hume did not know of this convention.)

Hardin, despite his verdict that "a social theorist must reckon Hume's analysis of convention and his use of it to explain social order the greatest contribution of all of Hume's work in moral and political theory,"[6] seems to have dipped into Hume to find game-theoretical accounts, not read him consecutively or carefully. Hume may, by *EPM*, have changed his mind about when governors would be needed, but in the *Treatise* it is a late invention, whose function is to align short- and long-term interest, and give extra incentive to conformity to the previous conventions, of which property is the first.

Hardin sees Hume's grounding convention, recognizing private property rights, as limited to such goods as are "moveable" and so easily seized.[7] In fact, Hume requires only that these goods be "external" to our minds and bodies, and that their *possession* be transferable without the transfer destroying their value. He gives the huts of Indians as among their possessions, of which they might be dispossessed, and he gives land as an example of the kind of property for whose transfer by consent special ceremonies are adopted. As border residents knew, land can be seized by invasion and "occupation." The only "fixed" goods Hume rec-

6. Ibid., 225.
7. Ibid., 145.

ognizes are those of mind and body, which can be attacked, but (before the trade in body parts) not transferred to the attacker in a usable state. Hardin even quotes Hume's clear statement about which possessions become property, namely anything whose possession can be transferred without suffering loss or alteration, but for some obscure reason takes this to exclude land. Hume's first convention establishes what, in the way of external goods, are mine, what thine.[8] The convention includes land, as is made clear when Hume explains what is meant by "possession, or occupation," in T 507. He gives the case of the occupation of an unoccupied island. Title to land is one of the most important sorts of entitlement, property in land is "*real* estate," and land is covered in what Hume regards as the ur-convention, inventing entitlement. He may later, in *EPM,* have realized that some property rights, say, to the use of wells, may have been recognized by wandering tribes like the ancient Israelites before rights to land, so property in land has to wait till we have a settled agrarian society, not a hunter-gatherer or a herding one, and even then may not be freehold, but involve a "feu," a remnant of a feudal due. But in the *Treatise* he is supposing that land will be among the goods "partitioned" into private holdings. The goods whose possession is frozen into ownership, or rightful possession, after the first convention is adopted, include much more than what one has made for oneself, and include food supplies and land. Even acute readers of Hume, such as David Wiggins, like Hardin seem reluctant to accept his view that it takes convention to establish what, beyond my personal qualities, counts as mine. That I have spun the wool and knitted it into my jacket does not make it my property, unless some convention gives me the right to the wool from which the jacket was made. Locke's view that mixing my labor with the wool makes its added value mine is dismissed by Hume, in a note to T 505, as a "needless circuit," since any kind of "accession," not merely being worked on, gives a right to what is added, but the Lockean view seems to retain its attraction. Thus Wiggins can write of "a convention or compact that enjoins us to keep our hands off what others have made, or had assigned to them by those who have made it, or had assigned to them by those who had had it assigned to them . . . by those who have made it," as if this supposed convention is one that Hume mentions, like

8. Ibid., 147.

that of the binding force of "I promise."[9] Like Hardin, Wiggins underestimates the scope of Hume's property convention, so underestimates the force of his claim that ownership is "artificial," not natural. In some societies indeed, making something or improving it may constitute a claim to keep it, but Hume explicitly rules out this construal of the ownership convention he supposes our ancestors to have adopted. He does at one point speak of the possessions which become stabilized into property as those acquired by a person's "fortune or industry" (T 489), but the industry could have been gathering nuts in the forest, or sowing crops in fields one owns, rather than "making" something.

The first convention is that whereby the interested passion restrains itself, to avoid violence and destruction of goods (and possible injury to their former possessors), and each self-interested person "concurs" with like persons to advance their common interest in stabilizing possession by inventing ownership, initially on the basis solely of present possession, and so inventing the possibility of theft, and of possession of stolen goods. Hume regards this as the work of our human understanding, our ability to envisage alternative futures, under alternative social conditions, and to make cost/benefit assessments. It is the interested passion at its most intelligent, and cooperative. It is "self-love," but a form of it which prefers working with others to working against them. The circumstances of justice include "selfishness and limited generosity" (T 494), but it is not the interested passion in the form of selfishness that is the origin of justice: it is enlightened, cooperative, inventive, and "oblique" self-interest.

"Selfishness," along with "avidity," "avarice," "greed," "extortion," and "rapacity," are terms implying condemnation, and part of the subtlety of Hume's account of the interested passion is showing how some forms of it can be bad and troublesome, others perfectly fine, indeed essential for a flourishing commercial society. Among the latter is, of course, the profit motive, as well as a taste for luxury. He is rapacious, you are greedy, I am rationally self-interested? As Mandeville had it in "The Fable of the Bees," "Millions endeavouring to supply each other's lust and vanity . . . thus every part was full of vice, yet the whole mass a paradise." Hume had learned from Mandeville about unintended conse-

9. David Wiggins, *Ethics: Twelve Lectures on the Philosophy of Morals* (Harvard, 2006), 71.

quences, both good and bad. A flourishing society requires intelligent self-interest to operate, as well as some taste for luxury. He anticipated Smith's "invisible hand," both in what he wrote about the price of corn,[10] and in his essay "Of refinement in the arts," originally called "Of luxury." Indeed, he saw relative religious toleration in England as the unintended outcome of intolerance for Catholic monarchs, and advocated religious establishment as a way to prevent the competitive zeal of warring sects, each headed by clergy supported by their followers, a way of bribing clerics, or at least those of the dominant church, to indolence. His strategic thinking went beyond what Hardin surveys.

Besides "concurrence" on a scheme to end disorderly seizing of one another's possessions, the first convention involves both "imitation" and "example." This is how justice differs from other social virtues like beneficence. "The social virtues of humanity and benevolence exert their influence immediately, by a direct tendency or instinct, which chiefly keeps in view the simple object, moving the affections, and comprehends not any scheme or system, nor the consequences resulting from the concurrence, imitation, or example of others" (E 303). Unless one person's just acts are imitating and imitated, they will be pointless; like the stone put up unsupported into an incomplete arch, it will "fall to the ground." There is no point in being, indeed it would be foolish to be, the only person restraining the urge to take what one wants, when it is in another's possession. Such an act only becomes wrong, and counts as theft, once possession is transformed into property by *general* acceptance of the convention declaring each to have a right to keep what is in her present possession. Indeed, Hume may be overoptimistic in thinking that the hypothetical first performer, under the new scheme, will have his exemplary conduct imitated. "Every member of society is sensible of this interest [the common interest in ending the scramble for possessions, in adopting property rights, based on present possession]: everyone expresses this sense to his fellows, along with the resolution he has taken of squaring his actions by it, on condition that others will do the same. No more is requisite to induce any one of them to perform an act of justice, who has the first opportunity. This becomes an example to others. And thus justice establishes itself by a kind of convention"

10. See David Raynor, "Who Invented the Invisible Hand: Hume's Praise of Laissez-Faire in a Newly Discovered Manuscript," *Times Literary Supplement* (August 1998), 22.

(T 498). This first "act of justice" presumably will be a refraining or abstaining, not, like loan repayment,[11] the example Hume has used in the previous section to generate his puzzle about the motive to just acts, a real "active" action. This first convention creates rights, perhaps the first rights, and seeing its adoption as a rational strategy, motivated by enlightened self-interest, in itself does not explain how *rights* get created by the solution to a coordination problem. (Hardin is silent on what gives rise to rights.)[12] Customs like saying "Grussti mit einander" to anyone one meets, as they do in some Swiss valleys, do solve a coordination problem, but do not generate any right to be thus greeted. Some simple customs, such as taking turns, or queuing, do give rise to a proto-right, namely, "my turn." Hume's first convenors, inventers of property, may have already been taking their turn at the well or water hole, before private property is invented, so already have recognized something like rights. Pushing in or out of turn could be called the display of a primitive case of an artificial vice. Anscombe, in her account of promising,[13] sees this link between keeping one's promise and keeping one's place in a queue. She describes the game in which several people put their hands on top of one another, and it is for the bottom hand to move to the top. Many games involve turns, and rights are merely a cross-temporal version of a turn. My turn to possess what I own ends at death, when some convention of "succession" decides who will be the next turn-taker at possessing it. When we do things together, turns are often involved. They were involved in Hume's example of two neighbors agreeing to help each other bring in the harvest. One harvest ripens before the other, so each has his turn at helping and at being helped. Contract may add security to such an agreement, but the idea of a turn does not require the acceptance of a forfeit for not doing what it becomes one's turn to do, as Hume thinks promise and contract do. These artifices anticipate magistrates, by introducing penalty and forfeit. Forfeit is also introduced by loans, and both penalty and forfeit come into play when it is anticipated that later performers (promise-givers, loan-repayers) may renege on their part of the agreed game, so need some extra incentive, one not needed in simultaneous agreed exchanges. But there is a sense in which

11. I discuss this case in Chapter 1, "A Solemn Bonfire? Hume on Loan Repayment."
12. The only rights he discusses are legal rights: Hardin, 190–191.
13. G. E. M. Anscombe, "Rules, Rights, and Promises," in *Midwest Studies in Philosophy*, vol. 3, *Studies in Ethical Theory* (Minnesota, 1980).

the penalty of withdrawal of trust will be inflicted on all those who do not do their part in some convention, so rob, and do not wait their turns. It is a penalty many are, however, quite willing to risk, especially if they do not expect to re-encounter those they robbed, or be in a queue with the same people again. In some Muslim societies thieves and robbers had their hands cut off, to stigmatize them as much as to prevent reoffending, but that usually involves the equivalent of magistrates. There is no scarlet letter "Q" to attach to queue-jumpers.

Waiting one's turn is a virtue (not one Hume lists, unless it is included in "patience"), performance of what one promised is a virtue, as is respect for exclusive property rights, and allegiance to magistrates. These are all forms of the interested passion, when it acts cooperatively and in coordination with others. I come now to consider which other virtues, in Hume's catalogue, are forms of the interested affection, that strongest of all human passions. Justice in all its Humean forms is the most interesting such virtue, and it involves a passion for increase in public as well as private goods. Hume claims that family self-interest can outweigh individual self-interest, as a typical human motive, and so it is for the sake of their loved ones and children, as well as for their own sake, that Hume thinks our ancestors agreed to accept property rights, and rules for the orderly transfer of property by consent. Other virtuous forms of the interested passion are frugality, or avoidance of waste, prudence or long-sightedness and caution in advancing our own and our family's interests, and some smaller matters, such as common courtesy, which Hume describes as like justice in preventing conflicts among different persons' pride and vanity. A large group of virtues come under his heading of virtues "useful to ourselves." Besides frugality, there is discretion, industry, enterprise, forethought, perseverance, economy, sobriety, presence of mind, "and a thousand more of the same kind" (E 243). So it is very clear that there need be nothing vicious, for Hume, about a concern for our own good, or for accumulation of well-chosen goods.

Hardin wonders why Hume spoke of obligations, when it was self-interest that required the obligated action.[14] This usage had precedent: the interested obligation to virtue had been discussed in Shaftesbury's *Inquiry,* and, as Hardin notes, Hutcheson recognizes that obligation can be interested. Hume does not, as far as I have noted, speak of *obligations*

14. Hardin, 52.

to benevolence, or to patience, or to frugality. He tends to reserve the term for what the artificial virtues demand. (He could have spoken of an obligation to wait till it is one's turn, and to take one's turn.) Sometimes he speaks of duty, where a natural virtue requires some action: parents have duties. He speaks of the sense of obligation a beneficiary would feel, if he lacked spontaneous gratitude, yet felt he should feel it, and so makes himself pretend to it. Obligations are what we have, and feel we have, when there is some inclination to neglect them, as well as a push to fulfill them. Justice is often like this, especially when it comes to loan repayment. Few of us may be tempted to steal, or become burglars, but we may, as Hardin says, cheat on our taxes. Natural virtues motivate us to do the right thing spontaneously. Artificial virtues are, in their nature, against the grain, at least some of the time, so they impose obligations. Even waiting in line is difficult, when one is in a hurry. When Hume comes, in the second part of his conclusion to *EPM,* to discuss "the interested obligation to virtue," it is, contrary to what Hardin says,[15] not beneficence and generosity, but mainly honesty and justice that he anticipates may be against the grain for clever self-interested people, even those who enjoy helping selected others, but who think they can get away with tax fraud, or other fraud or dishonesty. It is because of the temptation to sensible knavery that there is an *obligation* to justice, as well as a virtue of justice, so justice can count as, in the words of J. V. Lucas, an "unwilling virtue."[16] The really virtuous just person, however, is not unwilling to be just, and will not even consider dishonesty, so will not see any choice or feel any against-the-grain obligation. The one who feels tempted, and resists the temptation, is like Aristotle's continent man. Compared with the temperate man, he has a second-class virtue, one dependent on a nonadmirable temptation. Better to resist than to indulge a bad impulse, but best of all not to feel the temptation. The admirable honest man will never feel tempted to knavery, while the one who experiences honesty as an against-the-grain obligation, and shows his self-command in resisting temptations to dishonesty, will exhibit no vice, but fail to be exemplary. Hume thinks well-brought-up people will

15. Hardin, 209, says that Hume thinks peace of mind and consciousness of one's own integrity will be lacking in those who lack cheerful beneficence, but it is justice, the virtue the sensible knave lacks, which Hume is discussing here, at the end of the conclusion to *EPM,* not beneficence.

16. J. V. Lucas, *On Justice* (Oxford, 1980), 3.

never dream of being dishonest, any more than they will be tempted to discourtesy. Some offensive behavior is just beyond the pale. "What will become of the world, if such practices prevail?" such decent people may say, if challenged as to why they do not consider profitable dishonesty, why they, in Hume's words, "mechanically," out of trained habit, pay their bills, and their rent, and never consider committing theft or fraud.

Whatever may be the case for people in a civilized and commercial society, who have been in the hands of educators and politicians, and drilled to be polite and honest, this would not have been the position of their hypothetical ancestors, when the first convention was adopted. They must have felt very uncertain of the advantage they gained from abstaining from taking goods in others' possession, especially if those goods had once been in their own possession, or produced by their own labor. If their neighbor took their goat, or their hand-knitted jacket, the day before the convention was adopted (if we may so speak, since Hume says the convention becomes adopted slowly, as a natural language comes to be), then they may have had little of value in their present possession, so came out badly from the new arrangement. Of course they would have felt tempted to get back their goat, or their jacket, by force if necessary. They may have seen the long-term advantages of ending violent seizure and occupation, and replacing insecure temporary possession with stable property rights, but resented their unlucky small initial holdings. They may have felt an obligation to conform to the new convention, but they would scarcely have done so easily, as a matter of course, like the honest person in later generations. Hume tells us what Hardin calls a just-so story about how and why a sequence of artifices are adopted, and Hume distinguishes between treating an adopted convention as merely a mutually advantageous custom, giving rise to a "law of nature," and so creating a "natural obligation," the motive for which is interest, and treating such originally interested obligations as also moral ones, after they have passed the test of moral survey, which involves sympathy with the public interest.

"Sympathy with the public interest" is an odd and artificial thing, as artificial as the public interest itself. What Hume normally means by sympathy is that awareness of what those around us are feeling, that we today now know involves our possession of "mirror neurons." We can in this way sympathize with each other's self-interest, or feelings of group interest. But as the "public" has no expressive face to tell us, by a "presensation," what it feels—indeed, since it does not feel at all—sympathy with the public interest must be a degenerate case of sympathy, perhaps best thought of as sympathy with public officials, those whose job it is to look after the public interest. Since Hume believes that such officials, magistrates, and their helpers need not be invented till long after property rights are invented, it remains very unclear just what sort of sympathy is to prompt approbation of honest behavior, and promote the natural obligation to honesty into a moral obligation. A general point of view can be adopted, and must have already been adopted to see parental solicitude, kindness, and other natural virtues to *be* virtues, but the only sort of sympathy, in Hume's usual sense, there can be is sympathy with right-holders, with victims of theft or fraud, and those who fear it. In *EPM* he seems to make this sympathy with victims of injustice, after an appreciation of the utility of justice, an important ground of approbation of honesty, and disapprobation of dishonesty. Sympathy with the public interest is not invoked at all in *EPM,* and it may well be that Hume saw the incoherence of that notion. The public interest requires some things, like refraining from counterfeiting, and from milking the coinage, which have no particular individual victims. For victimless crime, sympathy is the wrong explanation of why we take such things as counterfeiting to be wrong.

Sympathy with right-holders is not prominent in the *Treatise,* because of the way Hume has stacked the deck with his initial example, in which the selfish miser who is owed money is a deliberately unsympathetic figure. That selfish miser survives into *EPM* (E 305) to show how inflexible rules must be, applied even when other considerations make us sympathize more with the one who has to transfer goods to the miser, than with the miser. (In *EPM* it is not loan repayment to the miser, but transfer of goods, perhaps inherited ones, to which the one who makes the transfer has no proper title.) But usually we do sympathize with those whose property rights are violated. Utility is served by inflexible application of the rules of property, and utility is "the sole source of the approbation paid to fidelity, justice, veracity and integrity" (E 204). In Hume's *EPM* answer to why utility, including the utility of justice as respect for property rights, pleases us, he still invokes sympathy—for example, with the one who stutters—and he speaks of the man of "cold insensibility" as atypical. Even Timon the man-hater loved Alcibiades, and sympathized with his ambitions. So sympathy with particular persons still is involved, but the main emphasis is on the appreciation of the utility of virtues such as justice: utility, that is, for most right-holders, and for the whole group. And when Hume gives his general account of moral approbation, in the conclusion to *EPM*, it is first described without invoking sympathy, as simply a view to what is beneficial to society and to individuals. It is later said that such a version of morality displays "the force of many sympathies" (E 276), but the role of sympathy is not as crucial as it is in the *Treatise*. This could be because Hume saw what a strange thing sympathy with the public interest would have to be, especially before official guardians of it were created, so changed his account of the moral sentiment to make even corrected sympathy less central to it. Sympathies with actual persons still come in, but for virtues like justice, direct appreciation of the utility and need for the cooperative scheme is invoked, as well as sympathy with individual right-holders under the scheme.

There is a difference between sympathizing with a right-holder qua right-holder, and sympathizing with him tout court. The vicious wealthy lender will not evoke much sympathy, as a person. But insofar as he, as lender, has a right to repayment, we, if taking up the general point of view, must sympathize with him as much as we sympathize with any right-holder, any owner, any loaner, any hirer out of wanted goods, for an agreed price. It is in the interest of any right-holder to be jealous of the protection of all right-holders, and justice is a "jealous" virtue. It is concerned with "mine and thine," insofar as these arise within an accepted scheme of entitlement.

Hume refers to self-interest as becoming "oblique" when it sees that it will be better satisfied by its self-restraint, in a cooperative scheme of rights, than in its direct or shortest route to gain. It sees that pursuing gain within an orderly society will get it more than it could expect if remaining in a disorderly "state of nature," where gains cannot be expected to be kept for long. Hume's version of this pre-artifice state is not nearly as dire as Hobbes's: he does not mention risk to life, only risk to stable possession. Indeed, he thinks the worst state, when relations with others do become "dangerous," and so perhaps we would be driven to be solitary, would be a reversion to violence, after property accumulation by contract, and breach of contract. That is the state which the invention of magistrates prevents, a state of noncompliance to previously accepted customs, both of recognizing property rights, and of keeping contracts.

Magistrates presumably will punish murder, as well as theft and fraud, but Hume mentions no customary rights to life preceding the invention of magistrates. The interested affection might have been construed as aiming at a longer life, as well as accumulated wealth or goods, but Hume treats "love of life" as a passion separate from the "love of gain." As indeed it is, since some who have lost the one persist in the other. Some, who are willing and ready to die, spend their last energies looking after the wealth they will have to leave their heirs. Others, who never cared much about wealth accumulation, try desperately to postpone death. Nevertheless, most versions of morality recognize disrespect for the right to keep on living as an even graver wrong than theft or other misappropriation.[17] I think Hume did see killing each other as an activity regulated by local convention, rather than seeing non-murderousness as a natural virtue, but that is a topic for a different essay. (He did recognize kindness as a natural virtue, cruelty as the worst vice, but killing others painlessly need not involve cruelty, except to their loved ones. Hume regularly defends killing in self-defense.)

I have tried, in this chapter, to bring out the great range of forms Hume saw self-interest to take, and its foundational role in getting us to accept the conventions of property, its transfer by consent, and promise—that is, of the rules of what he called "justice"—as well as getting us to see the advantage there was in inventing "magistrates," who will protect our rights by detecting and punishing those who violate them, and coordinate large-scale cooperative enterprises, such as draining swamps, building prisons, and raising armies. Some forms of self-interest are vicious, because destructive and antisocial. Others show us at our best, most intelligent, and most inventive. There is therefore no reason whatever to think, as some have,[18] that self-interest could only provisionally be an approved motive to justice. At the very end of the *Treatise* Hume repeats that justice is based on the "strongest interest imaginable" (T 620). As long as self-interest takes an intelligent and cooperative form, it is what Hume is sometimes willing to call "reason," and it is the reason to which "all the advantages of art" are due (T 610). Our social

17. I discuss Hume's treatment of other injustices than property crimes in Chapter 4, "Hume's Enlargement of His Conception of Justice."

18. See Rachel Cohon, "Hume's Difficulty with the Virtue of Honesty," *Hume Studies* 23, 1 (1997): 91–112; and David Norton's introduction to the Oxford (2000) student edition of Hume's *Treatise* (183–188).

inventions are the most advantageous of all the forms of this reason, since there our strongest passion, self-interest, is what gives liveliness and inventiveness to that long-sighted reason. "Nothing is more vigilant nor inventive than our passions" (T 526). Speaking of the rules of justice, Hume writes, "'Tis self-love which is their real origin; and as the self-love of one person is naturally contrary to that of another, these several interested passions are oblig'd to adjust themselves after such a manner as to concur in some system of conduct and behaviour. This system, therefore, comprehending the interest of each individual, is of course advantageous to the public; tho it be not intended for that purpose by the inventors" (T 529).

I have not yet answered the question of what it takes to invent *rights,* the question I noted that Hardin does not address. Not every solution to some social problem gives rise to rights. Standard time, and time zones, one of Hardin's examples, do not. Many cultural practices connected with time, like days of the week, do help us coordinate our lives with other people, make appointments and keep them, but do not get included under "justice," and do not create rights. If I chose to refer to "the day after tomorrow," rather than "Friday," in making a lunch date with you, your rights would not be infringed upon, and nor would they be if I forgot and did not turn up. That would be inconsiderate of me, not unjust. Hume is concerned with conventions that do give rise to rights, and the only time references in his discussion of justice are *EPM*'s observation that eating meat on Thursday may be lawful, but on Friday forbidden, and to the special prohibitions during Lent. So what, in game-theoretical or strategic terms, is special about conventions giving rise to rights and obligations? Of course, I have some obligation, in a weak sense, to turn up at lunch appointments I have agreed to, but only in that I may hate myself if I do not, and that the let-down person may not make appointments with me in future. But no magistrate would ever enforce such obligations, and the peace of society does not depend either on keeping them, or on punctuality in keeping them. Hume selects for his consideration not the myriad of cultural customs we have, customs of greeting, standard measures for various magnitudes, including those for time, dividing it into minutes, hours, days with names, weeks, years with numbers, conventions for indicating places on the earth's surface by latitude and longitude, for giving each other proper names, and using them to refer to one another. He does liken justice to accepting a common measure of wealth, in some currency like guineas. He is trying to explain justice, a person's due, what is owed to her. So he concentrates on those customs which are such that one person's breach of custom injures another in an unfair way. Justice and equity go together, for him, although equity is a natural virtue. Not keeping appointments inconveniences others, rather than injures them. Refusing to divide time into weeks, or length into feet (or meters), would be eccentric, not unfair to others. Orthodox Christians celebrate Easter at a different time than other Christians, and no one is injured thereby. Uniformity matters where diversity of custom within one society would be fatal either to communication, or to life and minimal social order, matters like a common language, common measures, common traffic rules and property rules. If one speaks only a language that others around one do not, or recognizes eccentric measures and measures of time, one will be gravely incommoded, but one's "eccentricities" will not be unfair to conformers to the standard customs, as they would be if one lived by one's own property rules or traffic rules. Justice requires the circumstances of justice, and these include some scarcity. (Traffic rules also require scarcity of room for movement, and are minimal or nonexistent on the high seas.) The greatest achievement of Hume's theory of justice, in my view, is not his anticipation of game theory, but his anticipation and advance correction of Kantian ethics, with its version of moral rectitude as acting in conformity to maxims one could will as law in a kingdom of rational beings. The question "Can I will that others do the same?" can be answered in the affirmative by the eccentric, who refuses to recognize weeks, and may welcome imitators, and maybe it can also be answered affirmatively by some sadomasochistic criminals. Hume saw clearly that the Kantian question (if we may so speak, before Kant formulated it) is unnecessary for actions like kindness and parental solicitude, where the action does good whether or not it is, or should be, the general practice, and where the vicious parent, who beats his child, may well be able to will that others do likewise. This is not to deny that the person with the natural virtues is exemplary, but the goodness of her act does not, like artificially virtuous acts, depend on others doing likewise, or on her willing that they should. The question that has to be asked in the circumstances of justice, circumstances of scarcity, is "What am I counting on being the general practice, in order to have the maxim I have, in this action, and can I will that others follow my example?" This question only need arise when some restraint has been imposed on natural impulse, and when there has been an agreed-upon convention as to what each may and may not do. It arises whenever something has been partitioned: possessions, food rations, right of way on the roads, right to speak. It arises, as Hume saw so clearly, in conditions of scarcity. Hume thinks that only when self-interest is restrained will such rules be needed, but in fact he describes similar ones for vanity (that it be concealed in company; there is a sort of scarcity of room to preen and boast). It arises whenever we have to take turns at something, but many conventions have other purposes, so do not give rise to a feeling of unfairness, if someone acts against them, if someone insists on measuring in feet when her society has switched to meters. She will be the main sufferer, if she does this, as her statements about measurements will not be understood. (Habermas, with his theory of communicative action, may see those who do not conform to usual systems of communication as violating rights, but linking justice so closely with communication can be seen as an eccentricity of his moral theory.) When a person fails to conform to conventions of justice, to conventions creating or involving rights, that person gains at others' expense. This is as true when one jumps the queue as when one steals or refuses to return what one borrowed, or breaks a promise. (It may also be true of one who refuses to observe the rules of debate, so shouts down his opponent, not allowing him his turn to speak.)[19] Justice, with its rights and obligations, comes in only when some scarce resource that all self-interested persons want is partitioned or allocated, for the advantage of all. Once that is done, magistrates come in to enforce justice, and so we have criminal justice. Justice is what magistrates enforce, but inventing them, for Hume, is not a convention of *justice,* and the rights it creates are much more conditional than property rights or contractual rights. With property rights, the obligation to respect them is conditional on most others doing so, and in the case of contract, on one's contractual partner also conforming. But with allegiance to magistrates, the obligation is also conditional on the proper performance of the magistrates. (Hume recognizes a right to rebel against tyrannical rulers, but not against unfair or oppressive property conventions.)

Hume's theory of justice is part of his moral philosophy, not part of his

19. I linked rights with norms for speech, perhaps too closely, in "Claims, Rights, Responsibilities," in *Moral Prejudices* (Harvard, 1994), 224–246. Property rights were not mentioned there by me, nor indeed were they plausibly covered by the theses I advanced there.

political philosophy. (Hardin denies that Hume has any moral views, only an explanatory moral psychology,[20] but Hume certainly believes that property rights should be respected, and cruelty avoided.) Hume originally intended to add a book on politics, and one on criticism, to the three books of the *Treatise,* of which the third is "Of morals." He has later essays on politics, and has a theory of law, its purpose, and the different "institutions of justice," such as trials and appeal courts, and about the more and less barbaric punishments levied, and methods of trial used, from trial by water or by combat to trial by jury, but this is found mainly in his *History,* especially its appendices. But since allegiance to magistrates, to governors and the judges they appoint, is for him a virtue, the convention involved in creating such authorities is included in his book about morals.

Hardin thinks that Hume was stuck with the terminology of virtues, but he was not:[21] he chose it, and includes conformity to some conventions among the virtues in his rather unconventional catalogue. (Balfour was incensed by it.) Kant in effect treated all virtues as if they were conformity to laws, and so artificial. In Kant's theory, questions about possible law (or "concurrence" in obedience to law), "imitation," and example-setting come in, not only when they are relevant (property), but also when they are not (benevolence). He then tries to distinguish the two sorts of requirement by the categories of perfect and imperfect duty, where the latter allows room for discretion, while the former is strict and punctilious. He sees us all as pretend-legislators of pretend-laws that cover almost all of life. Hume sees the reference to rules and laws to be needed for the artificial virtues, but, if dragged in for the natural virtues, to involve what he would term an "unnecessary circuit." In some parts of life we need to be able to rely on others doing the expected thing, not assaulting us, not robbing us, keeping promises and contracts. Only beggars need rely on our benevolence. The areas where we need to be fairly sure what others will and will not do define the areas where universal rules are called for, and to get definite rules we need social artifice. For the rest, we can hope for considerate treatment, since con-

20. Hardin, 8, 32–3, 230.

21. We do not find catalogues of virtues in Shaftesbury, Hutcheson, or Butler. It was lists of commandments, not lists of virtues, that Hume grew up with. Hobbes has a list of virtues, paralleling his laws of nature, so in a sense it was those interested in social artifices who found the terminology of different virtues and vices helpful. Certainly Hume in the *Treatise* needed his distinctions between natural and artificial, or convention-dependent, virtues. A deontological vocabulary would not have suited his moral theory at all.

siderateness is a virtue, but can live with a range of degrees of consider-
ateness. Of course, the very considerate person does set an example one
might *hope* others would follow. But the honest person sets an example
one *trusts* most others are also setting.[22]

The interested affection, and its strength, is one of the circumstances
of justice; the other is scarcity of wanted resources. (If Jiwei Ci is right,
we should add a capacity for resentment when we do not get our share
of the scarce partitioned goods, and also respect for other persons, leading to indignation if they suffer injustice, and it can be argued that
Hume recognizes at least the former in *EPM*.)[23] These circumstances
combine to motivate the conventions of justice, which give rise to rights,
and do so before magistrates, and criminal justice, are established. The
priority is conceptual as well as temporal, on Hume's conjectural history.
Justice is a matter of one's share, one's turn, what one deserves, according to some rule informally adopted for mutual advantage, to settle just
what is due one in an orderly manner. When magistrates become oppressive tyrants, or enforce their own wills rather than common law and
community custom, then Hume thinks allegiance to them not merely is
likely to cease, but also can rightfully cease. He is very cautious on this
matter, not wanting to encourage revolt and revolution, but he saw that
it can become justified, and he thought it was, in the case of the American colonies. (I think he also would have supported the North, in the
American Civil War, and supported the civil rights movement.) The
American rebels against Britain had the right sort of grievance—the injustice of taxation without representation—and the civil rights supporters had that of the tyranny and injustice of slavery, and of discrimination
against former slaves and the descendents of former slaves. Justice begins in the self-regulation of self-interest in cooperative conventions,
then establishes its own standards, which can be used to criticize governments. Justice, on Hume's account, is intelligent self-interest's first
and most important invention. It also leads to the invention of government, but government's task is "the execution and decision of justice,"
justice as already determined, in its main lines, by more basic conventions. Positive law is sometimes needed to settle what is whose, and

22. I discuss the difference between trust and hope in "Putting Hope in Its Place," in
*Reflections on How We Live: Essays on Ethics* (Oxford, 2010), 216–229.
23. Jiwei Ci, *The Two Faces of Justice* (Harvard, 2008), 14–16. He is influenced on this point
by P. F. Strawson, *Freedom and Resentment* (Methuen, 1974).

whether unwritten contracts bind, but the main lines of justice are, especially in the English tradition, a matter of common law, of community expectation, interpreted and not decreed by legislators and judges. As Hume says in his late essay "Of the origin of government," the main purpose of the whole complex scheme of the state, in England of the rule of the monarch in Parliament, was the maintenance of "twelve judges." It is only if that purpose is served that the invention of government will be "one of the finest and most subtle inventions imaginable" (T 539). Its subtlety lies, for him, in the way the very troublesome passion which makes governments necessary, preference for the close rather than the remote good, becomes a remedy to itself, by social engineering ensuring that the costs of quick dishonest gains will be too high, so that long-term and short-term interest come to coincide. It is another case of self-interest regulating itself, showing itself as reasonable and eminently approvable. The origin of justice lies in intelligent self-interest, and the same reasoned self-interest provides its continuing rationale, and also the reason why in large societies we need magistrates to declare and enforce it.

> And as this interest, which all men have in the upholding of society, and the observation of the rules of justice, is so great, so it is palpable and evident. . . . Since then men are so sincerely attach'd to their interest, and their interest is so much concern'd in the observance of justice, and this interest is so certain and avow'd; it may be asked how any disorder can ever arise in society, and what principle there is in human nature so powerful as to overcome so strong a passion, or so *violent* as to obscure so clear a knowledge? (T 534)

Hume appeals to his earlier Book 2 account of violence in passions, and the special appeal of close goods, to answer this question of why men sometimes act in contradiction to their known greatest interest, the "palpable and evident" interest in justice. Magistrates are invented to align this "greatest interest" also with what seems a feasible short-term interest, in other words, to make theft and fraud into obviously bad ideas. That it is "interest" that justice serves is said at the start, and at the finish, of Hume's long account of justice, of what it is, why we invent it in its first form, as property rights, and how it serves our sincerely felt and greatest interests. What its relation is to equity will be considered in the following chapter.

# 3

# Nature and Artifice,
# Equity and Justice

No virtue is more esteem'd than justice, and no vice more detested
than injustice. . . . Now justice is a moral virtue merely because it has
that tendency to the good of mankind, and indeed is nothing but an
artificial invention to that purpose.

—Hume, A Treatise of Human Nature, 577

Is justice more esteemed than equity? What exactly is their relation? The
courts of equity adjusted the rulings of lower courts when their outcome
was judged harsh or unfair. Equity is a feature of some but not all legal
judgments. Hume occasionally speaks of the virtue of equity, and never
calls it an artificial virtue. It is listed, along with generosity and clemency and other natural virtues, as a natural "social" virtue, at T 578, in
the paragraph following that which I have chosen as epigraph, where the
artificiality of justice is stressed. Equity, though it has a close link with
justice, is not said to be artificial.[1] In a late essay, "Of the origin of government," Hume refers to the "degrees of equity" (Es 38), whereas he
does not, in the Treatise, speak of degrees of justice, which has to be "entire" (T 530). We might speak of one person being more dishonest than
another, or more prone to break promises, but Hume says that both the
rights and obligations involved in justice, and justice itself, are "entire."

1. Neither Selby-Bigge/Nidditch, nor the Nortons in the Clarendon critical edition, 2007,
include equity in their index. Tom Beauchamp, in the Clarendon critical edition of EPM, is
much more helpful about its occurrences in EPM. It is never said there to be natural, but of
course that contrast, between natural virtues and artificial ones, is no longer drawn, replaced
by the contrast between wall-like and vault-like virtues. Equity is not said to be wall-like, doing
good act by act, but is usually paired with justice. Even bands of pirates or robbers, Hume says,
have to introduce "laws of equity" to maintain their confederacy (E 209).

If he means this of justice the virtue, not just of the justice of a particular act,[2] then a person's dishonesty for him is like a person's criminal record or sexual experience: either he has that, or he does not. Or he may mean merely that either a person has a certain right, or she does not. Hume admits that in common life we do "*secretly* embrace the contrary principle," and recognize half-rights, and may have an urge to share an estate between two claimants, each with a plausible case. And, as he does not note, we do recognize more or less honest people, and the dishonesty of some, as well as their sexual license, is much greater than that of others.[3] Those who steal, not from a private owner, but from the government or from some other communal owner, may be regarded as less dishonest than other thieves.[4] Hume says the rules of property are strict and inviolable, so either a person has ever violated them, or she has not. Taken this way, honesty no more admits of degrees than does a right. Equity, including the equity of a particular rule or custom, or of a court judgment, has degrees, but justice or honesty may not. Yet sometimes, as in his initial puzzle about the natural motive for justice, or even when discussing our "secret" belief that "justice and equity" may seem evenly divided between two claimants to a property, Hume seems to equate equity and justice, and speaks of "rules of equity." Equity does come in degrees. And it is breaches of equity, not of justice, that are said to set the stage for the invention of magistrates, whose task, however, is "the execution and decision of justice" (T 538). Clearly there is, for Hume, some close link between justice and equity. Yet if equity is a natural virtue, depen-

2. Jonathan Harrison, *Hume's Theory of Justice* (Oxford, 1981), 158, takes it to be limited to the justice of acts.

3. I discuss this greater similarity, for Hume, between honesty and virginity than between it and modesty, in Chapter 9, "Good Men's Women." But clearly modesty, chastity, and honesty do admit of degrees.

4. New Zealand property rights are complicated by the native Maori claims to ancestral land and fisheries. A recent prosecution and imprisonment for theft was that of David and Morgan Saxton, father and son, found guilty of taking valuable greenstone (jade) from land owned by a particular Maori tribe or iwi, Nga Tahu, to which they do not belong. (They do, like so many New Zealanders, claim some Maori association. Morgan Saxton's partner, the mother of his children, has a Maori father, who himself mined the greenstone, and taught Morgan how to cut it.) Both Saxtons were respected helicopter pilots, who had taken part in many search and rescue missions in the mountainous area where they lived. There was great public outcry at their imprisonment; helicopters flew over the prison in protest the day they entered it. So New Zealanders, although they have high standards for honesty regarding private property, are more flexible when it comes to community property, such as precious stone owned by particular tribes.

dent on our fellow-feeling with others, as well as our resentment of unfairness to ourselves, then its demands could affect what we accept as
"justice," and any natural motive to equity could be at least part of the
approved motive to justice.

What is the relation of equity to that "probity and honour" which
Hume thinks demands that the "rules of justice" become "inviolable
laws" to a person? Bernard de Mandeville had made great fun of "honour," which in any case seems more a concern with one's own standing,
than any sort of concern for fairness, impartiality, or equity. Concern for
fairness is concern for oneself as one among others, concern for fair
shares for all, when some good or some burden is distributed. It is not
the same as honor, and seems to arise quite naturally, without needing
inculcation from politicians and educators. Young children, who become upset if one of their number is left out in some general handout,
and are upset when they see beggars, seem to have some natural sense of
fairness, or at least of unfairness. Of course, a passion for fairness or equity is a fairly faint passion, often drowned out by competitive zeal, or
by selfishness, but it seems to be a component of human nature. It certainly is a trait we tend to admire, when we find a marked degree of it in
a person. Hume's perfect character, the fictional Cleanthes, is described
as "fair and kind" to all with whom he has dealings (E 269). And it can
provide a motive not to deprive another of what is her due, both when
that due is determined by some artifice, and in natural cases, like food
servings in a large family. It makes us disapprove of the one who cheats
at cards, or breaks any rule of a game, just in order to seem to win, or the
one who grabs another's bread, in addition to his own share. This is not
merely greedy; it is unfair. A sense of fairness involves sympathy with
the one done out of something, but also comparison with how different
people are being treated, and resentment of unfairness. It is not the same
as egalitarianism, but it does have an element of that in it. Why did
Hume both associate equity with the conformity to property rules that
he arguably misnames "justice,"[5] and yet fail to invoke it to answer his
question of what could be an approved motive for paying one's debts? I

---

5. Hume, by the time he has charted the history of jurisprudence in England, and comes to
write his last essay, "Of the origin of government," is fully aware that "the distribution of justice" is a lot more than guaranteeing property rights. I discuss this in Chapter 4, "Hume's Enlargement of His Conception of Justice."

shall look at some recent treatments of what Hume says about justice, before returning to this question of the relation of justice to equity.

Lorraine Besser-Jones, in "The Role of Justice in Hume's Theory of Psychological Development,"[6] which was influenced by earlier writings by Jacqueline Taylor and Stephen Darwall, discusses what she calls a "psychological transformation" that the Humean agent undergoes when she (as Taylor had it) becomes capable of taking up a general point of view, and so approves of any beneficial scheme of customary rights and obligations, and, as Darwall and Besser-Jones have it, "morally commits" to the rules of justice, and internalizes their requirements.[7] Hume himself never speaks either of a transformation, or of such a general moral commitment.[8] Indeed, he is rather scathing about acts of inner commitment, such as that which the one who gives a promise might be supposed to enact, to make her promise binding, or that which Henry VIII claimed he had not made when marrying Anne of Cleves, thus, he suggested, invalidating the marriage. The will, for Hume, can affect only what one does next, not whether one is bound in the future, so acts of commitment, unless express and witnessed, are pretend-commitments for him, not real ones. Certainly he does not talk of any community-wide express act of commitment to the local rules of justice, any kind of salute to the flag. The convention inventing property might be seen as a mutual commitment, but it comes before the supposed transformation, taken to occur when the new arrangements get surveyed whenever moral approbation is given to the scheme. Hume does speak of a transition from recognizing customary "natural obligations" not to take others' property, to regarding these as *moral* obligations. To do the latter one has to sympathize with "public interest," and with each property owner, who will feel aggrieved if deprived of what she had taken as securely her own.

It is not clear just what Hume supposes happens when the supposedly first convention is adopted. He spells out its terms, but also says it "ac-

6. *Hume Studies* 32, 2 (November 2007): 253–276.

7. Don Garrett, in "The First Motive to Justice: Hume's Circle Argument Squared," *Hume Studies* 33, 2 (November 2007): 257–288, also takes the motive to be a desire to stick to a policy of being honest. But he does not call it a moral commitment.

8. Indeed, he is criticized by Jiwei Ci, in *The Two Faces of Justice* (Harvard, 2006), for lacking just this notion of what Schopenhauer called "voluntary justice," and Habermas calls "solidarity" (Jurgen Habermas, "Justice and Solidarity," *Philosophical Forum* 21, 12 [1989]: 32–52).

quires force by a slow progression" (T 490), and likens accepting its terms to coming to speak a common language. What happens first is that each gets the right to keep what is currently in her possession; then other grounds of entitlement are added in: prescription, accession, succession, and various sorts of transfer from previous owners, with their consent, that is, barter, gift, sale, rent, hire, and loan. By the time Hume is writing, and raising his puzzle about the approved motive for loan repayment, the English and Scottish property conventions had such baroque complexity that it would be difficult to imagine anyone morally committing herself to them, as a total package. (Hume in his *Enquiry Concerning the Principles of Morals* [EPM] calls them "whimsical, unnatural, and even superstitious" [E 198].) To morally commit oneself to primogeniture, entailment of land, eminent domain, feus, blench (or blanch) holdings, women's loss of property on marriage, and the details of the law concerning ownership of islands in rivers and sea beaches, would take a real rule-fetishist, and a lawyer at that, given their complexity. It is one thing to say that a decent person does not steal his neighbor's ass, and does not even consider it, and another to say he never infringes on any part of property law.

One of the difficulties we have in understanding Hume's account of property is that its rules are, for us, enforced by law, while Hume supposes that they could have become accepted before there was any penalty for theft, other than indignation and natural distrust if the theft was detected. For us to understand what he is supposing it was like when the first cooperative scheme was accepted, before magistrates were invented, it would be better to think of some of our own voluntary cooperative schemes, such as recycling. If I fail to put out my recyclable bottles and other household containers for curbside recycling, my neighbors may notice and disapprove of me, but no other penalty will be incurred. This is what Hume, somewhat improbably, supposes was the origin of property conventions. For us, to steal is to risk detection, prosecution, and imprisonment, but for our ancestors, in his story, this was not the case. All they had to deter them from dishonesty was the disapprobation of their community, and the thought that, if too many others followed a dishonest person's example, security of possession would be threatened. Many otherwise decent people fail to put out their recyclables, and some keep the wallets they find on the street, rather than return them to their owners. Once on the airport shuttle from Ann Arbor, I was delayed while the driver went into the student union to pick up his wallet, turned in there after he had lost it. He came back exclaiming, "There still are some honest people! Of course the cash is gone, but my cards and driver's license are still here." Standards of voluntary honesty vary—in New Zealand I have several times, the most recent last week, had a lost wallet returned to me with the cash still there. But some communities, and individuals, do have lower or different standards. Some cheat on their income tax returns, a form of stealing from the public, of accepting the benefits government provides, without paying their assessed dues. Degrees of dishonesty exist, even if perfect honesty is an either-or matter, just as degrees of promiscuity exist, even if virginity is an either-or matter. Hume may have had impossibly high standards for justice the personal virtue, if any breach on anyone's property rights, including trespass on land, or forgetting to pay one's bills on time, makes one unjust and dishonest.

Some tax cheats disapprove of the way taxes are assessed, so cheat conscientiously. But then some also find the property law arbitrary and unfair, and have Robin Hood as their hero. And some trespassers claim old traditional rights of way. If the just person, on the Darwall-Besser-Jones version, has morally committed to the property rules of the society she finds herself in, she will need to have taken courses in property law and tax law to be sure what those are, and to check if she really approves of them. As Hume stresses, "justice" as he uses the term in the *Treatise* applies primarily to property, and its transfer by consent.[9] Sometimes he calls this "honesty." He has a separate term, "fidelity," for keeping promises and contracts, but sometimes includes this in "justice," treating promise as voluntary transfer of the right to future goods or service. (His "Some farther reflections on justice and injustice," in Section 6, comes after, not before, his treatment of promises, although it is mainly property he discusses in the "Some farther reflections.") His *Treatise* section on the rules that determine property is dense with footnotes on how the imagination, not public interest, has decided the details of what in *EPM* he calls "the punctilious distinction of *mine* and *thine*" (E 189). There

9. I discuss the changes in what he takes justice to be, in his later writings, in Chapter 5, "The Janus Face of Hume's 'Justice.'"

are no such footnotes to his account of promise, where, to fix the rules, there is less scope for the imagination.[10] There is nothing very noble about what Hume calls "justice"; it is simply the common law governing rightful ownership, and its transfer by consent and contract. What is needed, in the interests of all, he thinks, is some set of precise rules determining ownership, not the precise set we are born into. Just imagine the position of Hume's supposed pre-justice people, when "present possession" gets frozen into rightful property. The man who has just grabbed his neighbor's fine self-made cloak, and abducted his pregnant goat, gets to keep them. It would take a very long-sighted person not to even think of trying to get them back, to put the common interest in having property rights ahead of the question of what he personally is to get, and to lose, from the new scheme. To talk of moral commitment in these circumstances seems very optimistic. The most one could hope for would be reluctant agreement to give the new scheme a trial.

Even later, when "present possession" and present occupation have been supplemented, as bases of a right to property, by prescription, accession, succession, and positive law, the whole scheme might well strike one as unfair, especially if one were a woman whose property becomes her husband's if she marries. Hume in *EPM* shows sympathy with the levelers, who wanted property redistributed on a more egalitarian basis. It is only because it would take "rigorous inquisition" and "severe jurisdiction" to keep redistributing it, and because industry would be discouraged, that he rules out attempting to match property with need, and keep it so matched. He grants that, as things are, "the slight gratification of a frivolous vanity, in one individual, frequently costs more than bread to many families, and even provinces" (E 194). He mentions Sparta, and Roman agrarian laws, which did something to prevent such inequalities, without too severe a jurisdiction, or too much threat to freedom. His man of "probity and honor," in his own society, who respects the customary arbitrary rights, does so more out of resignation, or concern for law and order, than out of moral commitment to the details

10. Indeed, those who dispute Hume's claim that promise-keeping is an artificial virtue point to the absence of rules on how to promise as a sign that a promise is no real institution at all, but a natural act giving rise to a natural obligation. See Oswald Hanfling, "How We Trust One Another," *Philosophy* 83 (2008): 161–177, for a persuasive argument to this effect. Earlier Stanley Cavell had raised similar objections to Hume's view. I discuss Cavell's objections in Chapter 8, "Promises, Promises, Promises," and to some degree agree with Hanfling in Chapter 5, "The Janus Face of Hume's 'Justice.'"

of his country's property law. Indeed, one reason Hume gives against equality of possessions is that it, by "destroying all subordination, weakens extremely the authority of magistrates, and must reduce all power nearly to a level, as well as property" (ibid.). It seems the poor will always be with us, if we are to have freedom, incentive to industry, and allegiance to magistrates. Governments may, like Rome, attempt some egalitarian measures, even tax the wealthy to feed the poor, but perfect equality is deemed impractical, or too costly in other social values.

As for the rules of marriage in Hume's society, he did not even dare raise the question of what the approved motive was for conformity to them, or even if the natural obligation does get promoted into a moral one. Love may motivate marital chastity, and wives who feel obligated to be chaste may indeed feel a moral commitment, if they took a vow to "cleave to him only." But husbands took the same vow, and Hume does not expect them to feel any more morally committed to chastity than princes are to keep treaties. There is a lot more of Mandeville, and his cynicism, in Hume's account of the artificial virtues than some readers find.[11] In any case, marriage is unlike justice in that it does not seem to exhibit the self-regulation of a socially troublesome passion, unless we see this to be lust. But Hume expects brothels and prostitution to continue, alongside marriage. It is true he stresses the strength of "the amorous passion," and of female weakness to sexual temptation, so "modesty" is for him a singularly unnatural quality, an induced reluctance to indulge in "so capital an enjoyment." But the rationale for marriage is the care of children, not, as for St. Paul, the containment of lust,[12] so it is not presented as a case of some strong troublesome passion restraining itself.

Readers of Hume who do not notice the cynicism of his account of chastity and modesty, and do not see how all his artifices are supposed to show how self-interest and other troublesome passions, such as desire for easy quick gain (the passion Hume thinks government serves and regulates, by aligning our long-term with our short-term gains), can regulate themselves, will be encouraged by the introductory commentary to

11. For an estimate of the influence of Hobbes and Mandeville on the content of Hume's ethics, see Paul Russell, *The Riddle of Hume's Treatise: Skepticism, Naturalism, and Irreligion* (Oxford, 2008), ch. 17, "Morality without Religion," 239–266.

12. I discuss the difference between marriage and Hume's other social artifices in Chapter 9, "Good Men's Women."

the Norton and Norton student edition (Oxford, 2000) of the *Treatise*.
For there the approved motive for justice, and presumably for conformity to the rules of all the other artifices, is not any form of self-interest,
such as having one's possessions secure, and fear of being found out and
labeled a thief, a promise-breaker, or an adulteress, or of losing a husband's support for one's children, but rather an other-regarding concern
for the public interest. It is assumed that self-interest could only provisionally be a morally approved motive for justice. After noting that
Hume's view is different from Hutcheson's, David Norton goes on: "He
[Hume] too may be said to hold that actions are morally good only if
motivated by a regard for others" (183). But, as Norton of course allows,
Hume includes prudence[13] and due pride among the virtues, and one
large class of virtues is of those useful to their possessors. Norton also
takes regard for the public interest to be the same as "general benevolence" (184), and seems to equate the reason for approving of justice
with the motive which is approved, what he takes to be "an other-
regarding concern" (188). Some "moral sentiment"[14] must not only approve the motive, but also help constitute it, in his view. Rachel Cohon
also seems to take a similar view.[15] "The motive that makes honesty a virtue is a moral motive, approval of conforming acts and disapproval of violations, which has been strengthened and reinforced by habituation to

13. Prudence is considered as well as cautious self-interest. Hume never calls self-interest
itself a virtue, but neither is it a vice. "Interest" is return on investment. Self-interest, and public interest, are desires for increase of some good. The term "avidity," like "avarice," seems to
mean desire for endless and possibly pointless increase. I discuss these variants in Chapter 2,
"The Interested Affection and Its Variants."

14. This term is ambiguous. Its usual meaning for Hume is approbation or disapprobation,
but some of his commentators use it to refer to any passion or sentiment that gets approbation.
Hume, I think, never uses "sentiment" for any direct (or indirectly motivating) passion. Sentiments determine our taste, including moral taste in passions, while passions, especially direct
ones, determine our motivation. See his essay "Of the delicacy of taste and passion" for this
contrast. Hume's *Treatise* argument against the rationalists, in Part 1 of Book 3, however, seems
to require that morals motivate, so passion, as well as sentiment, must be somehow involved.
Hume wisely does not repeat this argument in *EPM*.

15. See Rachel Cohon, "Hume's Difficulty with the Virtue of Honesty," *Hume Studies* 23, 1
(1997): 91–112. See also her entry on Hume's moral philosophy in the Stanford online *Encyclo-
pedia of Philosophy*, and her book *Hume's Morality, Feeling and Fabrication* (Oxford, 2008).
Cohon sees the rationale for adopting property conventions to be to enable mutually helpful
cooperative social practices, but of course adopting property rules is itself a helpful cooperative
practice, and the crucial one, in Hume's story. The dishonest person whose own possessions are
secure is uncooperative, while reaping the benefits of others' cooperation in keeping possessions secure, that is, in treating them as rightful property.

become a motivating sentiment."[16] Now Hume explicitly says, in a sentence he added after the *Treatise* was published,[17] that sympathy with the public interest, which is what makes one approve of conformity to property conventions, is too weak to motivate; all it determines is our "taste," in this case taste in habits of behavior and motives for conforming to customary rules. And it would be arguing in a (virtuous?) circle to say that sympathy with the public interest leads us to approve of the (very rare) motive of concern for the public interest. So if some "moral sentiment" motivates honest acts, it is not that based on sympathy with the public interest, and it is hard to see what exactly it could be, if it is not that virtue for virtue's sake which Hume had declared to be "sophistry and reasoning in a circle" (T 483). Hume himself does not say that the approved motivation for honesty is some moral sentiment. It is a moral sentiment which does the approving, and its function is not to approve of itself, but to approve of some natural passions and abilities. He does allow that concern with one's own probity and honor may have to come in to bolster long-term self-interest, and one's own share in the public interest, and any or all of these can be approved. If probity and honor are equated with a concern for duty for duty's sake, then they seem as much gullibility as virtue. Hume never says we feel approbation for those who let themselves be trained to "honesty," or to any other sort of conformity to conventions whose point they cannot articulate. One's share in the public interest is what prompts one to give recognition to, and respect for, property rights, and should be enough to motivate one to show such respect. As Hume puts it, one finds one is a gainer from honesty, when one balances the account. This claim is made quite generally, not restricted to the initial conditions when the convention is adopted in a small group, and is repeated when Hume discusses the reason magistrates become necessary: not to make us gainers by our honesty, when we had been losers, but to eliminate the temptation to go for tempting dishonest gains, despite our knowing where our greatest interest lies. Magistrates' incentives to honest behavior eliminate temptations to neglect our greatest interest for the sake of quick temporary gains. It is as if some guardian of the female sex were appointed to remind young women what they risk if, before marriage, they succumb to "the stron-

16. Cohon, "Hume's Difficulty with the Virtue of Honesty," 107.

17. It is ironic that Norton and Norton supply this sentence, which Selby-Bigge/Nidditch left in their textual notes, but Norton and Norton seem not to take its point seriously.

gest imaginable temptation," perhaps also handing out antilust patches, or chastity belts, so they will not be tempted to forget what they stand to lose, if they forfeit their reputation for modesty. In the conclusion of Book 3 of the *Treatise,* Hume writes that "the interest upon which justice is founded is the strongest imaginable, and extends to all times and places" (T 620). This makes it perfectly clear that the approvable motive to justice is a sense of common interest.

When one repays a loan, one shows respect for the lender's rights, and this is of course an "other regarding concern," as is the concern not to let down the one to whom one promised some service. But neither loan re-payment nor promise-keeping show benevolence. Making the promise may have been benevolent, but keeping it is only right, and is in one's own interest, if one values one's reputation. Concern for the other's right, in such cases, cannot be prized apart from concern for one's own rights and reputation, since it is the scheme as a whole that is in the interest of "the whole and every part," and when anyone becomes known as dishonest, or not a promise-keeper, that one loses the trust of others. When we sympathize with the interest of the whole, with the public interest, we approve of conforming acts showing respect for property rights and contractual rights. Sometimes we also sympathize with individual right-holders, with the "parts," as we usually do with victims of theft, burglary, and broken promises. But in cases like repayment of a loan to a loan shark, there may be more sympathy with the borrower than with the lender, and yet we still approve of repayment, since the public interest requires that all rights be respected.

That long-term self-interest, and one's share in a common interest, can be an approved motive to honesty is made very clear when Hume comes to explain why we invent magistrates, as official punishers of the dishonest. Our "natural infirmity" makes us prefer close tempting goods to greater more remote ones. We might agree that "safe commerce" is a greater good than what we can get from some dishonest act, but nevertheless be tempted to dishonesty, especially if others are yielding to such temptations. Hume calls such dishonest acts "breaches of equity" as well as "acts of injustice," and clearly endorses the view that justice or honesty is supported by long-term self-interest, "what in an improper sense we call *reason*" (T 536). He clearly thinks "reason"-motivated honesty approvable, but when the honest person becomes "the cully of his integrity," when he is surrounded by "the licentiousness of others," then it is time to create magistrates, to make "the observance of the rules of justice our nearest interest, and their violation our most remote" (T 537). This account of the rationale for magistrates quite clearly takes long-term self-interest, once we balance our accounts, to be an approved motive to just behavior, in a premagistrate society. It need not be the only motive—indeed, respect for rights should be the main motive—but it is hoped that we will see how rights-recognition benefits all of us, and such appreciation of how it serves our own interests is also approved, when it is found. As I argued in the preceding chapter, it is a special form of prudence, prudent cooperation with others to advance a common interest. Rachel Cohon thinks it "a bad move for a virtue theorist" to identify the virtue of honesty with the virtue of prudence, as it takes shape in a social context.[18] But Hume is not your average virtue theorist,[19] and part of Cohon's own message is that the artificial virtues are not your typical virtues, especially if virtues are taken to be the ones recognized by Hutcheson rather than Cicero. "Thus for Hume, honesty is a virtue in roughly the sense that an artificial leg is a leg."[20] (Would she say the same of all the virtues which are abilities? They too involve no motive, natural or unnatural, but they affect the way we act on the motives we have, just as prudence, honesty, and good sense also affect that. Hume speaks of "natural abilities," but some of these may be affected by artifices, as when self-command takes the form of regular payment of one's debts, or wit and imagination take the form of making up tales to entertain one's small children, within a marriage.) Honesty is, however, more than prudence in a social setting; it is prudence in the context of accepted property conventions determining rightful ownership. Other forms of prudence in a social setting will be keeping on nonhostile terms with one's neighbors, avoiding public nudity, giving polite greetings to acquaintances, showing common courtesy, and so on. Usually consideration for others will combine with prudence in such cases, and there will be a shared interest in things like good relations with neighbors. The interested affection takes very many approved forms, and often combines with other passions, including forms of concern for others. Hume writes

18. Cohon, "Hume's Difficulty with the Virtue of Honesty," 104.

19. See my "Kinds of Virtue Theorist: A Reply to Christine Swanton, 'What Kind of Virtue Theorist Is Hume?'" in *Hume on Motivation and Virtue,* edited by Charles Pigden (Palgrave, forthcoming).

20. Cohon, "Hume's Difficulty with the Virtue of Honesty," 96.

in Appendix 4 of *EPM* that "the prudence explained in Cicero's *Offices* is that sagacity which leads to the discovery of truth, and preserves us from error and mistake" (E 318). The form of it shown in "common honesty" preserves us from dangerous mistakes of a special sort. Hume, in a footnote to this passage, says Cicero would have no patience with "narrow systems" that limit what can be called virtues to qualities of the will, excluding abilities such as wisdom, and strength and invention of intellect. Many of Hume's virtues are not motives; some are abilities and habits of action, and some, such as serenity and patience, are habits of reaction. Some, like considerate forgetting of the last shared debauch, involve both abilities and motives. Hume certainly does not limit virtues to approved *motives,* but lets in a large class of abilities, including wit and charm. Nor is he concerned to sharply separate virtues from each other. He has many virtue names that overlap in what they cover, as do prudence and honesty. Frugality and discretion are other forms of prudence. Generosity is a variant of benevolence, as is compassion. Many of Hume's "natural abilities" overlap each other, and he is no more committed to the separateness of each virtue than he is to the unity of all virtues. His undoubted maxim demanded that some natural human propensity be expressed in the approved act, but in the case of conscientious rule obedience—say, observing the highway code—many such natural propensities can come in: our mighty addiction to general rules, our pleasure in the game alone, our cautious self-interest or prudence in avoiding not merely collision, but also detection as a rule-breaker. So in the case of honesty, some may have made it an ingrained habit, while others have to work out the costs and benefits, have to discern their "strong interest" in justice before they pay their taxes, or their other debts, while yet others are honest because dishonesty is too risky. There are many explanations of honest behavior, and many human propensities expressed in it. Not all of them are especially admirable, but neither are they so shameful. Shaftesbury expressed distaste for the person whose main reason for honesty was fear of the gibbet, but he was a very fastidious moralist. As Hume says, when explaining how self-interest motivates acceptance of property rules, "For whether the passion of self-interest be esteem'd vicious or virtuous, 'tis all of a case, since it itself restrains it: so that if it be virtuous men become social by their virtue; if vicious, their vice has the same effect" (T 492). As quite often in these contexts, echoes of Mandeville can be heard in Hume's words. Avidity may be a private vice, but its self-regulation yields public virtue.

In fact, I do not think that Hume believes that the natural self-interest of his pre-justice people is necessarily a private vice. We can sympathize with a parent's wish to increase her store of grain to feed her family throughout the winter. Hume attributes to these pre-justice people not ruthless rapacity, but self-interest in the form of "confin'd generosity," given material scarcity. Qua prudent concern for the future, it is approvable. Qua generous to family, it is also approvable. Qua leading to violent seizure, it is deplorable, and that is why measures have to be taken to prevent that. What motivates the acceptance of the new scheme of settled rights and voluntary transfer of them is enlightened self-interest, and qua enlightened, and "reasonable," that self-interest too is approvable.

Why did Hume not say that a desire for equity, as well as reasoned self-interest, is among the natural, morally approved motives for keeping the rules of social artifices we are benefiting from? Desire for equity would seem to be one which would come into play quite naturally, whenever we are tempted to act in ways we hope others will refrain from. Equity as fairness does rule out self-serving exceptions of oneself from rules one depends on others keeping. (One might call it the Kantian virtue.) The sensible knave makes an exception of himself, and depends on others not following his example. Does the unchaste wife depend on others not following her example? Not so clearly. Does she expect her husband to be chaste? Not according to Hume. In her case, perhaps she has to ask if she expects other wives, her own mother, say, or her daughter, to be chaste. If she does not, as many of Hume's women friends in Paris clearly did not, then there may be nothing unfair, or in any other way wrong, in what she does. It is unclear what motive (or motives) to chastity Hume thinks is (or are) morally approved, as he is clearly rather scathing about the "preceding backwardness" to sexual advances which he takes induced modesty to involve. As an artificial social virtue, chastity seems to lack that vault-like structure the other artificial virtues have, since one woman's occasional lapses from chastity do not bring any social practice into danger of collapse.[21] Hume may be

---

21. Of course, one dishonest act does not do this either, as Hume concedes in his discussion of the sensible knave. The sensible adulteress, however, injures only the "vault" of her own trustworthiness, not that of other women. It is an interesting question whether the artifice of marriage is injured when women become more promiscuous. New Zealand women are said to be the most promiscuous in the world, and many are avoiding marriage at present, whether because no man wants a promiscuous wife, or because no promiscuous woman wants a hus-

wrong in thinking female modesty and chastity to be "conspicuous instances of the operations of those principles, which I have insisted on"
(T 570).Conspicuous instances of the non-natural, maybe, but conspicuous examples of the self-interested adoption of a social scheme in
which some passion restrains itself, the better to satisfy itself, not so obviously. If any passion restrains itself in marriage, as Hume construes it,
it is sexual love, but it is the care of children, not a better sex life, and
mothers' wish that their children get a father's as well as a mother's care,
which is the rationale he gives for the institution of marriage. Nor is it
clear that uniformity of behavior in this respect is needed. Society contains, quite harmoniously, some strictly faithful couples, some couples
where the wife is faithful, the husband not, and some with "open marriages," as well as with the toleration of prostitution. And, as Hume in
his essays pointed out, the deal women get from marriage with a double
standard can scarcely be called fair. The approved motive for female
chastity, whatever it is, can rarely be a sense of equity, since the system
Hume describes seems so obviously unfair. I think Hume took the approved motive for female chastity to be concern for their children's care,
combined with marital love, even of husbands who were not so chaste. If
the case were really to be like the other conventions and other artificial
virtues, then the approved motive would be respect for the husband's
rights. But since the woman has no return rights of the same kind, the
case is not one where one's own rights and those which one respects are
entwined with one another in one cooperative scheme, where there is
some "degree of equality" (E 190). To use Hume's words when he says
that justice requires some "degree of equality," marriage with a double
standard is an "unequal confederacy." He goes on to consider if women
are full partners in the conventions of justice, but significantly does not
include marriage as part of "justice" in *EPM*. It is touched on, briefly, under "political society," and its rationale is there clearly said to be "the
long and helpless infancy of man," and the need to give fathers a way of
knowing who are their own children, to whom they owe care. In the
*Treatise* chastity is an artificial virtue, included in Part 2, "Of justice and
injustice," where these are taken as conformity and nonconformity to
socially useful rules or conventions. In *EPM* it is part of the grimmer re-

band, is not so clear. There are many single mothers, and many more career women than when
marriage was the norm for women.

ality of political society, along with boxing matches and other "sportive wars." I think Hume never, in his theories, really did justice to mothers, despite his obvious love for and admiration of his own mother. Agnes Galbraith haunts his account of chastity.[22]

Hume is initially unclear just how he thinks that seeing justice as an artificial virtue solves the puzzle about what motive there can be to just acts, whether "sophistry and reasoning in a circle" is allowed, with artifices. As Frank Snare put it, the account of convention in the *Treatise* Book 2, Part 2, Section 2 seems "the wrong solution to the wrong problem."[23] (The wrong problem is that of finding a natural motive, when the only right motive, in these cases, is regard to justice. Snare also sees the same account of convention, and our approbation of conformity to it, as "the right solution to the right problem," where the right problem is specifying the sentiment which approves of just conduct.) The idea of property and that of honesty are mutually implying, as are those of promise and expected fidelity to them. At T 483 Hume may be conceding, as Rachel Cohon thinks he is,[24] that only with natural virtues must there be a motive separate from a sense of duty, that with social artifices, duty or regard to justice may come to be all the motive there is, or should be, in addition to the self-interest first served by adoption of the new scheme, an interest that lasts, but can be hard to discern as time goes on, as inequalities of property increase, and the honest may seem to become the cullies of their integrity. When discussing promises, and saying he is repeating the pattern of argument that proved justice to be an artificial virtue, he goes on:

> No action can be requir'd of us as our duty, unless there be implanted in human nature some actuating passion or motive, capable of producing the action. *This motive cannot be a sense of duty.* A sense of duty presupposes an antecedent obligation: And where an action is not requir'd by any natural passion, it cannot be requir'd by any natural obligation, since it may be omitted without proving any defect or imperfection in the mind and temper, and consequently without any vice. *Now 'tis evi-*

22. Agnes Galbraith in 1734 named David Hume to the Chirnside presbytery as the father of one of her illegitimate children. He had left home by then, and she wore sackcloth and was put in the pillory. See E. C. Mossner, *Life of David Hume* (Oxford, 1980), 81–83.

23. Frank Snare, *Moral, Motivation, and Convention* (Cambridge, 1991), ch. 7.

24. Tito Magri, in "Hume's Justice," forthcoming in the *Cambridge Companion to Hume's Treatise*, edited by Donald Ainslie, also takes this view, taking the artificiality of justice as ruling out there being a natural motive to it.

*dent we have no motive leading us to the performance of promises, distinct from a sense of duty.* If we thought, that promises had no moral obligation, we shou'd never feel any inclination to perform them. (T 518, my emphases)[25]

This passage seems both to deny and to affirm that a sense of moral obligation, of duty, can motivate promise-keeping. Understandably do commentators like Snare think Hume has muddled up several problems for his sentimentalist and naturalist account of morality. Honest acts, and promise-keeping, are "hard cases" for such a theory, especially if, like Norton and Cohon, we confuse the approved motivation for such acts with our reasons for approbation. The passage also seems to use "natural obligation" in a way different from formerly, when natural obligations arose from the "three fundamental laws of nature," namely, three socially beneficial conventions creating property, and regulating its transfer by consent and contract. They had redirected and enlightened self-interest as their initial motive. Here "natural obligations" seem to be for such things as gratitude for favors and care of offspring, where there is a natural passion prompting most people to do these things. The passage does not actually require a "natural motive" to promise-keeping, but some "actuating principle" in our nature. This could be our sensible willingness to adopt beneficial cooperative schemes, our enlightened self-interest. But this passage also seems to leave out of account both the motive of self-interest or prudence there always is for keeping promises, even if it is not always there to prevent easy unobserved theft, and also some natural concern for the one who has been induced to rely on one. In a promise, according to Hume, one subjects oneself to the severe conditional penalty of never being trusted again. There may be thefts one reasonably thinks one will get away with, but broken promises (unless made to those on their deathbed) are bound to be known to the victim, so the penalty of loss of trust, with the victim at least, and with many more if she spreads the word, will be automatically incurred. When Hume sums the matter up again, in the next section, looking back at

25. This is the passage that David Gauthier begins with, in his "Artificial Virtues and the Sensible Knave," *Hume: Moral and Political Philosophy*, edited by Rachel Cohon (Ashgate, 2001), 311–339, and he notes all the oddities of the passage, the use of "natural obligation" to contrast with "artificial" rather than with "moral" obligation, the clashing claims about a sense of duty as a possible motive, the ignoring of the self-interested reason not to break promises, given that the penalty for that is withdrawal of trust.

what makes justice, honesty, and fidelity artificial, and how these virtues differ from natural ones, in such matters as not admitting of degrees, and varying in their details from time to time, and from society to society, he ends:

> Upon the whole, we are to consider this distinction betwixt justice and injustice, as having two different foundations, viz. that of *self-interest* when men observe, that 'tis impossible to live in society without restraining themselves by certain rules; and that of *morality,* when this interest is observ'd to be common to all mankind, and men receive a pleasure from the view of such actions as tend to the peace of society, and an uneasiness from such as are contrary to it. 'Tis the voluntary conventions and artifice of men, which make the first interest take place; and therefore those laws of justice are to be consider'd as artificial. (T 533)

This passage clearly separates the approved self-interested willingness to conform to conventions with the reasons for approving such willingness, so separates the two problems Snare wanted separated, but it overlooks the special self-interest there always is in not becoming known as a thief or promise-breaker, an interest especially strong in the case of promises, where wrongful behavior can scarcely go undetected. Hume goes on to say that the sense of morality in the observance of these rules is certainly augmented by "a new *artifice,*" that contrived by parents and politicians, to give us "a sense of honour and duty in the strict regulation of our actions with regard to the property of others" (ibid.). These extra artifices will be needed more to get one to be honest than to get one to keep one's promises, given promises' inbuilt penalty for breach of obligation.[26] This passage seems to allow that there can, at least in the gullible, be an artificially induced sense of duty for duty's sake, just what his "undoubted maxim" had seemed to rule out. (The undoubted maxim seems to have become doubted in *EPM,* or at any rate is not pronounced.) But why cannot the approved motive to justice be duty for *equity's* sake? If equity is a natural virtue, then there is an approved natural desire not to get more than one's fair share, in any matter, property included. And the conclusion of the argument in T 483 is couched in terms of equity:

---

26. Once magistrates are invented to enforce obligations, as I point out in Chapter 5, theft is dealt with by the criminal courts, breach of contract by the civil courts. We need magistrates to get the detection and punishment of thieves, but contract-breakers present less of a detection problem, and in a sense no penalty problem, as long as their record follows them.

"From all this it follows that we have naturally no real or universal motive for observing the laws of equity but the very equity and merit of that observation."

How did equity get so entangled with justice? It is the concern for merit, not equity, in the last passage, which leads to the sophistry and circularity. To have merit, we must have an approved motive, and this cannot be just the wish to have merit, to be dutiful. But regard for equity is an approved motive, which shows itself quite naturally, outside the sphere of artifices, say, in parents' treatment of their several children. It rules out unfair favoritism, including favoring oneself. It will also come into play once there are social regulations, preventing a person from making an exception either of herself, or of her loved ones. Johnson gives "justice" as his first sense of "equity," "impartiality" as the second, and as the third, what the Courts of Chancery administer. Hume seems to vacillate between the first two senses, but it is no accident that they became associated, since one main place for equity as impartiality will be in the observation, decision, and execution of rules of justice.

In *EPM* Hume still speaks of "justice or equity." He does not repeat the puzzle about the motive to justice, nor endorse the "undoubted maxim" that all approbation is of natural motives. He does not call justice "artificial," and in a footnote to Appendix 3 says it is a purely verbal question whether to call it natural or artificial. It is contrived, but it is natural for us to contrive property conventions, contract, and some form of marriage, and all societies do. He does not there say exactly what motive is the approved motive to conformity to the rules of justice. Perhaps he thinks several could be approved. To return to the *Treatise*, "*Let those motives, therefore, be what they will*, they must accommodate themselves to circumstances, and must admit of all the variations, which human affairs, in their incessant revolutions are susceptible of" (T 533, my emphasis). These incessant revolutions are more common with the artifice of government, and of marriage, than with property and contract, but the rules concerning all of them can change. In *EPM* Hume says that the ideas of inheritance and contract are "infinitely complicated," and it takes hundreds of volumes of law, and thousands of commentaries on them, to attempt to define them (E 202).

If we suppose Hume really does take equity to be a natural social virtue, perhaps dependent on our capacity for sympathy with any who do not get a fair deal, then the motive to equitable conduct would be a desire that each get an equitable share of some distributed good. This natural virtue will get new application whenever there is a social scheme decreeing individual rights. To be minimally equitable in such a context is to let each get what the scheme allocates him. By most established schemes, it is not the saints who inherit the earth—indeed, they may not get anything in any way fitting. (As Hume relates in *EPM* Appendix 3, Cyrus, young and inexperienced, tried to ensure that tall boys got long tunics, short ones shorter ones, but soon gave up on that.) To conform to existent property conventions, or existent marriage conventions, one must be willing to say, "That's the deal," and make do with it. This is prudent and sensible, but scarcely noble and public-spirited. The public-spirited person makes donations to public hospitals and other public institutions; she must do a lot more than merely keep herself from any danger of arrest as a thief, from being sued as a contract-breaker, or divorced on grounds of infidelity. As Hume says in ruling the public interest out as a motive for repaying a loan, "That is a motive too remote and sublime to affect the generality of mankind" (T 481), so it cannot be the motive to "common honesty."

Hume in *EPM* says, "Qualities often derive their merit from complicated sources. *Honesty, fidelity, truth,* are praised for their immediate tendency to promote the interests of society; but after these virtues are established upon this foundation, they are also considered as advantageous to the person himself, and as the source of that trust and confidence, which alone give a man any consideration in life. One becomes contemptible, no less than odious, when he forgets the duty, which, in this particular, he owes himself as well as society" (E 238). This repeats the *Treatise* claim that it is society's interest that makes one *praise* conformity to its rules, but not concern for that interest that must motivate the honest person, and be the motive which is approved. He adds that new artifices of upbringing may bolster the self-interest there always was in conformity, by making a person want to be seen as trustworthy, to avoid being found odious or contemptible. Hume now treats the artifices of educators as part of the whole social contrivance—since in *EPM* he is avoiding the offensive Hobbesian term "artificial," he need not sharply distinguish the original artifice of property, or promise, from the "new" supplementary artifices of politicians and educators, which make a person feel he cannot, for his own sake, afford to disregard society's rules in these matters. He speaks of laws and statutes regarding property, as if government is part of the whole deal which makes justice possible. Could the complicated sources of justice, as the just man displays it, include a passion for equity? Marcia Barron, in her challenging essay "Hume's Noble Lie," writes, "No natural virtue would impel an agent who wanted the rules of justice to be inflexible to adhere rigidly to them."[27] This ignores the natural virtue of equity. But it should not be ignored. Hume himself may have ignored it when it could have solved his puzzle, but just what the role of that puzzle was is itself a puzzle.

Some think he did not want his puzzle solved,[28] that its point was that justice is not a real individual virtue at all, but is simply artificially induced conformity to socially useful rules, where there need be no real virtue at all, no meritorious character trait, shown in such docility. I think Hume did think he had solved his puzzle, by his talk of "oblique" and enlightened self-interest in willingness to cooperate with others in a beneficial scheme for the recognition of property rights, a version of the virtue Hobbes called being "tractable," and this is confirmed by his discussion of the clash of immediate and remote goods when he comes to say why magistrates are invented. Equity is connected with such reasonable cooperativeness: it rules out taking advantages of the social scheme without doing one's part in it. In the loan repayment case, it is unfair to the honest but otherwise possibly nonadmirable miser to keep what is rightly his, however much good one might do with the withheld funds. It is also unfair to all those others who do repay their loans. Qua debt, it is fair to repay it. Qua what will further impoverish a poor man to repay, it is money that a benevolent person might wish did not have to be repaid, and, if really benevolent, will help him to repay. Benevolence and equity can clash, just as Cato's justice offends the tenderhearted.

Hume has several related terms in his moral vocabulary: justice, equity, honesty, truth, trustworthiness, veracity, integrity, fidelity. The last is especially interesting, as Hume understands it to take several forms, for several sorts of "agreement" there can be between persons. There is the "fidelity of printers and copyists," the "constancy" of good friends, there is "fidelity" to promises and contracts, and there is "fidelity to the marriage bed." Fidelity to promises and contract comes in, as Hume

27. Marcia Barron, "Hume's Noble Lie," in Cohon, ed., *Hume: Moral and Political Philosophy*, 288.

28. See James Harris, "Hume on the Obligation to Justice: The Argument of T 3.2.1," talk to Hume Society, 2008, and its later version, *Hume's Definition of Justice* (forthcoming).

presents it, as an extension of the reciprocal services that good friends perform for each other, where the first performer acts "without any prospect of advantage," and her friend then "recompenses" her by similar services. Being a good friend was a natural virtue before fidelity was given its artificial extension with the invention of contract, and of marriage. Trustworthiness also gets an artificial extension by the artifices, all of which enlarge the field of sensible trust, and give opportunities also for new forms of untrustworthiness. Friends and family members would have trusted each other on many matters, before the hypothetical first introduction of property conventions and conventions for transferal of property and making contracts. Before them, nothing counted as theft or breach of promise, but of course if a trusted family member destroyed one's valued possession—say, burned one's coat—one would feel let down, just as one would later if some stranger, let into one's house, stole it, and just as lovers may have felt let down if deserted, especially when there were children to be cared for. Trust is extended by artifices, but not created by them. What artifices create are rights, and so new grounds for trust, as well as new areas where trust can exist. Also created are new opportunities for untrustworthiness, for new sorts of knavery. Does equity in a similar way get extended from its natural contexts, such as the natural family, to justice as honesty in matters of property?

Honesty in matters of property is reciprocity, doing one's bit in a scheme from which one benefits, not denying others the benefit one values—namely, security of possession. "Honesty" has application to the way we speak, as well as to our respect for others' property rights, speaking to others in the way we hope they speak to us. Hume usually terms honesty in speech "veracity," not "honesty," but it may also be that "truth" which, like honesty and fidelity, has complicated sources. If Hume sees the willingness to abide by the rules of accepted or "agreed" society-wide schemes of cooperation as always an extension of other more natural virtues of trustworthiness or "truth," virtues such as equity or fairness, not excluding some unfairly from the benefits of some cooperative practice, constancy and reliability in friendships, and in community relationships, and avoidance of deceit and lies, then any or all of these could come in to help provide the approved motives for justice. Many thieves are sneak-thieves. The one who breaks a promise may all along have intended to do so, so gave a lying promise. Like the unreliable copyist, his later acts do not square with the content of his original undertaking. The person who acts dishonestly takes unfair advantage of others' trust, and of their honesty, which is depended upon to keep the "vault" of justice from collapse. All Hume's artificial virtues are forms of trustworthiness, since all his artifices extend the areas in which trust of others is not foolhardy.

Hume's account of justice has been criticized, for example, by Raphael,[29] but before him by Broad[30] and Balfour,[31] for leaving out traditional concerns for some degree of equality, desert, and fairness, for making it no more than social docility to a distributive scheme, adopted in conditions of moderate scarcity. Broad thought it should apply also in extreme scarcity, getting us to share the last biscuit in a life boat before we all starve. Rawls[32] sees justice as fairness, as being able to stand apart from actual social schemes and criticize them. He takes over Hume's account of the circumstances of justice—moderate material scarcity and confined generosity—but thinks some social responses to these, in the form of recognized rights, may be unfair and so unjust. Hume cannot call them unjust, but he has the demands of equity in reserve. Since it is a virtue that applies to all distributive actions, it can come in not just to prevent a person from disregarding the existent rights of others, in her own favor, but also from attempting to reform the distributive scheme, in the name of greater equality, and of equity. Just as the approved motives to honesty and contract-keeping can include fairness, constancy, and truth, Hume's cautious, jealous virtue, "justice," needs equity, both for its own working, and for its reflective reform. The sensible knave has the virtue of good sense, so will not want to undermine any valuable social practice. He simply wants to exempt himself from its costs, as some try to cheat on their taxes, and do not bother to recycle their bottles. What all such secret rule-breakers lack is not only the artificial virtue Hume calls "justice," but also the natural virtue of equity. Jiwei Ci compares Hume's version of justice, as cautious and jealous, and tied to self-interest, with other versions, such as Schopenhauer's, which give it a nobler and less conditional character. Jiwei Ci has no entry for equity in his

29. David Daiches Raphael, *Concepts of Justice* (Clarendon, 2001), 87ff. Raphael notes, 99, that a sense of fairness should have been at least considered by Hume as a natural motive for just acts.

30. C. D. Broad, *Five Types of Ethical Theory* (Kegan Paul, 1944), 98.

31. James Balfour, *A Delineation of the Nature and Obligation of Morality* (Hamilton, Balfour and Neill, 1753; reprint Thoemmes Antiquarian, 1989), 80–81.

32. John Rawls, *A Theory of Justice* (Harvard, 1971).

index. But because of its tie with equity, Hume's justice can become less cautious, his just man concerned with the rights of others, not merely jealous of his own. When Henry VII enacted a law forbidding the abduction of women, he acted in the name of both justice and equity. Jiwei Ci sees justice as sometimes seeming to have an unconditional aspect, as a conscious virtue, as well as having its seeds and source in a conditional willingness to restrain immediate self-interest, provided others do likewise. Hume kept what he termed "justice" conditional, but the equity which he paired with it is more unconditional in its demands, both for self, and for others.

I have not answered my question of why Hume does not take our natural demand for equity to give us an approvable reason to recognize others' property rights, and so pay our debts. One plausible answer is that in that first section of *Treatise* Book 3, Part 2 he is merely preparing the ground for the second and subsequent sections, so wants there to be an unsolved puzzle. He may take it that only by understanding how "artificial" property is can we distinguish it from the mere fact of "possession," itself not easy to define. We need to appeal to a "convention" which makes the distinction between what is in our possession and what we *own*, to see why we should pay our debts. We can then, armed with this distinction between the fact of possession and the right of property, say that the poor debtor may have, in his *possession,* the funds to pay his debt, or the goods he agreed to forfeit, if he did not repay in time, but the *right* to those funds, or those goods—the *property*—lies with the lender, once the loan is due. Hume uses the concept of property in phrasing his initial question, *"Wherein lies this honesty and justice, which you find in restoring a loan, and abstaining from the property of others?"* (T 480), but he leaves the clarification of the distinction between possession and property for the next section, and that on binding agreements to the next but one. The conclusion of the first section is simply that we will not understand honesty until we understand social artifice, oblique self-interest, and convention. It would have spoiled the drama of his account if there had been an easy answer to the question of what natural motive we have to repay loans. And even if he had invoked equity, it would not have explained what honesty is, as honesty is only one variant of equity, and its special features require the account of convention, to which he is leading up. In that account, temporary possessions are all we have, before the convention, and so its own provisions refer to possessions, not to property. Property comes into existence only *after* possession has been made stable, by the convention. "After this convention is enter'd into, and every one has acquir'd a stability in his *possessions,* there immediately arise the ideas of justice and injustice, as also those of property, right, and obligation" (T 490–491, my emphasis).

In *EPM,* all that drama is dispensed with, and there is no conjectural origin of justice given, no story about how we first agree to make possessions stable, so invent property, then agree to make them less stable, so agree to transfer by owner's consent. (Loan would not be possible till after this second convention, if then, since it takes contract for the precise interest and length of loan to be specified, and the forfeit agreed on.) Hume's original *Treatise* puzzle, about what is approvable in repaying a loan, does not really get answered till three conventions have been explained, and it is interesting that only when Hume looks back on all these artifices, in his "Some farther reflections on justice and injustice," does he again refer to anything like a loan. The man who hires a horse for a day is like the borrower who is loaned funds, at some agreed interest, for an agreed time. The lender, and the horse-owner, are the "proprietors," and the rights of the borrower and hirer, however "entire," are of limited temporal duration. In *EPM* we get no sequential story about which invention comes first, and "laws" of property, statutes as well as customs, are appealed to, to explain the special features of justice as a virtue. It is a package deal, of property, its transfer by consent and by contract, along with magistrates to settle quarrels, that we are offered as "justice" in *EPM.* Indeed, it is only in Appendix 3 that fidelity to promises is separated out from the rest of "justice." We tend to read the *Treatise* into *EPM,*[33] but in fact the treatment of justice there is very different—no puzzle about motive, no maxim about approval being of some natural motive, no sequential story. It is almost as if magistrates and statutes are there to "partition" shared possession or property[34] into private

33. I say "we" advisedly. For the continuities between the two accounts, see Chapter 10, "Incomparably the Best?"

34. *EPM* shows some implicit recognition that there can be common ownership, "community of goods" in some families, and Hume speculates that the "rules to preserve peace and order" of extended families and tribes might precede that of larger groups. In some such groups, such as the Maori, community of goods was the norm, before Europeans appeared with their "selfish" insistence on private property rights. Hume says selfishness will always reassert itself over the communitarian ideals of "imprudent fanatics." He is thinking of the English fanatics at the time of the Commonwealth, not of Polynesian tribes, in these somewhat insular reflections.

property, and prosecute "injury," right from the start, although this suggestion is taken back at the beginning of Section 4, when the theoretical possibility of "natural justice," accepted customs without magistrates to interpret and enforce them, is recognized. In the *Treatise*, that possibility gives the story line of the whole conjectural history "Of justice and injustice." What is emphasized in *EPM* is the utility of justice, the difference between it and benevolence, the vault-like nature of the good it brings, the circumstances of justice (when taken as "partition of property"), the fact that cooperative conventions are involved, and that some, such as women and slaves, may be neither parties to them nor beneficiaries from them. Hume might at this point have spoken of the inequity of such exclusionary schemes, but he does not. He speaks instead of inhumanity and tyranny. Equity is bracketed with justice, in *EPM*, not given any role in criticizing the provisions of social schemes, or laws. This seems to me a real fault in Hume's *EPM* account of justice and equity. Justice as he there construes it is "a cautious, jealous virtue," but equity is not so jealous, and could "enlarge"[35] our understanding of justice. Did he not invoke equity to explain why most of us are honest because he was well aware how low a degree of equity our property conventions possess, and so had some sympathy with the Robin Hoods of this world, who think equity demands that we take from the rich, to give to the poor? He himself was reputed to be generous to the needy, but he was certainly, in his writings, no prophet for socialism. Still, if he thought there was any inequity in the property conventions he lived under (that Ninewells went to his older brother, was not shared between the three children of the former owner, for example), then to appeal to a sense of equity to motivate respect for private property rights would raise awkward questions about the degree of equity in the established property rules. But why bring equity in at all, in the discussion of justice, if its mention is embarrassing? I reiterate what I suggested earlier, that minimal equity does require that we not deny anyone his customary rights, for that would be invidious. There is not much equity involved in Humean justice, as sketched in the *Treatise*, but there would certainly be

---

Maori, however, could be just as "jealous" of their group rights as any individual is of his private rights.

35. Hume speaks of the gradual "enlargement" of our views of justice from the rules of one small community to those of a larger group at E 192. I discuss other enlargements in the following chapter.

inequity in denying the moneylender the repayment of the debt due to him.[36]

By nature we have some concern for equity. So when we adopt conventions determining property rights, or contractual rights, or rights to govern, or marital rights, we will have some inclination to ask if the distribution of these rights is fair and equitable. Rawls saw justice as fairness. Hume chose to keep fairness or equity as a value relevant to what he calls "the distribution of justice," demanding, at the least, that each get what the established scheme allots him, at the most, what an improved scheme, reformed in the name of equity, would allot him. Artifice enlarges trust, but artifices like polygamous marriage and feudal property laws can also oppress. Natural regard for equity requires periodic checks on traditional rights, on what Hume terms justice, just as the English courts of equity adjusted the rulings of the courts of justice, and in Hume's perfect commonwealth any emergent inequalities are to be corrected every hundred years. That is a little infrequent for equity to have its say, and if, as I have suggested, some regard for it can help motivate common honesty, and if its voice is regularly heard in any family, or any classroom, then its tones may not be at all unfamiliar. And they surely should be regularly listened to.

36. I discuss this case in Chapter 1, "A Solemn Bonfire? Hume on Loan Repayment."

4

# Hume's Enlargement of His Conception of Justice

We are, therefore, to look upon all the vast apparatus of our
government as having, ultimately, no other purpose but the
distribution of justice, or, in other words, the support of twelve judges.
—*Hume, "Of the origin of government," Es 37*

In the *Treatise* Hume has a very narrow notion of justice, as comprising
merely honesty in property matters, and fidelity to promises and contracts.[1] Refraining from assaulting or killing a person is not included in
it, any more than is distributive justice in the usual sense of a fair share
of publicly disbursed benefits and burdens, or criminal justice—namely,
being arrested only with warrant, getting a fair trial, and, if found guilty,
a fair sentence. This undue emphasis on security of property is slightly
modified in his *Enquiry Concerning the Principles of Morals (EPM)*, where
being just comes to mean keeping the law, and informal precursors to
law, on all matters, including respect for others' persons as well as their
property. Hume writes, at E 187, that a law-breaker may be punished in
his "goods and person: that is, the ordinary rules of justice are, with regard to him, suspended for a moment, and it becomes equitable to inflict
on him, for the *benefit* of society, what otherwise he could not suffer
without wrong or injury." Rules of justice and equity have here come to
include rules against assault and confinement. Other examples Hume
gives of what may be unlawful, by local custom, include eating meat on
Friday, building a house across the river from where one is permitted to,

1. Duncan Forbes, *Hume's Philosophical Politics* (Cambridge, 1975), 89, points out that
Hume is giving a conjectural history of which social conventions were first adopted, so does
not need, for his purposes in the *Treatise,* to go on to look at later adopted conventions.

83

as well as theft of a coat or horse. Where Hume's first account of justice supposed that customs or conventions grew up in a definite order, property before promise and contract, and all of these before official law-declarers and law-enforcers, *EPM* is noncommittal on that. Praetors, chancellors, and juries are mentioned in the section on justice, so magistrates seem to have become coeval with property rules and rules against assault. Marriage as a custom may be present in a wandering tribe with communal possessions, and no possessions in land, and leaders may emerge in battle, and go on to serve as rule-enforcers. As the first appendix to Hume's *History* later allowed, Germanic tribes may have had leaders before much private property. Even a Moses, a leader of wandering tribes who emerges from the mountain with a tablet of laws which he then enforces, becomes a possibility in *EPM*. But allegiance to leaders, whether military or civilian or religious, was never included by Hume in what justice comprised. Keeping the rules they enforce is what justice is, and he thinks that usually those rules will be recognized before leadership is. And of course those rules usually forbid insult and injury against persons, as well as destruction and theft of property. "Thou shalt not kill" was high on Moses's list. Not that we call murderers unjust. What we would call unjust is denying protection of the law against murder to some group, such as gypsies or Jews in Nazi Germany, or letting some, such as the rich and influential, get away with murder. Justice, as we understand it, requires that there be *equal* protection against murderers, as well as against thieves and cheats, and equal prosecution of all lawbreakers.

Another advance in *EPM* is the reference to some basic equality, that of power to make resentment felt, in all those covered by the rules of justice. This point is made in answering the question of who is owed justice, if any are excluded from the advantages it is claimed to give those it protects. Animals are excluded, and some ruthless colonizers have tried to exclude some "barbarous Indians" (E 191), sometimes tried to enslave them and so to treat them *as* property. Some have also tried this with women, presumably the most obvious case of rational creatures "intermingled with men" who are deemed of "inferior strength, both of body and mind," so unable to show resistance to bad treatment. Hume goes on to say that women "are commonly able to break the confederacy" and then points out their special role in enabling a man to know he has "propagated his kind." Self-sufficient creatures who could singly propagate their kind would not need the justice Hume has outlined, nor be capable of it. So, if women are ruled out, it is only children, or domestic slaves, who could possibly be those rational creatures intermingled with men, of such inferior strength that the rules of justice may be suspended with regard to them, although Hume does not mention children. The whole passage is enigmatic in intent. Hume takes "kindness to children" to be instinctive in our species, so he will not expect fathers to exert "severe tyranny" over their children, but such tyranny has of course often been exerted, as it has also over women. Hume knows that there have been times and societies when "the female sex are reduced to like slavery" (like to that inflicted on "inferior" races), so his claims about their power to break "unequal confederacies" is not implausibly taken, as I have in the past taken it, as a call to women to break free of their social shackles. The whole passage is a great advance over the *Treatise* for raising the question of whom justice serves, and for recognizing resentment of bad treatment, and power to make that resentment felt, as almost a third circumstance of justice—his discussion of it follows from his discussion of the other two. One implication of it is that if, say, in one household some "lordly master" maltreats both his hounds, who have insufficient power to make resentment felt, and his wife and children, who can make it felt, then the latter inhumane treatment counts as unjust, as well as inhumane, while that of the animals is inhumane but not unjust. The "confederacy" between man and dog is necessarily "unequal," but that with the rest of a man's family has at least the potential for equality.

That justice might seem to demand some approximation to equality of property is also acknowledged by Hume, in *EPM*. But he deems it too costly in other values. Even if we started with equal property, one person's superior industry and enterprise would soon give her more, and it would take "rigorous inquisition" and "severe jurisdiction" to stop inequality from developing, as well as such official interference deterring industry and so failing to encourage increase in wealth (E 194). At least Hume does see that great inequality is a *prima facie* reason for some redistributive measures, and mentions those of Sparta and Rome.[2]

2. Howard Sobel, in *Walls and Vaults* (Wiley, 2009), 202, says that he finds "*nothing* in Hume's texts that has anything to do with when social arrangements are just, fair or equitable." This seems to ignore not just the *History*, but also such texts as T 498, where Hume says that the experience necessary to bring about agreement to social practices that come to count as the conventions of justice, is that they be "infinitely advantageous to the whole and to every part" of society. Sobel would interpret this as a claim merely about the "origin" of justice, not an ongoing constraint on it.

Throughout the *History* Hume treats justice as including much of what we take it to include, not merely honesty and contract-keeping, but some approximation to equality of protection, and equality before the law in prosecution of law-breaking. It comes to be the subject matter of jurisprudence, discussed fairly extensively by Hume when looking at the achievements of Alfred, and of Edward I, "the English Justinian." I shall survey some of the *History's* references to justice, acts of justice, and acts of injustice, beginning with what Hume wrote first, the Stuart volumes, then working back through the Tudor volumes to the medieval, the last that he wrote. By the time he wrote his last essay, "Of the origin of government," what governments exist for is not simply to protect property rights and contractual rights, but to maintain twelve judges, and so protect all the rights the courts protect.

That there is such a thing as a right not to be dispossessed, or assaulted, or imprisoned without trial, for Hume, is always a matter of "artifice," of a society-wide agreement to recognize and protect such a right. Justice is an artificial virtue. At first he overconcentrated on the right not to be dispossessed, and the right not to be killed, or injured in ways other than dispossession, was slow to be carefully investigated by him, but in the *History* these wrongs certainly get acknowledged.[3] He refers at the end of Chapter 66 to James I's introduction of "justice" to Ireland, certainly not meaning introducing property rights, since, as noted earlier, what James did was change the traditional ones of "gavelkinde," whereby property, at the death of an owner, was shared between all his children, legitimate or not, then reshared out by the local chieftain if any of them died, so parcels of land diminished with rise in population, and no one had incentive to build on, or to improve what land he had, as its tenure was only temporary. James changed this for English customs (presumably including primogeniture) so that any improvements an owner made to his land would not be "so much lost labour." Justice here meant a fair return on one's labor, as well as fixed tenure of one's land. James also ended the practice of fines for killings, whereby each person,

---

3. Eugenio Lecaldano, in "Hume's Theory of Justice, or Artificial Virtue," in the Blackwell *Companion to Hume*, edited by Elizabeth S. Radcliffe (Blackwell, 2008), notes how justice for Hume did not include any rule against assault and murder, but says that the natural virtues of consideration and gentleness will prevent assault (270). They may not, however, prevent infliction of painless death, and I think Hume does take the rules about killing to be a matter of "convention," varying in content from group to group.

according to rank and sex, had an "eric" or price to be paid by his or her killer. Changing this "barbarous" custom was part of what counted as James's introduction of "justice." In another "laudable act of justice," James insisted on "the severity of the law" in Scotland when friends of Lord Sanquhir, who had murdered a fencing master, had tried to prevent his judicial sentence of death. So James's justice included insisting on the death sentence for murder, without fear or favor, and altering the property law so as to give incentive for improving land which one owned. Criminal justice, and the redesign of property laws so as to reward labor, since "who sees not, that whatever is produced or improved by a man's art and industry ought, for ever, be secured to him, in order to give encouragement to such *useful* habits and accomplishments?" (E 195), now get included under justice, the latter even at the cost of dispossessing illegitimate children of their time-honored rights. Hume seemed to mean his question in *EPM* as a rhetorical one, but the answer is that Brehon law in Ireland, with its gavelkinde, had not seen that truth. Nor indeed had Hume in the *Treatise,* when he dismissed Locke's claim that one owned one's own labor, and had a property right to anything one had mixed one's labor with, saying that this was figurative talk, and any improved value was better called "accession," which in any case presupposes that one already owned what one worked on, so talk of a right to one's own labor, and what it was mixed with, was a "needless circuit" (T 505, note).

Once wrongful death counts as an injustice, of course, English history becomes a long string of injustices, since many who ended on the scaffold or the gibbet can be seen as wrongly convicted, and of course many died at the hands of ordinary murderers. Sir Walter Raleigh, who had been sentenced to death under Elizabeth, for treason, had been thirteen years imprisoned in the Tower, but was freed by James to search for a fabled goldmine in Guiana. The sentence of death had been long delayed, and this had led to popular sympathy for the proud and once-hated Raleigh, whose original sentence now seemed not only harsh but also unjust. The expedition was unsuccessful in finding gold, and led to the sack of St. Thomas, at the mouth of the Orinoco River, thereby offending Spain. James was trying to arrange for his son to marry a Spanish princess, so was angry with Raleigh, and ordered his old sentence of death to be carried out. Raleigh, the soldier poet, met his death bravely, first testing the sharpness of the executioner's sword. "'Tis a sharp remedy, but a sure one for all ills." Hume refers to Raleigh's "unbroken magnanimity" and his "extensive genius." He writes: "No measure of James's reign was attended with more public dissatisfaction than the punishment of Sir Walter Raleigh. To execute a sentence, which had been originally so hard, which had been so long suspended, and which seemed to have been tacitly pardoned by conferring on him a new trust and commission, was deemed an instance of cruelty and injustice" (H 5.48.79). Hume refers to the principle of law which prevented Raleigh from being tried for his new offense, the sacking of St. Thomas, when still under sentence for treason, so the justice of his death depended on the rightfulness of the king's power to order an old sentence of death to be carried out.

The next possible miscarriage of justice in James's reign was his pardon to the Duke of Somerset, his former favorite, to whom he had given Latin lessons, who, with his wife, was found guilty of the slow poisoning of Somerset's old friend, Overbury. The court, headed by Sir Edward Coke, sentenced him to death, but James intervened. Hume excuses this case of unfair favor, on James's part, by talking of the remains of tenderness James felt for Somerset, his anxiety at his own role in having Somerset brought to trial, and his fear that Somerset might have revealed secrets from the days of their great mutual confidence, if he were not pardoned. "James was sensible, that the pardoning of so great a criminal . . . was of itself invidious" (H 5.47.63). Somerset had slowly and bunglingly killed the friend who had helped him with his illicit amours with his countess, while she, Frances Howard, was still the wife of another man, Essex, so Overbury knew too much. Somerset himself may have known too much about James's own amatory tastes, and may have threatened to tell all unless James pardoned him. Somerset and his countess lived into old age, Hume tells us, under one roof, with their former guilty passion turned to deadly mutual hatred, in "infamy and obscurity," but with a royal pension. This is a most unsavory bit of English history, but Hume seems almost to relish its salacious details. (He tells how, when the countess was divorcing her first husband, Essex, to marry her lover, Somerset, the grounds of divorce were that the marriage to Essex was unconsummated. Hume says this was true, as she had rebuffed him from the wedding night. But now, to procure a divorce, she had to prove herself a virgin, which of course, after her "guilty love" for Somerset, she was not. A young masked virgin was substituted for her, to undergo the examination by a "jury of matrons." The jury system had spread, it seems, from criminal law into matrimonial law.) Hume calls James's conduct in pardoning Somerset "invidious" rather than unjust. He prefers to see it as an act of mercy, a gesture to recognize his old tenderness for his favorite, rather than a straight miscarriage of justice. When he sums up James's character, he says it would be difficult to find, in all history, a reign "less illustrious, yet more unspotted and unblemished" (H 5.49.121). James's qualities, he later says, as if having second thoughts, were "sullied with weakness, and embellished by humanity" (122). He had shown "magnanimity" in protecting innocent Catholics after the gunpowder plot, so had shown humanity. But his concern for criminal justice was intermittent. He had begun by insisting that the full severity of the law against murder be carried out against a nobleman he did not know, Sanquhir, and had a delayed sentence carried out against the gallant and eloquent Raleigh, but he had not insisted on the death penalty when it was his own former intimate whose life was at stake. This particular expression of his fondness for young male favorites may surely be deemed verging on the "criminal and flagitious." Taking the birch to the young Robert Carre, who became the Duke of Somerset, to teach him Latin, was not, Hume judges, criminal. But pardoning Somerset, from the mixed motives of fear, guilt, and tenderness toward a former intimate, convicted of slow poisoning—that should, I think, count as "flagitious" as well as weak and "invidious."

The next wrongful death Hume considers at length is that of the Earl of Strafford, accused of treason, found guilty, and beheaded. Hume quotes at length from his speeches in his own defense, in which he accuses the court of trying him for offenses invented there and then, and for treating an accumulation of small offenses as "constructively" amounting to a capital one. "Where has this species of guilt lain so long concealed?" asks Strafford. "Where has this fire been so long buried, during so many centuries, that no smoke should appear, till it burst out at once, to consume me and my children? Better it were to live under no law at all . . . than fancy we have a law on which we can rely, and find at last that this law shall inflict a punishment precedent to the promulgation, and try us by maxims unheard of till the very moment of the prosecution" (H 5.54.316). Hume is clearly very moved by the manifest injustice of Strafford's trial and conviction, but the injustice of it has nothing whatever to do with the infringement of property rights. Criminal justice, and that formal principle of law, that promulgation of law precede prosecution for it breach, is what is at issue here. Hume refers to the "enormity" of Strafford's conviction and death, and the nobility with which he died, after writing to the king, who was irresolute about whether to try to help him, entreating him, for the sake of peace, not to intervene. Charles did not intervene, so Strafford died advising others: "Put not your trust in princes." (When he wrote his generous letter to the king, was he trusting him to disregard it?)

Hume also waxes indignant about the trial and death of Archbishop Laud. Earlier Laud had referred to his age and infirmity, when, from the Tower, he blessed his younger friend Strafford on his way to the scaffold. His trial for popery and treason showed "the same illegality of an accumulative crime and a constructive evidence" as that of Strafford, and to Hume showed how popular assemblies can be "exempt from the restraint of shame, so, when they overleap the bounds of the law, naturally break out into acts of the greatest tyranny and injustice" (H 5.57.457). Passages like this show that Hume, had he lived to know of it, would not have been surprised at the reign of terror in revolutionary France. The English "rebellion" did foreshadow the French Revolution. These two treason trials, of Strafford and Laud, led up that of Charles I himself, beheaded for tyranny and treason, for taking up arms against his parliament and his people. Hume allows that there are two sides to the matter of whether Charles had overstepped his authority enough to justify resistance, but points out that resistance need not mean dethronement, nor dethronement punishment by death. He seems to sympathize with those who thought Charles's trial was a mockery of justice, since, in a monarchy, only a monarch could charge anyone with treason. Whether or not one agrees with him about that, at least Hume is acknowledging that trials and verdicts can be unjust, against the rules that have been established in a community. He issues his usual warnings against attempting to say precisely when resistance to authorities is justified, and contrasts a clear case of tyranny, Nero, with that of Charles. "When we pass from the case of Nero to that of Charles, the great disproportion, or rather total contrariety of character immediately strikes us, and we stand astonished, that, among a civilized people, so much virtue could ever meet with so fatal a catastrophe" (H 5.59.545). It is "catastrophe," not injustice, that Charles suffered, and Hume knows that Charles's judges did have a case. When discussing the gunpowder plot to rid England of Stuart rule, he calls the plot a "nobler and more extensive plan of treason" than merely assassinating the king: to kill all his family and supporters in one explosion (H 5.46.26). Had Charles I merely been banished, his supporters would have rallied around him, and Jacobite rebellions would have been predictable, so the death of Charles may have seemed necessary—not as extensive a plan as the gunpowder plotters', but more extensive than mere banishment. Of course, Hume is ironical in his treatment of the gunpowder plot, but he does show some admiration for the character of Catesby and Digby, for their bravery and even for their clear-headed ruthlessness.

Hume speaks of Oliver Cromwell's "justice and clemency," once he was in power, that is, once his part in the "atrocious murder" of the king was over, and he became Lord Protector. He does not mean Cromwell's respect for property rights, which was not very noticeable in Ireland, when he seized Catholic lands after the 1641 massacre of Protestants, but his regard for due process in criminal proceedings. Later in his second Stuart volume, Hume gives much attention to the "violent and inhuman" Judge Jefferies, and his persecution both of popish plotters and of republican rebels like Algernon Sidney. When Sidney complained of the irregularity of the proceedings against him—for example, that only one witness deposed against him—he was told that the same irregularities had occurred in prosecuting the papists. Hume comments, "A topic more fit to condemn the one party than to justify the other" (H 6.69.436). That equal injustice was done both to papist plotters and republican rebels may have an element of equity, showing how even-handed was Judge Jefferies's violence, but clearly Hume sees all these proceedings under Charles II as part of what leads him to say of that king that his character was "dangerous to his people, and dishonourable to himself" (447). But the injustices to individuals during his reign, the executions and the near-fatal floggings of Titus Oates, had nothing to do with property rights, and everything to do with personal rights.

Similarly, in his Tudor history, the references to property rights fade in comparison with references to criminal justice, the constitutional rights of parliaments, and even the rights of dispossessed nuns. Henry VII is praised as a legislator, for improving policing, but is condemned for those of his laws which interfered with market forces in Britain. Hume writes, "The more simple ideas of order and equity are sufficient to guide a legislator in everything that regards the internal administration of justice. But the principles of commerce are much more complicated, and require long experience and deep reflection to be understood in any state" (H 3.26.74). Henry, wanting to encourage archery in England, had put a limit on the price of bows and arrows, thus ensuring "either that the people would be supplied with bad bows or none at all" (78). But he had also done such things as introduce a law forbidding the abduction of women, one of those measures Hume sees to be obviously required by equity. Refraining from interfering with the law of supply and demand is not so obvious. Between the two, perhaps, lies Henry's law forbidding his nobles to dress their retainers in livery. But Hume sees the power of the barons more effectively reduced by letting entail be broken, and so altering the property laws. Clearly the customary rules are not being regarded as sacrosanct by Hume.

Henry VIII also made a huge difference in England by dissolving the monasteries, and appropriating church land. Hume calls this unjust and even rapacious, but it is not included in what gets mentioned as his worst vices, when Hume sums up his reign. (The beheading of Ann Boleyn, on trumped-up charges, of the Countess of Salisbury, without any trial, and the deaths of Lambert, Fisher, and More, for daring to disagree with Henry on theology, were his worst injustices.) The state had always had some power to take land, for public purposes. As Hume says, "The good of mankind" is the only object of all law (E 192). The right of eminent domain, defended by Grotius, has a long history. But this supreme law, and the state's right of eminent domain, did not cover what Henry did when he took over a quarter of the cultivated land in England from the church, without compensating the former owners. That was an injustice, but abolishing canon law, so clergy were subjected to the same criminal justice as anyone else, for such crimes as murder, was an advance in justice. Hume does not regard the seizing of the church's land as a more important injustice than the travesties of criminal justice enacted under Henry. And one of his expressed concerns was for the fate of all those homeless evicted nuns, when the nunneries were seized. Some concern for their rights, including their welfare rights, is expressed. Monks might learn a useful trade, but what became of the nuns? An unmarried woman, if not of the servant class, "really had no rank which she properly filled: and a convent was a retreat both honourable and agreeable, from the inutility, and even want, that attended her situation" (H 3.3.252). How far we have come, from the monkish pseudo-virtues!

Middle- and upper-class nuns, turned out on the street, or sent back to their families, evoke Hume's sympathy, and inspire him to denounce Henry's rapacity and violence. In his antipapist frenzy, Henry had the shrine of Becket destroyed, and even enacted a treason trial of him. His bones were burned, his ashes cast in the air. Hume himself does not treat Becket very respectfully, but this travesty of justice, accusing a man's bones of treason, and finding them guilty, which set an example for the later posthumous beheading of Cromwell, makes Hume almost approve of Pope Clement's denunciation of Henry, and dispatch of his soul to hell, for "making war on the dead," a practice which even pagans had not engaged in. Henry dissolved 645 monasteries and 110 hospitals. Some favored abbots and priors were given royal pensions, and the revenue of one nunnery was bestowed on a woman "as a reward for making a pudding that happened to gratify his palate" (255). Hume seems to prefer the persecuted and dispossessed church to Henry, whose caprices and theological niceties kept his enemies guessing, and his parliaments cowed into submission. Henry ruled by fear and favor, and some, like Anne Boleyn and Catherine Howard, passed fairly quickly from the extreme of the latter to the extreme of the former.

Edward VI is said to have had "an attachment to equity and justice," by which Hume does not mean that, unlike his father, he seized no estates, but that, convinced by Norfolk that his sister Mary should not succeed him, because of her Catholic bigotry, he also excluded Elizabeth, for whom he had a tender affection, since the official ground of exclusion was the same: their declared illegitimacy. So the reluctant Lady Jane Grey was made to succeed him, for nine days, and was later beheaded at the command of Mary, thus becoming the only monarch of England before Charles I to die that way,[4] so Edward's "equity" in his treatment of his sisters had a heavy cost.

In his treatment of the reign of Elizabeth, Hume stresses her assumption of more rights than her predecessors had claimed, and also discusses her use of the Star Chamber, and Court of High Commission. He calls the former "illegal and despotic" and the latter a jurisdiction "yet more terrible." This was where trials for heresy were conducted, by

4. She was not yet crowned, so Charles was the only crowned monarch to die this way. Others, like Edward II, had met violent ends, but not been tried and found guilty of high treason, like Jane. Richard II had been charged and found guilty of tyranny, but was not beheaded. (He probably died of starvation.)

methods Hume calls "contrary to all the most simple ideas of justice and equity" (H 4.App 3.356). The simplest idea of justice has come to include a fair trial for any accused offense. So his Tudor volumes, like the Stuart volumes, show an inclusion of criminal justice in the simple core of the idea of justice, and even some attention to the welfare rights of unmarried women and dispossessed nuns. Property rights, even those of the church, are still included in justice, but certainly do not constitute its core.

In the medieval volumes there is an extended discussion of just what the Magna Carta did and did not achieve, as well as a detailing of the advances of criminal justice, from Alfred's invention of the jury system, and replacement of barbaric tests for guilt, like trial by water, with more reasonable measures, to Henry II's reform of the law regarding offenses against the person, which originally were treated either, if assault, as offenses against the king's peace, or, if manslaughter, as thefts of man-power or woman-power, with lesser fines for killing women than for killing men. It is hard for us, unless we are followers of Hammurabi, or Immanuel Kant, to see the death penalty for murder as an advance in justice, but the earlier system of simply fining the killer, and making the amount of the fine depend on the sex and status of the victim, certainly strikes most of us as barbaric. One would, however, expect one who had ever seriously believed justice was no more than respect for property rights to welcome this simplification of the criminal law, even at the cost of treating man-power as property. Hume, to his credit, does not, but enlarges his conception of justice to include appropriate differentiation of murder from theft, and fair punishment for each, after due process of law. He attends carefully to the improvements of Edward I, "a friend to law and justice," who reformed the provincial courts (H 2.13.142), and confirmed the provisions of the Great Charter. "The English nation have the honour of extorting, by their perseverance, this concession from the ablest, the most warlike, and the most ambitious of their princes" (122). Edward is condemned for his violations of equity and justice in his dealings with Scotland, and was guilty of "violent plunder and banishment of the Jews" (142), a measure which rebounded on him, as the Lombard merchants who took over the moneylending were thought to have robbed the Exchequer of 100,000 pounds.

Hume is often taken as having as one of his aims in his *History* to counter the Whig emphasis, in his own time, on the "ancient liberties" of the English, and on the Great Charter as the canonical proclamation of these. It is true he treats the Charter as benefiting mainly the barons, and as tacking on some rights of the people as a way of gaining their support against King John, but he is by no means dismissive of the importance of the Magna Carta, or of its confirmation during the rule of Edward I.

> It must be confessed that the former articles [those regulating what the barons owed the king] contained such mitigations and explanations of the feudal law as are reasonable and equitable; and that the latter [regulating the barons' rights over inferior vassals] involve all the chief outlines of a legal government, and provide for the equal distribution of justice, and free enjoyment of property, the great objects for which political society was first founded by men, and which people have the perpetual and inalienable right to recal, and which no time, nor precedent, nor positive institution ought to deter them from keeping ever uppermost in their thoughts and attention. (H 1.11.445)

Of note in this rather rare bit of proclamation on Hume's part is the separation of "the free enjoyment of property" from "the equal distribution of justice." Justice is no longer equated with respect for property rights. They are still important, but so are other rights, especially the right not to be seized and imprisoned. Hume had referred to the Great Charter, when discussing the completion of the protection it guaranteed, when the bill of Habeas Corpus was passed in 1679, saying that, thanks to these legal protections, the English alone enjoyed "absolute security" against arbitrary imprisonment" (H 6.67.366).

The first appendix to the *History* is largely concerned with the judicial procedures, or what Hume calls the "criminal jurisprudence" of the Anglo-Saxons. Property is acknowledged to be fairly equal among the bulk of the people, and only thanes held land. Indeed, under the later feudal system, the property rights of lesser thanes and vassals were conditional on service, and insecure. In the second appendix, indeed, we find the statement that property in land was, in the lands of German chieftains, "a kind of military pay, and might be resumed at the will of the king or general" (H 1.App 2.457). Then Hume points out that where land rather than other pay was given for military service, even though the tenure was insecure, "the attachment, naturally formed with a fixed portion of land, gradually begets the idea of something like property, and makes the possessor forget his dependant situation, and the condition which was first annexed to the grant. It seemed equitable, that one who had cultivated and sowed a field, should reap the harvest: Hence fiefs, which were at first entirely precarious, were soon made annual . . . they were next granted for a number of years." Then Hume tells how "a man would more willingly expose himself in battle, if assured that his family should inherit his possessions. . . . Hence fiefs were made hereditary in families. . . . The idea of property stole in gradually upon that of military pay" (458). Whereas, in the *Treatise,* Hume has our ancestors jump straight into land ownership, forgetting the feudal period, when only kings and superior chieftains had unconditional tenure of any lands, now in Appendix 2 property in land, for most people, steals in gradually, and is preceded by temporary leasehold, and military pay. And it is equity or justice, in the form of the recognized right to profit from one's labor, that helps transform insecure and temporary tenure into property. Property is now born out of justice, in the form of the right to pay for service, and to profit from labor, rather than being definitive of it. Locke could almost have agreed with Hume in Appendix 2.

It is worth comparing this treatment of private property in land, and its slow evolution, found in the last volumes of the *History* that were written, with what Hume says in the first volume he wrote, when he praises James I's reform of land tenure in Ireland. There he seems to assume that there was something unnatural about the temporary and insecure tenure the Irish had, that James made it what property should be. Now he realizes that tenure in land was typically temporary and insecure, before it became more secure. And what goes for land may go for other possessions too; hire and loan from a superior may precede private property rights. For such things as armor, soldiers may have depended on those they fought for, as soldiers typically do. Secure rights, to fairly unimportant things like cloaks and shoes, may have been the exception, not the rule. Hume grew up in the Scottish lowlands, where land tenure, and rights to animals and grain, were fairly secure, except on the border with England, when marauding invaders were a danger. Had he, like Adam Ferguson, grown up in the highlands, he might not have taken private property so readily for granted as the sine qua non of society. In Section 2 of his 1767 *Essay on the History of Civil Society,* Adam Ferguson points out that there can be no property until a way of defining possession is reached, so to him it is "evident that property is a matter of progress." Tomorrow's food, for the hunter, is still in the forest. If he hunts with others, the spoils are shared. Similarly with the fruits of the gardens or fields in which the women worked together—they will be "enjoyed in common." Ferguson takes communal property as more primitive than private property, and property in land as a late development. Bows, he says, will belong to individuals, huts to families, children to mothers. Leadership in war or prowess in hunting will not necessarily lead to any special position when the leader returns to the tribe (137). "The love of justice and the love of equality were originally the same" (144). These reflections of Ferguson draw on Charlevoix's travels in North America, where an Indian leader proudly refused goods from the French, saying, "I am a warrior, not a merchant. Your cloaths and utensils do not tempt me" (151). What Hume regarded as the strongest passion, love of gain, is not present in these "noble savages" of Ferguson, who are more like Rousseau's than Hume's. Independence and equality are more valued than accumulation of goods. Hume disliked Ferguson's essay, and maybe Rousseau's discourse, but by the time he writes the medieval volumes of the *History* he had pondered Tacitus's account of the early German customs, and maybe pondered Rousseau, so may be aware just how ahistorical was his version in the *Treatise* of our ancestors as greedy accumulators of goods. Of course, the brilliant account of convention given there can easily be adapted for restricted private property, such as clothes, bows and arrows, or even for communal sharing: that each who helps in fields or in the hunt gets to share in the yield, in the communal feasting. But given Hume's own stress on the importance of commerce and trade for human progress, the glorification of noble hunter-gatherers, let alone noble warriors, was not something he could be a party to. Killing and war are not the areas where he thought our best qualities were shown, so Ferguson's version of our ancestors, which included such claims as that male cowards would be put to death by the women they had failed to defend, would strike him, as he told Hugh Blair it did, as disagreeable in both form and matter. Rousseau's eloquence he never denied, but he found his theses "full of extravagance."

Of the 392 references to justice in Hume's *History,* most are to the execution of justice and the courts of justice, which ruled on far more than crimes against property. "Justice to" an individual, such as Henry V's to Richard II, at his funeral, gets 16 uses. And "law and justice" is a frequent combination, as is "humanity and justice."

Hume in his *History* has enlarged his conception of justice to include fair trials, fair return on labor, a fair chance at some station in life, a fair account of one's character, as well as protection of one's property rights. Even John Ball's rebellion is treated quite sympathetically, since the ideas of primitive equality "are engraven in the hearts of all men" (H 2.17.290). It was a resented tax that sparked the riots under Richard II, so property is still involved, and Hume always deplores violent protest, such as that of Wat Tyler. But some measure of social equality is coming to be seen by Hume as only just. His *History* is usually treated as the story of liberty in England, but it is also the story of justice, and of a monstrous series of injustices, of heresy trials and burnings, treason trials and beheadings, riot suppression, and poverty, as well as dispossession and unfair taxation. By the time Hume writes "Of the origin of government" he is quite clear that justice includes any matter, from treason and sedition, through theft and copyright infringement, to kidnap, rape, and murder, that the twelve judges of the high court may have to rule on. And he always has equity in reserve, to stand in judgment on customary rights and the processes by which they are protected. It is striking how, at crucial points when some change in law is being praised by Hume, it is "equity" which is the value promoted. It is almost as if justice is obedience to custom, while equity is what often demands reform of custom, just as courts of equity revised lower-court rulings. As T. E. Ritchie put it, Hume's aim in his *History* was to trace "the progress of legislation and civility."[5] That makes it a history of justice and equity, as much as of anything else. Hume is always at pains to link the changes in law with economic changes, and to trace the advance of the material culture, as well as of other advances. Not just the printing press, but the potato, other root vegetables, and Catherine Parr's revolutionary introduction of salads are detailed, since "Can we expect, that a government will be well modelled, by a people who know not how to make a spinning wheel, or employ a loom to advantage?" (Es 273). In the same essay ("Of refinement in the arts") he links, in a prophetically Kantian fashion, the neglect of ethics and that of astronomy, as both of them correlated, in a not-so-Kantian fashion, with the inability to make good woolen cloth. Justice and equity go with industry and commerce. If neither the starry heavens above nor the moral law within is scrutinized carefully enough, expect the tartan too to be inferior, and the meals mere

5. Thomas Edward Ritchie, *An Account of the Life and Writings of David Hume Esq.* (T. Cadell and W. Davies, 1807; reprint Thoemmes Antiquarian), 6. Ritchie thinks Hume's early study of law may have prepared him for this task.

porridge. In the *Treatise* Hume links justice and equity a bit too closely with possession of, and disputes about, material goods, to the neglect of other disagreements and grievances. This neglect he remedied, but he never stops being interested in the interdependence between material and immaterial culture. Artifice, in the sense of clever contrivance, transforms both, as shown most dramatically by the spinning wheel, the loom, and the printing press. Social artifice in the form of property rights, and procedures for their transfer by consent, transform the scope of natural equity, which before that would have been limited to fair use of things like common land, fair participation in the fruits of shared labor or collective hunting, and fair treatment within the natural family. As the youngest of three children, Hume must have had occasion to ponder equity in families, and he says every parent, to keep peace among her children, must decree some proto-property rights. He admired his mother, who apparently did this wisely and lovingly. The law decreed that the nine home wells not be shared out three to each child, at her death, but that the whole property of Ninewells go to Hume's older brother. There would be occasion for the young Hume to ponder the arbitrary features of justice in property distribution—though there is no indication he resented his "slender patrimony," or disagreed with the policy of primogeniture—and for him also to ponder the role of equity in adjusting the decrees of justice. (His family did support him and welcome him to live at home, right up beyond his mother's death in 1745 until his brother's marriage in 1751, when he wrote to Michael Ramsay that he had fifty pounds a year, and his sister Katty, who would move with him to Edinburgh, thirty pounds, so her patrimony was slenderer than his. Hume had written to Henry Home in June 1747, expressing his shame that he was not "fixed in any way of life" and his resignation to "continuing a poor Philosopher for ever,"[6] not merely poor, but dependent on his brother for a home at Ninewells.) It is not surprising that he invokes equity as well as justice, or that he regards equity as a natural virtue, one magnificently displayed, it seems, by his mother and his brother. But, as we have seen in the previous chapter, he left it for his readers to work out the precise relation of natural equity to artificial justice.

6. *New Letters of David Hume,* edited by Raymond Klibansky and Ernest Campbell Mossner (Oxford, 1954), 35–36.

# 5

# The Janus Face of Hume's "Justice"

> The interest, on which justice is founded, is the strongest imaginable, and extends to all times and places.
> —*Hume, A Treatise of Human Nature, 620*

In the *Treatise*, justice for Hume is a matter of obedience to the rules of several social "artifices": those of property, promise, and perhaps marriage. Exactly what form do these rules take? We can distinguish the general moral rule of justice, that we respect others' rights, give each person her due, from what Hume calls the "rules that determine justice," rules that tell us exactly what those rights are, what exactly is due to a given person. It is these latter that vary from place to place, and that can be altered by positive law. Middle-level rules—such as "do not take others' property without their consent!" or "do not break promises!"—depend for their content on a spelling out of what exactly counts as a given person's property or as a promise. That is where Hume's claim that all such obligations are "artificial" comes in, since he regards property and promise to be social artifacts, invented for us for our convenience. They enable us to do things we otherwise could not: count on keeping our possessions without having to fight off those who would like to take them, count on what another person will do, where it affects our interests, and he has given us his word. "His word" is, if Hume is right, something that did not exist before promises and vows were invented. So the most important rules of justice are those that tell us exactly what counts as our property, and exactly how to transfer it, and to give our word. Such rules do not take the form of commands, but rather are what later thinkers such as H. L. A. Hart in *The Concept of Law* (1961) called "enabling rules" or "constitutive rules." They instruct us on how to make a binding promise or contract, how to buy or sell something that is ours, how make a will, and how to be sure exactly what is ours, in the first place.

Human beings have invented not merely social entities such as property and promise, for mutual advantage, but also games, for fun, and the constitutive rules of cricket, or of chess, tell us how to make moves that count as proper ones in such games. John Rawls, in his influential "Two Concepts of Rules,"[1] used the game of baseball to make his point about the difference between "summary rules," such as "No rough play!" and the rules defining a practice, such as the rule that a batter in the game of baseball has only three attempts at striking the ball. Once we have these constitutive rules of the game, we will also have some prohibitions telling us what counts as cheating or a foul, in such games.

Playing such games is voluntary, and takes up only part of the lives of their players, but the activities structured by what Hume calls social artifices are not all optional, or part time. One could, like Descartes, resolve never to bind oneself to another by any promise, or, like Diogenes, not want to own any property, but most people neither can nor want to live without property, nor without some reliance on promises. Still, familiar games can help us see the nature of the various sorts of rules of justice involved in Hume's *Treatise* account of it. Most important, both in games and in justice, are the enabling conventions, those that tell a player how to play chess, or a person how to make a promise, or a gift. Dependent on these enabling rules are what we might call the disabling warning rules: "If you move your pieces in the wrong way, no one will want to play with you" and "If you do not keep the promises you have made, no one will accept your promises." Such warnings get upped in force to commands and prohibitions, such as "Keep the rules of the game!" "No cheating!" "Do not steal!" "Keep your promises!"—the last two being enforced by magistrates. But such prohibitions would not have any meaning unless there were the more basic enabling rules, telling us how to promise, or how to give another something that had been our property.

Gift or bequest, one of Hume's second set of social artifices, under his general head of "transfer by consent," is more easily seen as requiring enabling rules than is his first social artifice, that inventing property. But

---

1. John Rawls, "Two Concepts of Rules," *Philosophical Review* 64, 1 (January 1955): 3–32.

we can also see property as enabling, if we attend to Hume's words about why he thinks our wise ancestors adopted his first convention. It was to end the tussle for one another's possessions, to end what he calls their "looseness and easy transition." He supposes parents to have already done this, within the natural family, creating proto-property among their children. (Marriage, a later version of the family, is itself an artifice, though Hume's description of its basic rules leaves the reader doubtful if it is of advantage to any except children, that is to say, to all of us, when children.) The agreement our ancestors made, outside the family, presumably echoed that within it: "I observe, that it will be in my interest to leave another in possession of his goods, *provided* he will act in the same manner with regard to me. He is sensible of a like interest in the regulation of his conduct. When this common sense of interest is mutually express'd, and is known to both, it produces a suitable resolution and behavior" (T 490). Such an agreement, especially with some parent or superparent to supervise us, transforms my "goods" and his "goods" into our separate private "property." Before such an agreement, nothing counted as property, only as temporary possessions and goods, so nothing counted as theft or trespass. So the rule to keep to this natural agreement is an enabling rule, enabling all of us to be owners (and a few of us to become thieves and trespassers). Hume stresses that this agreement is not a promise; it is a natural precursor of a promise, likened by him to the willingness to row in stroke, when sharing a rowboat with others and wishing to go in the same direction. It is a case where "The actions of each of us have a reference to those of the other, and are perform'd upon the supposition that something is to be performed on the other part" (ibid.). Contract and covenant, once invented, substitute assurance for supposition, in such a reciprocal act.

In Book 2 of the *Treatise* Hume had noted that prohibitions tend to be counterproductive, since "we naturally desire what is forbid." He wrote there that "the notion of duty, when opposite to the passions, is seldom able to overcome them; and when it fails of that effect, is apt rather to increase them" (T 421). Plain prohibitions, such as those that used to be seen on billboards in Singapore—such as "Don't spit!"—only encourage those who had no urge to spit to try it, to see what pleasure they were being denied. Hume's rules of justice are not counterproductive, first because they serve our interest, rather than oppose our passions, and second because they are not pure prohibitions, but instructions on how to get what we are presumed to want, to be an owner among owners, one who can engage in barter and gift, who can be a party to promises and contracts, so have much greater security of possession and of planning than would otherwise be possible.

Eventually, in his *History,* Hume extends "justice" to everything jurisprudence covers, so does let it include pure prohibitions such as those against murder and assault.[2] One could try to see the criminal law, and other branches of the law, as enabling us to live under law, rather than the arbitrary commands of magistrates or plain bullies, and so see all prohibitions as derivative ones, but it is much easier to see the law of property and contract this way, and I think Hume did well to make them the core of justice. It is not that not stealing is more important than not assaulting, but rather that, if purely disciplinary rules are to be kept to a minimum, lest they provoke their own infringements, then the core of the rules of justice are best seen as those that enable us to serve our interests, rather than those that thwart the passions some of us may have. There is a joke in German-speaking countries, where parks tend to have rules forbidding cycling, littering, walking on the grass, loud music, and so forth, about one such park which simply had the notice "Hier ist ja Alles Verboten" (Here Everything Is Forbidden). That is the ultimate in social silliness. Our pure prohibitions should be the minimal needed set, but our enabling rules, and the prohibitions deriving from them, can be much more extensive. With enabling rules, of course, always comes the general prohibition against cheating by those engaging in these enabled procedures, against becoming what Hume termed a "knave." Dishonest knaves are certainly no worse than rapists and killers, but the dishonest person, the one who perverts our cooperative social rules for her own gain, who is a free rider on others' compliance, and exploits their trust and honesty, is despised in a special way, if found out. For her victims are not only the direct ones, but also the social fabric itself. All of us suffer if the core rules of justice are disregarded.

Many of Hume's readers have criticized him for making property too central to justice.[3] The very concept of our "trespasses," in the Christian

2. I discuss this enlargement of his view of justice in Chapter 4.

3. Reid and Balfour made such objections, in Hume's lifetime. For more recent criticism of the narrowness of Hume's conception, see, for example, J. L. Mackie, *Hume's Moral Theory* (Routledge and Kegan Paul, 1980), 94; Jonathan Harrison, *Hume's Theory of Justice* (Clarendon, 1981), 28ff; and David Daiches Raphael, *Concepts of Justice* (Clarendon, 2001), ch. 9.

morality that Hume learned as a child, seems to be a metaphor, suggesting that property wrongs are seen as fairly basic. Hume had good reason to begin there,[4] not only because the traditional definition of justice—giving each his due—seems to require, as supplement, a way of determining exactly what is that due, and that most obviously with respect to what goods are due him, but also because Hume wanted to show what justice *enables* us to do, what it is we could not do without it. Hart, in *The Concept of Law* (1961), called enabling rules "secondary" in comparison with what he saw as the primary "mandatory" rules, those that form the criminal code and the law of torts. Such straight prohibitions may be legally primary, but in a pre-legal society, the sort Hume thought invented justice, the forms of cooperation will be as vital as any taboo. I shall go on, after a look at what he calls the "circumstances of justice," to suggest that he may have taken his third artifice, promise, to be more like property than it really is, since a binding agreement between two people could survive the breakdown of social order in a way that property conventions would not.

Hume takes justice as a virtue to be a willingness, in the circumstances of justice, to go along with agreed conventions decreeing what each person's rights are: property rights and contractual rights, later also rights to the protection of the law, and to due process in criminal proceedings. We do this, he says, for the sake of increased security, and in order to avoid violent disputes. Hume usually speaks of obligations, rather than rights, but if the rights in question are taken as what are correlative to the obligations his artifices create, what he sometimes calls a person's "due," then it is harmless, as well as convenient, to speak of them as created by social artifices. As noted, this account of justice has seemed, to many of Hume's readers, to make it too narrow in focus, even when it is in the *History* extended to criminal justice, since it seems to omit desert, and any claim to equal treatment.[5] The last is, I think, usually spoken of by Hume as a demand for "equity," rather than justice, though he often pairs the two. (He says equity is a natural virtue, so its

4. For other very plausible reasons why Hume began with property, see James Harris, "Hume's Peculiar Definition of Justice," forthcoming in a volume about the *Treatise,* edited by Peter Kail and Marina Frasca Spada (Oxford). Harris sees Hume to be particularly concerned to deny the claim of Frances Hutcheson that we have a "moral sense" which tells us what is and is not just.

5. Raphael, *Concepts of Justice,* is particularly concerned about these omissions.

frequent pairing with justice, which is artificial, is interesting.)[6] Desert is a notion Hume has little room for, given his determinism. He can allow that there can be truth, or falsity, in any claim about a person's causal and moral responsibility for some injury to another person, or to the public, such as that claimed when trials for treason were enacted in English courts. Methods of trial did change and improve over the course of English history, and Hume includes these, such as Alfred's reforms, and his invention of trial by jury, in his account of criminal justice. But he does not have much room for the idea that a person's virtue or vice makes him or her deserving of happiness or unhappiness, since he sees our character, and so our actions, as largely determined for us, and most of us to have a mixture of virtues and vices. "Were one to go round the world with an intention of giving a good supper to the righteous, and a sound drubbing to the wicked, he would frequently be embarrassed in his choice, and would find, that the merits and demerits of most men and women scarcely amount to the value of either" ("Of the immortality of the soul" [Es 594–595]).

Still, some judicial sentences were unfair and undeserved, given accepted grounds for criminal responsibility. Justice, as Hume understands it, is respecting rights that have been accepted in our community, rights to keep what is legally ours, and get what we have been promised, rights not to be assaulted, abducted, or raped, to have what say we have been granted in public matters, such as votes in elections to parliaments, to have a fair trial if arrested for some breach of law, and to be accused only of offenses declared to be such before the accusation. The trial of the Earl of Strafford was manifestly unfair, since he was tried for and found guilty of offenses invented there and then, not for breach of promulgated laws. The Countess of Somerset, during the reign of Henry VIII, and later the Duke of Monmouth, during that of James II, were beheaded for treason without any trial, as were all those against whom a bill of attainder was passed in Parliament. Hume notes these injustices. So his version of justice, by the time he has written his *History*, encompasses a lot more than respect for traditional property rights, and the circumstances of this enlarged justice are also enlarged. Not merely limited natural generosity, but also limited natural respect for others' *persons,* for their freedom, and for their reputations, make the full rules of justice necessary.

6. I discuss it in Chapter 3, "Nature and Artifice, Equity and Justice."

In a recent study of justice, Jiwei Ci's *The Two Faces of Justice,*[7] Hume's view is taken to be so strongly influenced by his version of the circumstances of justice—namely, moderate material scarcity and limited generosity—that not enough scope is given either for conflict which is not over material goods, or for the nobler motivations of some just persons, whose justice need not, it is claimed, be so cautious or so jealous. When indignation is felt at injustice to others, whose cause inspires one's actions on their behalf, or when forgiveness is given for injuries to oneself, there has been an overcoming or forgetting of the narrowly self-interested beginnings of justice, and it has grown into a more altruistic virtue. Jiwei Ci notes that the Chinese tradition has little to say about justice, so he has raided the Western tradition, from Hume to Schopenhauer, Nietzsche, Rawls, Barry, Buchanan, Strawson, Shklar, Kierkegaard, and even Paul Tillich. His is a remarkable synthesis. In the Chinese tradition, he tells us, both traditional and Marxist, the emphasis is on the need for altruism and public spirit, for doing things for the sake of the larger whole, rather than on enlightened egoism, of the sort he finds in Hume's account. Sometimes he calls it individualism, rather than egoism, but he seems unable to see, as really admirable and virtuous, any behavior whose motivation is wholly or even mainly self-interested. He quotes Hume's reference to benevolence as a "nobler virtue" than justice, and sees justice as "intermediate" between altruism and rational egoism, where the former is really virtuous, the latter not. So the "conditional motivation" of Hume's just person, who is willing to do his bit only if others are, and is concerned to "balance his accounts," is contrasted with the "unconditional motivation" which some achieve, when they have "overcome" or suppressed the memory of any self-interested roots their disposition to justice may have grown from.

What I find remarkable is that there is, among Hume commentators, a wish to find something very like this self-overcoming thesis within Hume's text itself, and so people like David Norton[8] find Hume to think that the approved motive to justice cannot possibly be any form of self-interest, but must be some concern for the group, and for others. So the concern for the public interest which prompts one to *approve* of honesty and justice, according to what Hume says, seeps down into what gets ap-

7. Jiwei Ci, *The Two Faces of Justice* (Harvard, 2006).

8. See his remarks about justice in the Norton and Norton introduction to the Oxford (2000) student edition of the *Treatise*.

proved, public-spirited justice, rather than prudent self-interested justice. I shall call this interpretation the Chinese one, with due acknowledgment that Jiwei Ci does not claim to find it plainly there in Hume's text, although he does consider it, in what he calls the "diachronic" interpretation of the *Treatise* Book 3, Part 2, Section 2.[9] There is no doubt Hume thinks that first property rights were respected out of a sense of "natural" and interested obligation; later these obligations get promoted into moral ones, when the whole scheme is found to merit moral approbation, and to serve the public interest, so there is something diachronic in Hume's account. But whether what is approved, as an individual virtue, is self-interested and cooperative conformity to property rules, or something "nobler," is what is disputed. In my own view, there is nothing at all "logically unbridgeable"[10] in supposing that sympathy with the public interest can lead us to give approbation to "oblique," intelligently self-corrected self-interest, when it takes the form of conformity to coordinative rules which all benefit from, so I accept what Jiwei Ci calls a "synchronic reading," one he grants is not incompatible with what Hume writes. This synchronism of moral approbation of conformity with a self-interested motive for it comes about diachronically after a pre-approbation social phase, when the only obligation to conform is "natural" and interested, rather than both moral and interested. What is typically Chinese, it seems, though not Jiwei Ci's own view, is the conviction that "one ought to rise above egoism,"[11] the conviction that self-interest cannot be virtuous, however intelligent it is, or however good for the community its workings might be. I could also call this attitude Christian, the demand that we love others, and if necessary sacrifice ourselves for them. It may be best to call it simply the C view of justice, and leave the detail of its origin vague. (This way it can include Rachel Cohon, who also rejects the view that it is oblique self-interest that could be the approved motive to justice.)[12]

First a clarification: Hume does have, in his catalogue of virtues, benevolence to others, generosity, and public spirit, so such "noble" traits are given their due. But he thinks justice does not reduce to forms of them. They are natural virtues, and justice is artificial, and he denies that

9. Jiwei Ci, 110–112.
10. Alastair MacIntyre is quoted on this point by Jiwei Ci, 113.
11. Ibid., 238, 242.
12. See Rachel Cohon, *Hume's Morality: Feeling and Fabrication* (Oxford, 2008), ch. 6.

it is a form, even an artificial form, of benevolence. He claims that only self-interest can correct self-interest, and that concern for the public interest can influence our taste in what we approve of, but not determine our motivation, when our own interest and the public's are opposed. Approbation does not, for Hume, require, in the approved, a "desire to be just for moral reasons,"[13] but only, in the approver, a special moral pleasure when just actions are done for some approvable natural reason, reinforced, perhaps, by the knowledge that it is approved. His claims about the insufficiency of anything except self-interest to curb self-interest, and the motivational weakness of concern for the public interest, along with its insufficiency to influence our approbation, are made quite categorically, not restricted in application to one phase in any "progress of sentiments" the history of justice displays. Nor would Hume regard it as noble to be the last honest person to pay one's debts, when no one else is doing so, and social order is in collapse. That would be stupid, not noble. For if justice really is an arch, if it is such that the good done by any just act requires the support of other persons' similar acts, then to keep on keeping the rules when they are generally disregarded would be like trying to play tennis with oneself, at best a whimsical exercise. There may indeed be conditions, intermediate between those when most others are keeping the rules of justice, and those when they are mostly not, and in such intermediate conditions some nobility may be shown by those who are restrained by the old rules, rather than imitating the "licentiousness" of others. But soon this effort to save the old cooperative scheme may degenerate into self-sacrificial foolishness. As Hume says, if one's just act is not imitated, it "falls to the ground," useless. This is more obviously the case with respect for property rules, less clear with promise. To be the last person to keep a promise seems quite an honorable achievement, and, unless it kills or badly affects one, in no way foolish. If no one else offers or accepts promises, they will die out, but there is no silliness in the idea of one last promise-keeping, as there is in the idea of keeping to property rules no one else respects. I shall return later to the rather special case of promising, and consent in general, for Hume.

Why does Jiwei Ci think unilateral, "principled," or "unconditional" just acts are morally praised? He does not himself say they are praise-

13. Jiwei Ci, 112.

worthy: what he tries to explain is why some societies and some philosophers, such as Schopenhauer, have praised, and seen to be socially necessary, an unconditional willingness to do what justice requires, even if
it is not being done toward oneself. Even Hume allows that the artifices
of educators may try to make us feel that the rules of justice must be "inviolable rules" to us. But we will justifiably feel this only as long as conformity to them is the rule, not the exception, in our own society. If I am
a victim of theft, in a society where social order has not broken down,
that certainly does not permit me to steal even from the one who stole
from me. Nor does it permit me to punish the thief, or seize back, by violence, what once was mine. Once we live under law, we leave all that to
the police and the justice department. Nietzsche's point that living with
a chip on one's shoulder merely spoils one's own life, so it is simply psychic hygiene to put the memory of old wrongs against one behind one,
and move on, leaving the punishment of the offender to public authorities, makes forgiveness of trespasses against us sensible, for the forgiver's
sake. These days this is often called "closure," as if a wound has healed
over. But such acts of acceptance or resignation to suffering injustice do
not make the justice of such a person unconditional—it never was conditional on there being no unjust acts, merely on justice being the norm,
not the exception. And honesty in property dealings still is the norm, in
most societies, unless they are war zones. Hume speaks of a convention of justice being established by "a slow progression, and our repeated experience of the inconveniences of transgressing it" (T 490).
Whether this means the inconvenience of others' transgressions, or of
one's own, if noted and disapproved of, is uncertain, but clearly he
does not make individual conformity conditional on universal conformity. What is needed is "confidence of the future regularity of their [oth-
ers'] conduct" (ibid.), and such regularity is compatible with occasional
transgressions. There will always be some sensible knaves, and some
foolish ones. So Hume's justice is not conditional on perfect conformity
within a group. There would be no need for magistrates, if there were no
nonconformers.

Rachel Cohon sees the approved motive to justice to be a sense of
duty to a cooperative scheme, even if it no longer benefits one in any
easily seen way. But then she sees duty as nearly always present, since
she thinks calling some trait a virtue is seeing it as our duty to have it.
"Hume says it is my duty to have a certain motivating sentiment just in

case my having it would elicit approval, and my failure to have it, or deficiency of it would elicit disapproval."[14] This makes virtue ethics resolve into deontology, a list of duties, in a most un-Humean fashion. Since Hume says that our characters are no more of our own decreeing than the motion of the heavens, it would be really strange to still say we have a duty to possess all the virtues. Hume does not say this: what he says is that we may feel a sense of duty when we hate ourselves for failing to have some approved character trait, so try to pretend to it. This does not amount to saying that such self-hatred is to be encouraged, nor that those who do have the virtue have done their duty in a way the ungrateful person has not. Hume is fairly sparing in his use of the term "duty," and his commentators should be cautious in extending its use on his behalf, or they will turn him into Kant. Hume does think parents have duties, and that all artifices impose obligations. Since what they, unlike the natural virtues, mainly require is conformity to rules telling us how to act, such conformity may be within the power of people with many different sorts of motivation, some more admirable than others. Some may pay their debts merely to keep out of debtors' prisons. Some may do so mindlessly, since they have been drilled to do so by parents and educators. Some few may reflect, "What is to become of the world, if we do not pay our debts?" Some may feel sympathy with the individual creditor. And many may have mixed motives, as most of our actions typically do. The virtue of justice may be a bit like the virtue of cleanliness: its point is both for oneself and for others, with no fine discriminations of whose sake is paramount. It is good policy to encourage cleanliness, and to let it become mere automatic habit, just as paying one's bills is, for most people. It does not seem to me a good social policy to encourage mindless conformity to all local customs. Such customs have often been pernicious, as when slaves were treated as property, or when women, by marrying, lost their property to their husbands. The question "Would the world be better, if this custom were changed?" is often the right one to ask.

Hume would also have us ask, "What would become of the world if everyone felt free to try to reform established customs in the way she thinks an improvement?"[15] "Rebellion" and "riot" were dread words, in

14. Cohon, 169.

15. Frank Snare entitles his chapter on Hume's theory of justice "The Conservative Theory of Justice" (ch. 8 of *Morals, Motivation, and Convention: Hume's Influential Doctrines* [Cambridge, 1991]).

his vocabulary, but he certainly did not approve of slavery, and seemed to want women to come to share some hitherto male privileges. The accepted practice of the age is the default practice, and changes to it must be done cautiously, without danger of violence and disorder. Many changes to the customs and rules in Britain were recorded and approved by Hume the historian, especially changes in the way changes could be made, by parliamentary initiative as well as monarch's say-so. In his essay "Idea of a perfect commonwealth," elaborate attention is given to change in laws, who can propose them, who can veto them, who sets the agenda. In a perfect commonwealth, Hume thinks, elected representatives from parishes will elect county magistrates who elect a national senate, and there will also be a "court of competitors" of defeated senate candidates who received a third or more of the vote, who can challenge senators, and keep them honest. Yearly elections will also do that, even if it makes Hume's commonwealth, in its yearly elections, as "inconvenient" as Harrington's *Oceana*. There is, in his "perfect commonwealth," a property qualification for being a voter, so every voter has some stake in the commonwealth. It is an elaborate scheme modeled partly on Cromwell's scheme, partly on the United Provinces of the Netherlands. It aims to give the people a say as to who makes their laws, but not really much say as to what their content is to be. Every century inequalities, of unspecified sorts, are to be remedied. Maybe he only means a redrawing of parish boundaries, but possibly other inequities may be the intended targets of these centennial adjustments.

So what did Hume think counted as the consent of the governed, or the consent of those regulated by some pre-legal convention? He calls the customs he thinks constitute justice "agreed" to by our hypothetical ancestors, and that agreement "expressed," but clearly none of us have had much say in the property customs we were born into, any more than we did about the traffic rules or the rules of tennis. If we find local customs too offensive, we can in theory emigrate, as many did from England from the time of the American colonies onward. As Hume stresses in "Of the original contract," we are not like butterflies, arriving on the scene a generation at a time, so the "agreement" to the going scheme has to be somehow won from each young person reaching adulthood. Nothing in particular counts as young people's giving a commitment to the going scheme, or to ways of proposing changes to it. And young people are very often those found guilty of property crimes. "The artifices of educators and politicians" have to try to keep this number of young offenders down. Even if they can be made to see that, when they accept *some* set of property rights, and of other rights, they are gainers, on balancing the account, they may still find the existing set objectionable. What then? What are dissenters to do? Emigrate? Stand for Parliament and try to change the laws? Dissent is an important act, given too little attention by Hume.

What Hume does describe is a series of more and more explicit consentings, from the "express" one involved in the acceptance of a convention, to explicit consent to transfer of a right, or to some simultaneous exchange, and on to fully explicit and sometimes signed contract. Consent is taken by him as "artificial" when it involves some conventional sign, be it a nod or a handing over of a sod of earth to signify consent to transfer the right to land. But surely consent can also be a natural act, once there is language, or even before it. "Yes" and "No" in reply to the question "Do you accept this proposal?" are basic words. Often assent is assumed unless dissent is expressed. Agreement itself need not be artificial; otherwise Hume's first convention could never get started. And it may be claimed that his second and third conventions, consent to transfer and promise or contract, as mutual conditional promise, neither need nor have the baroque and elaborate rules that the artifice of property, as Hume describes it, does have. There is something natural about doing what one said one would do, especially when one knows others are counting on that. Of course, there can be good reasons to let other considerations sometimes override that, as there can be for breaking explicit promises. The safety of the people, Hume says, is the supreme law, and in times of famine, grain stores may be stormed, and promises broken.

Hume sees the conditionality of the obligation to respect the rules of any social artifice as going along with its "artificial" character, its being the solution to some coordination problem, given the circumstances of justice. But conditionality attaches also to any obligation which is reciprocal, whether or not artifice is involved. For example, the services friends do each other depend, by Hume's own account, on the expectation of each that the other will reciprocate. "I may still [after the invention of promising] do services to such persons as I love, and am particularly acquainted with, without any prospect of advantage; and they may make me a return in the same manner, without any view but that of recompensing my past services" (T 521). Hume calls the services of friends "disinterested," but, should one get no return of services from one's friend, one will not feel badly in ceasing to do the things one used to do for that one. This is not revenge; it is the natural tit-for-tat workings of reciprocal relationships. Conventions oblige us, provided they are generally accepted. Promises oblige us, provided they are understood and accepted. Friendships oblige us, provided the mutual reciprocity continues. Individual explicit agreements seem intermediate between the general acceptance of property laws and governments, and the individual possibly unspoken commitments of friends to each other. Promises are in some respects not like Hume's other conventions, and are more like individual understandings between friends or neighbors.[16] If I find my neighbor's cat wounded by the roadside, of course I call a vet, just as I expect my neighbor would, were it one of my cats. But we have never spelled out this expectation. Some things do not need express promises. And where there is an express promise, its power to bind does not seem conditional on how many others are breaking their promises. Promises, because they are between two people, as is friendship, differ from the standing obligations we have to the community in general, to go along with its laws, or to use the approved ways to change them. There is something faceless about the obligation not to steal, or break other criminal laws: it is owed to anyone and everyone, and, short of social breakdown, for all times, and the protection one's property rights give one is against any would-be thief. But promises are made to individuals, for performance at some limited future time, and often sealed with a handshake. They create *special* obligations and *special* rights. Hume was rightly aware that provision has to be made to enable binding private commitments between individuals, both contract and marriage, as well as for general obedience to order-maintaining laws. But he may have overly assimilated the former to the latter. For him, keeping a promise, or a marriage vow, is not just doing what one led someone else to rely on one's doing, but also keeping a general standing commitment, with everyone else, to "be true to one's word." The latter commitment may be mythical, and is not needed to generate the former. Educators may well instill in one that one must be true to one's word, but the good reason one must do so is not the general agreement to this effect; it is the en-

16. I am influenced here by Oswald Hanfling, "How We Trust One Another," *Philosophy* 83 (2008): 161–177.

couraged reliance of the particular one to whom one gave one's word. Society-wide agreement is needed for the words "I promise" to have the force they do have, a force backed by the penalty of withdrawal of trust from any known promise-breaker. But if my promise is made in private, my breaking of it may not become generally known, so the withdrawal of trust from me will be only from my victim. I may not mind that, so may be quite willing to pay that penalty. Nor will I have significantly wronged the community by not taking one promise seriously, any more than I do by any other misuse of a common language. But I do wrong the one I encouraged to rely on me, just as I would by a false profession of love or friendship. The wrong of promise-breaking requires a social convention to be possible, but it is a wrong against the one to whom it was given, not against the community, as any breach of law would be. Breach of promise is not *law*-breaking. This difference is shown in the fact that theft is a breaking of the criminal law, while breach of contract is a civil offense. Only if serious fraud is involved are the criminal courts involved in breach of promise or contract.

The fact that we leave it to individuals to bring suit for breach of contract, while the state prosecutes thieves, may seem to make the former a lesser wrong than the latter. It is more that theft is a double wrong, against the community whose rules are broken, as well as against the one whose property was unlawfully taken. As Hume says about the imagined theft of his coat in *EPM* Appendix 3, the thief *doubly* displeases him, and offends every bystander (E 310). He is displeased to lose what he had counted on keeping, and displeased also that laws are being flouted. But if he had been promised the loan of a carriage, which then is not delivered, he would only be once displeased, and any bystanders, if ignorant of the promise, would not be at all offended at his carriageless state. Are not the rules of promising the community's rules, just as much as the property rules? Yes, but they are *special* enabling rules, set up to give individuals, *if they so choose,* the means to take on new special obligations, and acquire new special rights. And the magistrate does provide the civil courts to enable victims of breach of contract some redress. But since the wrong done in such acts is wrong only because of the prior promise, not in itself unlawful, like theft and assault, it is left to the aggrieved victim to take action against the wrongdoer. Before magistrates, the aggrieved victim of breach of promise, in the story Hume gives, leveled the penalty of withdrawal of trust, letting it be known that the wrongdoer is not to be relied upon. No such victim-initiated penalty is mentioned in the case of theft, nor is it easy to think of one that is as natural and appropriate. To attempt to seize back what was wrongly taken from one would lead to undesirable violence, so is not encouraged, and there is no nonviolent way to disable a thief from thieving again, as branding a promise-breaker as such disables him from future promise-givings. Any witnesses to the theft will help the victim let it be known that the thief is such an offender, so trust will be withdrawn from him, but that need not disable him from stealing again. Only incarceration by magistrates, or nastier penalties like lopping off the hand that stole, can disable thieves. There is no safe victim-initiated penalty, in part because the main victim is not the only victim; there is also the community whose laws have been flouted, and it is the community and its officials who must levy the penalty. When contract is used in serious fraud, there too the state steps in to prosecute, and does not leave the matter to the civil courts. For in that case the institution of contract is itself under threat of subversion: if it is to continue to enable firm commitments between two parties, criminal false pretense, what Kant called lying promises, must be prosecuted.

"Justice," in the *Treatise*, comprises first honesty in matters of property, so that, once magistrates are invented, some sorts of behavior, such as theft and trespass, will become criminal, and also comprises fidelity to promises and contracts, avoidance of behavior which, once we have courts and magistrates, may make one a defendant in the civil courts, where another individual, not the state, brings the suit against one, unless serious fraud is involved. When Hume looks back on his account, in his "Some farther reflections concerning justice and injustice" in the *Treatise* (T 526–524), it is not promises he looks at, but matters like hiring a horse for a day, or inheriting a property. Loan and hire of course do involve a contractual relationship between owner and borrower, so do, like sale and contract, depend on some fairly explicit special agreement between individuals. Keeping to such private agreements is one face of Hume's justice, and does not, despite its "interested" nature, seem very far away from the natural virtue of being a true friend, in that the basic thing is dependability, and a mutual understanding about what each expects from the other. It is conditional on the relevant other doing his or her part. Should the hired horse prove to need reshoeing, the deal is off. The other face of Hume's justice is conformity to general standing rules, such as those decreeing what is whose, and what sort of behavior is allowed, rules forbidding theft, fraud, counterfeiting, assault, libel, kidnap, and rape. Property rules oblige us only as long as there is general acceptance of them, and as long as the material circumstance of justice, moderate scarcity, holds. Often the two sorts of justice will come together: there will be customary rules about how much one can charge for one's horse for a day, and what condition it must be in, customary standards also about how hard the hirer may ride the horse. And there is the law of contract, which varies from place to place. In England but not Scotland some "consideration" was needed for a promise to bind. An agreement to hire, or rent, like a promise, is between two particular people. Hume thinks the free market will determine fair price, in most cases.

In criminal justice too there are both the community rules the criminal is claimed to have broken, and the relationship between a particular criminal and his victims, between a particular prisoner and a particular judge, and later between the prisoner and the ones appointed to carry out the court's decree. Hume gives one particularly ghastly example of an unjust killing, that of the Countess of Salisbury, the last Plantagenet, by order from Henry VIII. She was old and gray, but resisted what she saw as injustice being done her—no trial had been held, no prosecuting counsel or judge had been faced. She refused to lay her gray head on the block, but defied the executioner to catch her, and ran around the scaffold, while he levied what blows he could until he finally managed to subdue and behead her. Among the many atrocious murders Hume relates in his *History,* this is one of the worst. What was she charged with? Remaining true to the old religion, refusing to accept Henry as head of the church. Her executioner, one would think, must have felt ashamed of his part in this atrocity. To carry out sentence of death on someone found guilty after due process of law is a bad enough thing, to be Henry's private ax-man, and having to chase an old woman around the scaffold till he could bring her down quite another, and much worse. This killing was murderous assault on someone whose only fault was to have offended a tyrant king, and who had not been given her day in court, her chance to face her accusers. Another ghastly killing Hume documents is that of the charitable Anabaptist Elizabeth Gaunt, found guilty by Judge Jefferies of harboring the family of one of the supporters of the Monmouth Rebellion against James II, and burned alive. She embraced the faggots, as she died a terrible death for helping the destitute family of those deemed traitors to a Catholic king. The number of persons in England who died for having the wrong religious faith is of shocking magnitude. Dying for one's faith became almost the standard way of living for it, as kings and courts demanded proof of one's orthodoxy, even when kings were not so orthodox themselves. James was willing to tolerate Quakers, if they would tolerate Catholics, but was not willing to save Anabaptists from fiery fates, if they had supported the destitute families of rebels against his rule.

Justice regulates our actions both with those with whom we have individual understandings, giving rise to special rights and special obligations, and with the general public who form the community whose customs are the default laws regulating our behavior. Other virtues too come in with our individual relationships: we can be good or bad friends, good or bad parents, considerate or inconsiderate spouses, good- or bad-tempered, polite or rude. These are natural virtues, while Hume thinks fidelity to promises is artificial. But to enter into an undertaking seems not to need the help of artifice. What binding promise does is institute a form of words whereby one is enabled to subject oneself to conditional penalty for failure to do what one promises—it invites the other to take one to court if one fails to do what one contracted to. Not every undertaking does that, though one knows one risks one's reputation as trustworthy if one does not do what one assured another one would do. There may or may not be traditional signs and symbols, like handshakes, or oaths, used to seal an understanding. There usually will be a shared language. To be the last person keeping her promises would be tragic, but, since a promise is between individuals, any "arch" or conditionality it involves concerns mainly only those two. If the promise was accepted—if its currency, so to speak, was still operative—then to keep it is to do what one said one would, to prove trustworthy. But if, as one's country was overwhelmed with rising floodwaters, one dashed about repaying debts, before drowning with one's creditors, that would be at best whimsical, at worst senseless behavior. To drown while trying to hold up one's friend, whom one had promised not to leave, would be only right.

One face of justice is traditionally blindfolded, treating all alike, no favors or exceptions. This is justice as impartiality. But another face looks with clear vision at particular relationships between particular persons, and what each owes the other because of the relationship, and the undertakings given. This is justice as getting what was promised one. Criminal law is typically blindfolded. Civil, contract, matrimonial, and family law are concerned with the particularities of individual undertakings and understandings. Hume was a law student, and uses Scots legal terminology such as "prescription" (which could refer either to long-established use, or to a limitation on the length of time a legal action could be delayed) and "wakening"[17] (a revival of a court action, after a year and a day had passed). He knew the difference between the Court of Session and the High Court of Justiciary. We do not know if he was training to become an advocate, or to be a writer to the signet, concerned more with noncriminal cases. Both sorts of justice are important, but they vary in the degree of artificiality their rules involve. Hume in *EPM* stresses that there are hundreds of volumes of law regarding both contract and inheritance. Contract may be as complex as property, but promise is usually simpler, giving less scope for "finer turns and connexions of the imagination" than property law. The typical breach of promise cases to come before the courts were for breach of promise to marry, but Scots law differed from English in allowing action for breach of "gratuitous promise," one without any "consideration," provided there had been either "writ" or oath. Had Hume begun his studies with Scots property law, which in some ways his *Treatise* account of justice, especially the section on transfer by consent, might suggest, he could scarcely have avoided knowing of the remains of feudalism still in it, the existence of the "feu" for property ownership, which was only fully abolished in 2000. Then he could not have taken freehold as the normal sort of land ownership, but would have known of the feu, and of the blench (or blanch) holdings. So maybe it was precisely because he was so nauseated by all those volumes on property law that he could turn his back on it, generalize about its fanciful and superstitious features, and yet treat it as he did, as the core of a simple notion of justice, taken as conformity to possibly fanciful custom. Had it been criminal law he studied, he would have had theft, along with fraud, assault, homicide, abduction, rape, and defamation, as wrongs against a person which could be prosecuted. That would have given him a better core set of "inviolable laws" a person must keep, to keep out of the hands of the

17. He uses this term, ironically, in a letter to James Edmonstoune of Newton, September 29, 1757, in *New Letters of David Hume,* edited by Raymond Klibansky and Ernest Campbell Mossner (Oxford, 1954), 41.

criminal court, and it is these, as they apply to property, more than the civil law on promise, that he really takes to constitute the "rules of justice" that an honest person keeps. It is these that do show artifice, such as the very notion of a "feu," and of "prescription," for example, that five years' use of a path constitutes right of way, or that court actions lapse after a year and a day, and need to be "wakened" if they are to proceed. All these have the elements of arbitrary definiteness, which are precisely what Hume makes typical of artifice, and also the conditionality on general acceptance that he makes go along with this. But the law on promising was much less fanciful. What else could possibly count as a binding promise but a swearing to another that one will do something, at or by some specified future time? It is indeed conditional on the other understanding and accepting the promise, but it seems not conditional on other promise-givers keeping their promises, nor does it seem to require any special act that only cultural education could tell one how to perform. The only performance a promise requires is that future one it promises. How to make a promise seems to come quite naturally. As for the oath, or oath equivalent, which a promise in Scotland required, that in Hume's story is merely the staking of one's reputation as trustworthy, as a secular equivalent of the *interpositio fidei* required by canon law.[18] Not "may God damn me to hell if I break this promise," but rather, "may others know that promises from me are not to be accepted, that trust should not be placed in my promises," something like "Scouts' honor." Some artifice is involved in contriving oaths, but for binding individual commitments to specific others, no contrivance seems necessary.

Both faces of Hume's justice, both that which demands of us our due to the community who once formed and now protects us, and that which demands our due to specific other persons with whom we have come to particular understandings, are important, and different branches of law, and of our departments of justice, promote this on the one hand blindfolded, on the other hand keen-sighted, justice. The keen sight is needed for the decisions on the justice of private agreements, and how they were kept. The blindfold is needed when there is any danger that special treatment might favor some over others whose case is no different. Both sorts of justice—even-handed application of laws, and attention to the details of private agreements—are conditional, the former

18. I discuss this in Chapter 8, "Promises, Promises, Promises."

on the promulgation of the general law, and general acceptance of it, the latter on the specifics of the private agreement in question. And in both sorts of cases, considerations of equity, and courts of equity, may sometimes lead to revisions of what lower courts had found just. The only statue of equity I have been able to find is at the National Health Service University Hospital in Newham, East London. Mike Speller's fine statue shows a human figure, standing on a globe, whose arms join with a large inclusive circle above its head. That it should be a health service in East London which set up this statue shows how far Britain has come since Hume's day, since rights to health care were not included in his concept either of justice or of equity. It is only equitable that health services serve all residents, Indian and Cockney, and that some doctors speak the language of the patient, in a multicultural society like contemporary Britain. Hume himself complained of prejudice against him, because he was a Scot, and spoke English with a despised Scottish accent. He wrote to Ben Franklin that he might have to look to America for justice, and what he meant by "justice" in that context had nothing to do with property rights, or with promise, and everything to do with careful attention to the merits of a particular person and his writings. There was nothing very cautious or jealous about the justice Hume hoped for from his American readers. Cautious about getting his meaning right, yes; jealous of any superiority claimed over native American thinkers like Jonathan Edwards, maybe. But mainly simply keen-sighted Justicia, with her two-edged sword and her well-balanced scales.

# II

ASSOCIATED TOPICS

6

# Hume's Account of Social Artifice:
# Its Origins and Originality

## Why Hume's Theory Is Important

Hume makes his account of social artifices, and of the artificial virtues that consist in conformity to their constitutive rules, the centerpiece of Book 3 of the *Treatise*. He devotes to that topic twice as much space as to the natural virtues, and almost four times as much as to the anti-rationalist preliminaries of Part 1. I think that, had Hume written an abstract of Book 3 and raised there his questions of what might "intitle the author to so glorious a name as that of inventor" (T 661), he would have judged the best candidate in Book 3 to be the account of social artifice, of how what he half but only half ironically calls "the three laws of nature," namely, stability of possessions, their transfer by consent, and performance of promises, are "entirely artificial, and of human invention" (526). The originality is threefold: first, in the claims concerning what it is that we collectively invent—the very possibility of ownership, of loan, of gift and barter, of promise, of authority over others, and so of the obligations and rights these involve; second, in the details of the account of how we are able to do this inventing; and third, in the account of the relation of these rights and obligations to the rest of morality. My claims about originality are an invitation to correction, and I make them diffidently and tentatively. It is because I find the Humean account the best account we have of these rights and obligations and their relation to the wider field of morality when that is seen as cultivation of virtues that I am interested in its genesis. My corrigible and correction-inviting claim is that Hume's account of human collective "inventions" or artifices, along with his account of their relation to what we did not need to invent, makes him a glorious inventor in moral and social theory.

This assessment is of course influenced by my own evaluations and prejudices, and it is well if I make some of these explicit. What I look for in a moral theory is a demystifying account of the deontological component in morality as decent people recognize it, an account which does not subordinate the gentler tones of that morality to its sterner deontological voice, along with a plausible explanation of our persistent tendency to mystify moral matters. Hume's account satisfies these demands. Virtues theories such as Aristotle's typically fail to do justice to the deontological aspects of morality, fail to explain why some ways of behaving ("adultery, theft, murder" are Aristotle's examples at 1107a 11–12 of *Nicomachean Ethics*) are just plain ruled out, not, like vices, merely discouraged. But Natural Law and Kantian theories go to the other extreme, reducing all of morality to the stern voice of duty (perfect or imperfect) or to overtones of that voice. There were, of course, some mixed or nonreductive theories before Hume's—Aquinas's and Locke's—but these were theological or partly theological theories that derived the richness and manysidedness of morality, its combination of love and mercy with justice, from the stipulated amplitude of a divine creator who was both loving father and stern lawgiver and judge, demanding from us both obedience and freely given return love. Aquinas has a more or less coherent story about how we can be guided both by the virtues we have been helped to cultivate and by a moral law, but the coherence is bought at the cost of a theological foundation, and one that simply takes it for granted that fathers, and so divine fathers, have authority over the children they have sired. Authority, the most troubling moral concept, is assumed, not explained (or maybe it is merged into authorship), and all obligations are derived from that of obedience to authoritative commands. Hume's theory secularizes and demystifies the concepts of obligation and of authority, and does so in a nonreductive distinction-preserving way. The full variety and complex interdependence of different grounds of obligation are recognized, along with the fuller variety of the gentler moral pressures to be a decent person and a good companion as well as a conscientious doer of one's duty.[1] The most

1. I discuss this virtue of Hume's theory in Annette Baier, "Hume—the Women's Moral Theorist?" in *Women and Moral Theory,* edited by Eva Kittay and Diana Meyers (Rowman and Allanheld, 1987), reprinted in *Postures of the Mind* (Harvard, 1995), 51–75.

influential modern moral theories that avoid resting morality on a religious base are contractarian and so reductive theories, resting all obligations and sometimes all of morality on the obligation arising from contract or mutual voluntary agreement. Hume gives voluntary agreement its due as a source of obligation, but he also gives us a fine stock of anticontractarian arguments. His theory banishes not merely ancient but also modern superstitions in moral theory.

The demystification of property rights, promissory rights, and rights to command obedience that Hume provides is contained in his account of the social artifices whereby the problem caused by the fact that "the opposite passions of men impel them in contrary directions" (T 491) is given at least a partial solution, through a redirection and coordination of those same passions. Hume anticipates Feuerbach and Marx in his account of how "the mind has a great propensity to spread itself on external objects" (167), and then to fail to recognize its own handiwork, both when they are the "fictions of the understanding" and when they are the "artifices" of convention and social inventiveness. We typically fail to acknowledge our own collective handiwork, both in metaphysics and in morality. Hume is fully aware of the resistance his readers will put up to his shocking claim: "See if you can find that matter of fact or external existence which you call *vice* . . . you can never find it until you turn your reflexion into your own breast and find a sentiment of disapprobation which arises in you towards this action" (468–469), and he has an explanation for such resistance.[2] In the case of the "laws of justice," which in his account are "entirely artificial and of human invention" (526), our wish to see these as "Laws of Nature," or of God-or-Nature, as the work of some superhuman legislator, is easily explained if one of our major inventions is that of the special role of law declarer and enforcer. Having given the job of declaring law to a special functionary, and dignified that role, we plausibly then see all rules as stemming from a source external to and more awesome than the ordinary citizen and see the most fundamental rules as coming from as wise and equitable a magistrate as we can imagine. For Hume our religious propensities are the clearest proof of our mind's propensity to spread itself on external objects, and the

2. This resistance is found even among Hume's admirers, some of whom seem to think that to be a serious moralist one must be an objectivist. A striking example is D. F. Norton's version of Hume's ethics in *David Hume: Common-Sense Moralist, Sceptical Metaphysician* (Princeton, 1985).

Natural Law tradition exhibits this phenomenon. Hume plays up the link between the projections of purely religious or "priestly inventions" and the projections of our moral inventions by repeatedly likening the social artifices to the superstitions of religion (T 515, 524–525; E 198–199) while at the same time contrasting the usefulness and benefits of the one with the "uselessness" and "burdensomeness" of the other. The needed and "natural" artifices giving rise to the obligations of justice are freed from a religious base, yet shown to be like enough to purely religious artifices to explain the persistent illusions of the human mind concerning them. Hume, as Manfred Kuehn has pointed out, anticipates Kant's account of the unavoidable illusions we are subject to, and, as Kuehn does not point out, he sees the same propensity at work in our moral objectifications.[3]

## Hume's Originality: The Scope of His Moral Creationism

I now come to the respects in which Hume's theory picks up elements of some earlier theories but uses them in a new way. Those of his predecessors who came closest to anticipating his theory I take to be Hobbes, Pufendorf, and Locke. Among other influences on Hume's moral theory as a whole, and so on this part of it, I would of course include his own list in the *Treatise*'s introduction, which besides Locke lists "my lord Shaftesbury, Dr. Mandeville, Mr. Hutchison, Dr. Butler" and adds an *et cetera* (T xviii), as well as those cited or referred to in *Treatise*, Book 3, and the *Enquiry Concerning the Principles of Morals (EPM)*. In the latter, however, the earlier proud claims about artifice are prudently somewhat muffled, and the word "artificial," with its Hobbesian associations, is avoided except in one footnote. Those cited include Cicero, Justinian, Grotius, Malebranche, Bayle, and Montesquieu. Among influences on Hume I would also include Machiavelli, whom Hume seems to have read carefully.[4]

It is because I have not read all these authors as carefully as Hume did that my claims about originality must be tentative. I still have much to learn about Hume's relation to those voluminous writers he calls "the ci-

3. Manfred Kuehn, "Hume's Antinomies," *Hume Studies* 9, 1 (April 1983): 25–45.

4. See E. C. Mossner, "Hume's Early Memoranda, 1729–40: The Complete Text," *Journal of the History of Ideas* 9 (1949): 492–518. See also Mossner, *The Life of David Hume* (Oxford, 1889), 266, for an account of Hume's "loan" of a Machiavellian passage to Robert Wallace.

vilians."[5] In that connection, I want to quote what Hume's second biographer (third, if we count Hume's own as the first and Smellie's as the second) said about the link, for it still bears repeating. Writing in 1807, after quoting Hume's own autobiographical remarks about his reactions to Voet and Vinnuis, Ritchie goes on:

> Among men of letters a fashion has long prevailed of decrying the writings of the civilians, the usual magnitude of whose works is certainly not calculated to render them inviting. . . . It is probable, however, that the mere circumstance of directing his attention, although in a superficial degree, to the Roman Code and the municipal laws of his country gave a slight bias to his studies which, being seconded by favourable events, suggested at a future period the project of compiling his *History*, a task he understood not from a wish to detail battles and exhibit a tedious succession of political broils, but for the more dignified purpose of tracing the progress of legislation and civility.[6]

Ritchie is surely right, both about the influence of Hume's law studies and about the aim of his *History of England*. Thanks to Duncan Forbes and others, it is now becoming less fashionable to play down Hume's debt to the Natural Law jurisprudential tradition, and less fashionable also to try to separate his writings in social philosophy from his historical writings. The appendices of the *History of England* obviously continue, and sometimes revise,[7] the line of thought begun in *Treatise*, Book 3, Part 2. And as for "the civilians," even a superficial reading of Grotius and Pufendorf alerts one to the many echoes of their discussions in Hume's writings. Pufendorf, for example, says that part of the point of morality is "the polishing and methodizing of common life," and Hume borrows the phrase to describe philosophical judgments as "the reflec-

---

5. I learned first from Duncan Forbes, *Hume's Philosophical Politics* (Cambridge, 1975), and more recently from various writings and lectures by Istvan Hont and Knud Haakonssen. Among these are Istvan Hont, "From Pufendorf to Adam Smith," paper presented at the Conference on Political Thought of the Scottish Enlightenment in a European Context, Edinburgh, August 26, 1986; Knud Haakonssen, "Hugo Grotius and the History of Political Thought," *Political Theory* 13, 2 (May 1985); and "Natural Law and the Scottish Enlightenment," *Man and Nature* 4 (1985); as well as two anthologies, Istvan Hont and David Ignatieff, eds., *Wealth and Virtue* (Cambridge, 1983), and R. H. Campbell and Andrew S. Skinner, eds., *Natural Law and the Scottish Enlightenment* (Edinburgh, 1982).

6. T. E. Ritchie, *Account of the Life and Writings of David Hume* (London, 1807; reprint, Thoemmes Antiquarian, 1990).

7. The first appendix, dealing with the Saxon form of life, notes how allegiance to a leader preceded any recognized stable property rights, at least to land.

tions of common life, methodised and corrected" (E 162).[8] Like Hume, Pufendorf has a lengthy discussion of the ambiguities of the term "natural." Hume uses Pufendorf's near-technical term "imposition" in the *Treatise* (499), in his summary of his preliminary account of the artificial virtues. Hume follows Grotius in taking the basic rationale for the institution of marriage to derive from the underprivileged epistemological position of putative fathers. (In a section of *De Jure Belli et Pacis* concerned with "the rights of bastards," Grotius says that "the mother can be certain that the child is hers . . . but this certain cannot a father be . . . therefore some way was thought to be found whereby it might appear who the father of every child was: and this was marriage.")[9] Besides the influence of Roman, continental, and Scots law,[10] there is doubtless also some influence not just of maritime law, cited in *Enquiry Concerning the Principles of Morals,* but also of English common law, from Hume's brief time with a shipping firm in Bristol.

Let me come now to Hume's improvements on the accounts of social artifice that we find in Hobbes, Pufendorf, and Locke. The very term "artificial" would to Hume's first readers evoke Hobbes's version of Leviathan, the authoritative state, as an automaton, or artificial animal. In his introduction to *Leviathan,* Hobbes likens the making of this monster to "that *fiat,* or the *Let us make man* pronounced by God in the Creation." Hume seconds Hobbes's reappropriation of creative power from gods to human creators, but he also generalizes the scope of what we could call Hobbes's "creationism." Not merely does Hume correct (or revise Butler's correction of) Hobbes's version of the psychology of the human creators, but he also extends the range of their creation to include contract

8. Samuel Pufendorf, *Laws of Nature and Nations,* translated by Basil Kennet (R. Sare, 1717), bk. 1, ch. 1, sec. 3, p. 3.

9. Hugo Grotius, *Laws of War and Peace,* translated by William Evats (Ralph Smith, 1682), bk. 2, ch. 7, sec. 8.

10. Neil MacCormick has pointed out to me that Hume's words in *My Own Life* concerning his "unsurmountable aversion" to his legal studies, in particular to Voet and Vinnius, except those linked with "the pursuits of philosophy and general learning," may echo the words of James Dalrymple, Viscount Stair, *Institutions of the Laws of Scotland* (London, 1693), bk. 1, title 1, sec. 17, that the study of mere compilations of legal decisions, not linked to some general jurisprudential theory, may "exceedingly nauseate delicate ingines." Although Hume may not have continued his law studies to the point where Scots law was the prescribed field of study, he can be assumed to have at least browsed in Stair's *Institutions,* as he was a member of a family of lawyers, and a younger cousin of Henry Homes, Lord Kames, with whom he was in fairly frequent intellectual debate.

or covenant, and the very idea of authority and authoritative law. Where Hobbes took the concepts of authoritative law, and of contract, as somehow innate, waiting only to be analyzed and used, Hume takes them to be human inventions, having as it were to be synthesized before they can be analyzed. Hobbes takes the human tool for creating or inventing Leviathan to be covenant or contract. Hume saw that we must first, by some more natural means or by some more natural tool or tool equivalent (what he calls "convention"), create contract. We must create it before we can use it. As far as I am aware, no one before Hume saw obligations arising from prior promises or contracts to be just as problematic as any others, saw that they were in no sense more "primary" than the obligations to which social contract theorists, Hobbes included, tried to reduce to them. Hume sees, as others before him did not, that the very concepts of promise and contract are cultural achievements, themselves dependent on cultural invention or artifice. The precise form of contract, like that of the other artifices, will vary from community to community, not just because of their varying stages of development toward that commercial society where contract really comes into its own but also because social artifices are, as Hume says, "changeable by human law" (T 528). Historical contingencies will lead to variations in positive laws, just as they also lead to some variations in the customs and conventions whereby artifices first evolve. Scotland, for example, had, and to some extent still has, a different institution of marriage than England,[11] and supposedly the Tongans do not have any institution of promise.[12] (Hume would have been surprised at this, since he did believe that the artifices he described were "natural," that is, naturally needed, and such that some form of each would naturally evolve or be slowly "invented" in all human societies.)

Hume generalizes Hobbes's secular moral constructivism or creationism to include the full variety of our strict obligations and correlative rights, including the demand that men "perform their Covenants made." Both contract and authority are, for Hume, like property in being cul-

---

11. "Gretna Green marriages," or marriages *de praesenti* (namely, of minors without parental consent), were recognized, as was marriage without any ceremony, but merely by "cohabitation with habit and repute" (see the Right Honorable Lord Cooper, *The Scottish Legal Tradition,* rev. M. C. Meston, Saltire Society Pamphlet, N.S. (William Blackwood, 1982), 18–21.

12. See Fred Korn and Shulamit R. Decktor Korn, "Where People Don't Promise," *Ethics* 93, 3 (April 1983): 445–450.

tural products invented to solve the social problem caused by "the opposite passions of men" (T 491). The concept of obligation, he says, is "altogether unintelligible" without first understanding justice and its dependence on convention, and he accuses those who use it in their explication of justice of "a very great fallacy" (ibid.).

## An Aside on the Scope of Humean Obligations and Duties

In the important section "Some farther reflexions concerning justice and injustice," Hume contrasts the "entire" rights and obligations of property and promise, whose entirety and strictness are taken as a mark of artifice, with "half rights and obligations, so natural in common life" (T 531), but this occurs only in "our common *and negligent* way of thinking" (530, my emphasis), and Hume himself never, as far as I am aware, unequivocally endorses this looser and broader use of the term "obligation." In this passage, he is contrasting the "strictness" and "entirety" of obligations arising from social artifice with other moral concepts such as virtue(s) and vice(s) which do admit of degrees and gradation. He only twice appears to suggest that all talk of virtues can be translated into talk of obligations (or half obligations), and in both cases the appearance need not be taken as showing what he really thought. One of these two passages occurs during his discussion of promises. There he says:

> All morality depends upon our sentiment; and when any action, or quality of mind, pleases us *after a certain manner,* we say it is virtuous; and when the neglect, or nonperformance of it, displeases us *after a like manner,* we say we lie under an obligation to perform it. A change of the obligation supposes a change of the sentiment; and the creation of a new obligation supposes some new sentiment to arise. But 'tis certain we can naturally no more change our own sentiments than the motions of the heavens, nor by any single act of our will, that is by a promise, render any action agreeable or disagreeable, moral or immoral; which without that act wou'd have produc'd contrary impressions or have been endow'd with different qualities. (517)[13]

The claim about obligation may appear to imply that we have an obligation to avoid every vice or at least to avoid acting viciously. Such a gen-

13. Pall Ardal drew my attention to this passage when a version of this paper was given to the Hume Society, Edinburgh, August 29, 1986.

eral claim, covering natural as well as artificial virtues, would be hard to reconcile with Hume's earlier already quoted claim that those who use the term "obligation" without first showing its link with justice and with "its origin in the artifice and contrivance of men" are guilty of "a very gross fallacy" (491). The only way to reconcile the two passages would be to suppose, a bit implausibly, that Hume thinks that the artificial virtues swallow up the natural ones, that some convention or some legislator makes it our strict obligation to acquire the natural virtues. Before embracing such an interpretation, we should, however, note two things about the passage in the *Treatise* (517). First, the apparently general claim about obligation is not that there is an obligation to avoid having qualities of mind that would be morally disapproved of but, rather, to avoid *acting* to display such vices. Since Hume keeps repeating that, in general, actions are subject to moral evaluation only insofar as they display motives or qualities of mind (477, 575), this restriction of "obligation" to obligatory performance or non-neglect *of actions* is itself a sign that Hume is not really proposing that all attribution of virtue and vice can be translated into attribution of obligations. And, second, the main point of the passage is not to establish anything about the scope of obligation but, rather, to show the error of the view that promissory obligations are willed into existence by the promisor. Hume's concern here is primarily with the artificial virtue of fidelity to promises, the artificial vice of infidelity to promises. It seems to me a more charitable reading to suppose that he spoke a little carelessly here than to suppose that he spoke carelessly when he earlier made the very strong and general claim that obligation is "wholly unintelligible without first understanding justice" (490–491) and its dependence on artifice.

The other passage apparently recognizing a general obligation to avoid not merely artificial but also natural vices occurs in the *Treatise* (T 479), while Hume is explaining and defending his "undoubted maxim, *that no action can be virtuous or morally good unless there be in human nature some motive to produce it, distinct from the sense of its morality,*" and creating the puzzle about what the natural motive to justice is, a puzzle his theory of artifice is designed to solve. There, after stating the maxim, he concedes eventually that "on some occasions a man may perform an action merely out of regard to its obligation," and the example he first offers is this: "A man who feels no gratitude in his temper, is still pleas'd to perform grateful actions, and thinks he has, by that means fulfill'd his duty" (ibid.). More generally, he then says, "When any virtuous motive or principle is common in human nature, a person who feels his heart devoid of that principle may hate himself upon that account, and may perform the action without the motive, from a certain sense of duty, in order to acquire by practice that virtuous principle, or at least to disguise from himself, as much as possible, his want of it" (ibid.). I note, about this whole passage, that Hume uses the word "duty," not "obligation," when talking specifically of display of the natural virtue and vice of gratitude and ingratitude, and then makes the more general claim about acting "from a certain sense of duty" in order to "practice" the virtue, or at least to conceal its absence, before he shifts to the concession about acting out of regard to *obligation*. The latter is of course what is at issue for his discussion of the motivation to just actions, so it is understandable that he includes it in his concession, and in his explanation of how that concession is compatible with his "undoubted maxim," since the exceptional case "still supposes in human nature some distinct principles which are capable of producing the action, and whose moral beauty renders the action meritorious" (491). Does Hume use "duty" and "obligation" interchangeably? I think not, and will shortly give support for this finding. For the moment we simply need to note that Hume has not explicitly said that there is an obligation to show gratitude; rather, he has said that a man of ungrateful heart may feel a certain sense of duty to put on a display of (fake) gratitude. And we should also note how guarded Hume himself is about endorsing what the unnaturally ungrateful man thinks, when he thinks he can fulfill his duty by performing apparently grateful actions. Hume's concession here is to what people think and say, perhaps in their "common and negligent way of thinking" (530). I do not think that this passage shows that Hume wants to extend the scope of the concept of obligation to make it coextensive with that of action expressive of virtue or the absence of vice. What the passage shows about Hume's use of the term "duty" is another matter, to which I shall shortly turn.

I have said that Hume's theory has the resources to explain the errors of its opponents. I think that his account of obligation as arising from artifice, from social measures taken to redirect troublesome passions, can also show why some might think they have an obligation to try to rid themselves of any vice they detect in themselves, although he himself does not exploit these resources. If, say, Calvinists believe that a "sinfully" proud person (like Hume as a child proud of his achievements in letters) has an obligation to discipline his pride, or, to take Hume's example here, a coldhearted, unresponsive person feels he has an obligation to try to feel more gratitude to his benefactors, then he is reacting to his own individual idiosyncratic faults in a way parallel to the way a whole society reacts to the generally shared fault of avidity and limited generosity, trying by artifice to redirect a passion. Hume clearly thinks that the redirection of undue avidity, through a whole society-wide "scheme of actions," is an actualized possibility. But he expresses no optimism about *individual* attempts to redirect other passions which can in occasional individuals take socially pernicious forms. I have already quoted his claim that "'tis certain that we can naturally no more change our own sentiments than the motions of the heavens" (T 517), a claim that theoretically allows for the possibility that an individual might non-naturally, by an individual (as distinct from social) artifice, change his own sentiments. Later in Book 3, in discussing the limits of voluntary individual control, Hume praises the ancient moralists for treating as virtues qualities that are "equally involuntary and necessary, with the qualities of judgment and imagination. Of this nature are constancy, fortitude, magnanimity; and, in short, all the qualities of the great man. I might say the same, in some degree, for all the others; it being almost impossible for the mind to change itself in any considerable article, or cure itself of a passionate or splenetic temper when they are natural to it" (608). Clearly Hume thinks that the malleability of avidity by social artifice does not imply the general flexibility of other passions, certainly not by mere individual self-improvement regimens. For one who was as pessimistic as Hume about adult character reform it would be inhumane in the extreme to say that there is an obligation to change vices that cannot, in fact, be changed, and Hume does not say this. He limits obligation, on my reading of him, to the obligations arising from social artifice, to the sphere where cooperative redirection of passion is known to be possible.

The deontological family of moral concepts, the favorites of the Natural Law tradition, are authority, law, rights, obligations, duty, and right and wrong. I have discussed Hume's treatment of authority, law, rights, and obligations, and come now to duty and right and wrong. Hume only occasionally, and then usually ironically or derisively, speaks of right and wrong. The phrase from his pen tends to occur within such contexts as "the eternal rational measures of right and wrong" (T 466). He does at the start of the second *Enquiry* say that even the most insensitive human heart is not altogether untouched "with the images of Right and Wrong" (E 170), but then he goes on to analyze good and evil, virtues and vices, not right and wrong considered as such. He often includes "blame" and "censure" among the expressions of the workings of the moral sentiment, but this is blame and censure of mostly involuntary vices and defects, not of wrongful actions denominated as such. Hume says that even the altogether involuntary bad qualities, which the moderns prefer to call defects, not vices, are "blameable and censurable" (312), but "blame" and "censure" do not for him carry the special connotations the terms have for official punishers or for moral philosophers who are "divines in disguise," forever anticipating divine punishments and rewards. Hume gives no important place to moral indignation, for the sort of censure that has angry or resentful overtones. "Who would live amidst perpetual wrangling, and scolding, and mutual reproaches?" (257). If the moral sentiment motivated such mutual scolding, it would increase, not decrease, "harshness" and discord, and it would forfeit its title to be an improver of human life. A decent humane and Humean morality will minimize the sort of scolding and reproach where the term "wrong" is most at home. (It is of course at home in most games, and in simple arithmetic, where rules define what count as right and wrong moves, as the conventions of justice for Hume define morally right and wrong moves.)

I come now to Hume's use of "duty." He seems to use it beyond the field regulated by the social artifices. He can speak of a father's duty, although given his view that men need the artifice of marriage and the artificial virtue of female chastity to know to whom they are fathers, this may not count as an artifice-independent duty. Does Hume ever speak of a mother's duty? Not as far as I know. Wives and wives-to-be have "special duties" (T 570), as well as "obligations" (573), ones defined by the artifice of marriage, and citizens have "political duties" (542) and civil duties (543) as well as an obligation of obedience to magistrates (583). Hume in the *Treatise* (546) contrasts "our public and private duties," where the private duties in question are ones arising from promises or contracts a person has made as a private person. So in fact most of Hume's references to "duties" seem to be to artifice-defined ones. The exception is the putative "duty" to appear grateful, in the passage in the *Treatise* (479) whose significance I have already discounted. Nevertheless, I think that Hume does use "duty" differently than "obligation," and in a way that allows extension beyond the sphere of the artifices. I think his "duties" are Cicero's *officii,* and attach to roles which may be natural or artificial. So children can be said to have duties to their mothers and guardians, in virtue of their natural role as offspring and beneficiaries, and more generally, gratitude can be a duty for those who occupy the role of recipient of a free gift. In an artifice-regulated society, many roles which could be natural ones will be artifice-regulated (e.g., that of parents and children), and many roles will be artifice-created. The temporary role of promisor, and the role of citizen, are artifice-created, and so generate "duties." Not all Humean artifices design human roles with accompanying special duties; the artifice of property does not. It creates property owners, with rights, and with obligations to respect one another's rights, but not with special duties attaching to their status as property owners (or not duties that Hume mentions). I conclude that Hume reserves the word "duty" for a fairly definite moral requirement on action arising out of some (possibly natural) station a person occupies (parent, friend, teacher, wife, husband, promisor, citizen, magistrate) but uses "obligation" where and only where some artifice puts a requirement upon us. He does not use either term when he is speaking of role-independent natural virtues such as benevolence, cheerfulness, good temper, fortitude, patience—that is, in his discussion of most of the natural virtues. These, unlike obligations and duties, are not strictly required of us but, rather, encouraged and welcomed. That fact, however, does not make them a less important component in Humean morality than the artificial and other virtues that do require a conscientious doing of one's duty or fulfilling of one's obligations. Strictness need not correlate with importance.

## Hume's Originality, Continued—Giving Nature Its Due

The fact that Hume does make the concept of a virtue, not that of either obligation or duty, the primary one in his moral theory and does not, like Hobbes, take a virtue to be the same as obedience to some general rule, brings me to the second point I want to make about his originality. He sees, as Hobbes and Pufendorf and Locke did not see, that the thesis of moral creationism applies only to one *part* of morality, the deontological part. Hume does not merely generalize Hobbes's moral creationism to include contract, authority, and the very concept of obligation itself in its scope, but also recognizes what lies outside its scope, namely, the natural virtues, the vital part of morality that does not consist in authoritative rules and requirements but in welcomed and encouraged natural tendencies. Hume indeed sees, as I shall shortly elaborate, that unless there *were* more to morality than laws and obligations, there could not be any moral laws and obligations. Hume's very phrase "artificial virtues," and his peculiar special problem about what motive we approve when we approve of the honest man's actions, alert us to this important fact about his moral theory—that its central formal concepts are not Stoic but Aristotelian. Morality is fundamentally a matter of recognition and approval of virtues, of "that complication of mental qualities . . . we call personal Merit" (E 173). The Stoic concepts of law and action in obedience to it need to be brought in only for a special important subset of the moral virtues, those Hume calls "artificial."

In Hume's moral theory as a whole, deontology is circumscribed and subordinated to the main account of morality as the cultivation and welcoming of virtues, both natural virtues and artificial virtues. This fact brings me to Hume's difference from both Locke and Pufendorf. For, as far as moral creationism goes, they both have wider claims than Hobbes or Hume. Pufendorf's theory of "moral entities," imposed on physical nature and existing only as long as the imposing will recognizes them, and Locke's *Essay* doctrine that moral concepts, including that of obligation itself, are mixed modes made without external archetypes by "the human mind pursuing its own ends," both outdo Hobbes, and Hume too, in the explicit or implied scope of their creationism.[14] (As a matter of fact, neither Locke nor Pufendorf explicitly lists contract among these special moral entities, notions, or "modes." Although by general implication both must include it, they also both treat contract as more basic or "primary" than other moral modes, able itself to generate moral entities and new obligations.) Pufendorf's moral creationism is extremely comprehensive; among the examples he gives of such (in one sense) non-natural entities are *child, adult, man,* and *woman.*[15] Indeed, any term

14. See Pufendorf, pt. 1: "Of the Origin and Variety of Moral Entities"; and John Locke, *An Essay on Human Understanding,* bk. 3, ch. 5, sec. 6.

15. Pufendorf, bk. 1, ch. 1, sec. 12, p. 8, dealing with moral entities that are "moral persons," says that among the categories of private person are those stemming from distinctions arising from "Sex and Age, whence come the Differences of Men and Women . . . for though the

with any moral implications for Pufendorf names a moral entity, created by some will's imposition. Both Pufendorf and Locke, unlike Hume, want to be able to say that the honors for doing this creative imposition are to be shared between God and human beings. Pufendorf divides them out fairly straightforwardly, making some concepts depend on human legislation, other more basic ones on prior divine legislation.[16] But Locke seems to want to divide the responsibility in a less clear manner. He thinks, it seems, that we create the moral ideas—ideas such as adultery, theft, murder—but that it is God who forbids such actions. It is as if we give God the vocabulary with which He then enunciates the moral law. We think up the idea of obligation, and a range of possible obligations, but God decides what our obligations really are.[17] I can make little sense of Locke's theory, taken as a whole. Its tensions and incoherences derive from its attempt to combine a sort of secular moral creationism with a more traditionally theological Natural Law theory. Pufendorf makes the same attempt. The problems in his account are less glaring than in Locke's but are at root the same. The identity of the imposing will or wills is basically unclear in both theories, and both presuppose rather than explain the authority and power of these unclearly identified imposing wills. Hume, by contrast, is straightforwardly secular in his account, and he does try to show the evolution of the concept of legislative authority, as much as of any other deontological concept. The strength of his theory of artifice lies in its being embedded in an account of natural morality and the natural virtues, for it is to this he can and does turn to show just how human communities can invent the deontological entities they do, including eventually the artifice of magisterial authority. Hume's theory of human artifice is supported by a theory of human nature and, within that, an emphasis on our natural capacities for coopera-

---

Diversity of Sex and Number of Years are not of external Imposition, yet in the Method of Social Life they involve some kind of Moral Notion, in as much as different Actions are becoming in different Sexes." He can be read as here anticipating our distinction between sex and gender. Later in book 6 he develops his views about what actions are becoming and unbecoming to human males and females; he takes it that sexual initiative is becoming in males only and that women should agree to male sovereignty in marriage, and he characterizes as "Barbarous at least, if not Beastly" (34) the reported couplings of "Amazonian marriages" where these asymmetries were reversed, thus going against "the Genius and Character of both Sexes."

16. Pufendorf, bk. 1, ch. 1, sec. 3.

17. For a valiant attempt to make sense of Locke's theory, see John Colman, *John Locke's Moral Philosophy* (Edinburgh, 1983).

tion and coordination, displayed most importantly within the natural family. I turn now to that aspect of his theory.

## The Place of the Natural Family in Hume's Theory

In the story Hume tells in the *Treatise,* it is only because of our biologically given nature, and of some aspects of that which we can approve of and so call virtues, that we *can* make the moral creations or artifices that we do make. We do not create or invent ex nihilo but out of potentialities provided by nature, and our creations, although not directly modeled on them, do in fact reflect and repeat features present in that non-artificial social structure, the natural family. For our given biological nature, as Hume understands it, makes us not merely physically but also emotionally and motivationally beings who are essentially family members, linked by what he calls "the relation of blood" to both ancestors and descendents, the closest of whom we live with in intimacy and interdependency.[18] The relation of blood, Hume says, "creates the strongest tie the mind is capable of in the love of parents for their children" (T 352). Hume's account in Book 3 of how we can collectively invent artifices, society-wide schemes of cooperation, depends crucially on what he has already in Book 2 argued is our human psychology. It is only because of our way of procreating, of letting family lines continue, and the psychological preconditions and effects of that, that we are able to do any social creating. Hume's story of the genesis of the social artifice is centered on this key sociobiological fact about us, one that Adam Ferguson was to repeat, that we are from the start family members. We are mammals; we "propagate our kind" by cooperating with mates and offspring in the natural family. As Hume says, "in order to form society, 'tis requisite not only that it be advantageous but also that men be sensible

18. The place of love and family intimacy among our modern values has been the focus of some interesting recent discussions by social philosophers. Bernard Williams discusses it in *Ethics and the Limits of Philosophy* (Cambridge, 1985), and Charles Taylor in his essay "Legitimation Crisis?" sees family life as a currently threatened value. He writes: "This is particularly critical because the version of identity predominant in our society is one which aims towards a mobile subject, who loosens the ties of larger communities and finds himself on his own in the nuclear family. But this gives tremendously heightened significance to the nuclear family, which is now the main locus of strong, lasting, defining relations; and it has given the emotions of family love a uniquely important place in the modern conception of natural fulfillment. The eighteenth century already sees this positive valuation of family life, family ties, family feeling" (*Philosophy and the Human Sciences: Philosophical Papers* 2 [Cambridge, 1985]).

of its advantages. Most fortunately, therefore" there is the natural family, where such advantages become known (486). Human beings start with "a long and helpless infancy" (E 206) and, if they survive that, must have had a fair amount of parental care, and been able to cooperate enough to receive that, and so become accustomed to some forms of trust and trustworthiness. Hume's account of the artifices is a story of the enlargement and proliferation of forms of trust and cooperation, and its linchpin is some initial trust, some experience of the advantages of sustaining trust. For this reason it is scarcely coherent to deplore, as J. L. Mackie does, the fact that Hume's splendid account of moral artifice is accompanied by a different account of what he calls "natural" virtues.[19] Hume's theory of artifice needs the support of his account of our nature, our natural coordinative abilities, their easily perceived advantages, their natural limits, and their potential for artificial extension.

What is strictly needed in Hume's account is the fact and easily perceived advantage of natural cooperation within the natural family. But he also believes there is *love* there too. His version of family relationships in Book 2 is of mutual love and easy intimacy, not of tyranny, rivalry, jealousy, or hostility. It speaks volumes for his own childhood care by his devoted widowed mother, and for her ways of "keeping peace among her children." In his autobiography Hume tells us how impressed he was by the maternal care he experienced, and the dedication of his *Four Dissertations* to John Home, author of the play *Douglas,* which is largely concerned with the intensity of mother love, as well as his fervent support for the controversial first production of that play, may have been inspired as much by the matter as by the manner of that now not-much-admired dramatic work.

There is nothing at all novel in the general thesis that social ties beyond the family depend somehow on social ties within the family. Where Hume is interesting and original is in the details of his account. One striking feature is not just the emphasis on maternal devotion but also the total absence of patriarchal authority from his account of the natural family. Whereas Grotius takes "marriage in its natural terms for such cohabitation as places the woman under the custody or safeguard of the man," Hume does not take it that way.[20] Since his father died in his in-

---

19. See J. L. Mackie, *Hume's Moral Theory* (Oxford, 1980), 129.
20. Grotius, bk. 2, ch. 7, sec. 8.

fancy, and his mother did not remarry, he never experienced paternal authority. He had a firsthand empirical demonstration that some women could care for their children without being, in Grotius's phrase, under the "eye" and protection of a husband, a member of the "nobler sex," to whom women in their stories submit in return for protection (protection not from the elements but from other noble males).[21] Hume's widowed mother doubtless was dependent on some male relatives for the "expenses" of child rearing, but she seems to have managed home, estate, and children well enough without a husband as father and master. We know that this fact impressed Hume, and his theory is indebted to his own experience, in a way that confirms his own empiricism in epistemology.

Hume's model of family cooperation, which I am suggesting is to be seen as the original parent of the social artifices, is not of cooperation within a family that needs and has a male "head." Hume knew paternal authority to be unnecessary. What is essential for the family to play the role alloted it in Hume's theory of how social artifices get invented is, first, cooperation or at least continued cohabitation between a man and a woman, then some shared parental control over children, enough to "rub off" any "rough corners and untoward affections" (T 486) and to "preserve peace" among them (493). (The mention here of untoward affections signals Hume's continuing near-obsession with the question of incest and why it should be seen as "untoward." His *History of England* indulges his great fascination with canon law prohibitions and various breaches of them.) Such shared parental control will be a sort of family forerunner of that "mixed government" that he thought was the best version of the artifice of magisterial authority. Any male sovereignty in the family, he tells us in "Of polygamy and divorces," counts as "real usurpation" (Es 184). This is pretty radical, compared with Grotius and Pufendorf. Hume has come to be seen as a conservative in social theory, but on some root social issues, namely, on priestly power and male supremacy, he is no conserver but a reformer or a revolutionary.[22] If it was his aim to rid his society of "the Christian superstition," as he is reported to have said on his deathbed it was (while acknowledging that the work was unfinished), this alone makes the term "conservative" inappropri-

21. Ibid.
22. I have discussed this in "Hume on Women's Complexion," in *The Science of Man in the Scottish Enlightenment*, edited by Peter Jones (Edinburgh, 1990), 33–53.

ate. If, as I am suggesting, the demise of priestly power in a religion wor-shiping a God-father would mean the demise of one form of patriarchal power, then radicalism in religion and radicalism in male-female power relations are natural partners. Hume not merely wages a sustained and varied antireligious literary campaign, but he also diagnoses the root causes of patriarchal monotheism and attempts some subversion at that deeper level. His revised version of the natural family, as a family with-out male sovereignty, may owe something to Hobbes, who allocates power over the child to the mother, but Hobbes does not, as Hume does, give this nonpatriarchal version of the mini-society of the family a vital role to play in the explanation of wider-ranging social structures of co-operation.[23] The natural family provides experience of the benefits of co-operation and gives members of it the crucial knowledge that there can be conditions in which we can trust and work with others to mutual benefit. What is more, in Hume's account of it, we find within the natu-ral family "the rudiments of justice" (T 493), not just in cooperation itself, and in that unspoken agreement to coordination which prefig-ures what Hume calls "convention," but also in forerunners of specific artifices, of the content of specific conventions. In the family there is a primitive foreshadowing of property (ibid.), of fidelity to a sort of under-taking (571), and of mixed government, when "the parents govern by advantage of their superior strength and wisdom, and at the same time are restrained in the exercise of their authority by the natural affection which they bear their children" (486). I use the word "foreshadow" for these family anticipations of specific social artifices, following Hume's terminology in the *Treatise* (540), when he says that military leaders who assume command in time of war, before governments are insti-tuted, enjoy a "shadow of authority," so that "camps are the true moth-ers of cities," that is, of governed communities. (Hume's biological and feminine metaphor here is worthy of note.)

It needs to be made quite clear that these family shadows, or fore-shadowings, of the specific artifices do not, in the Humean story, directly generate or even serve as the model for those artifices themselves. The causal story is not that we make artifice copies of primitive rights and duties within the natural family. Hume's natural history of the artifices is much more complicated. In his account of the rise of property, it is fam-

23. See Thomas Hobbes, *Leviathan*, ch. 20.

ily cooperation in general, not the specific form of it that consists in recognition of children's proto-property rights to their "own" toys, beds, and so on, that is invoked. In the account of the rise of promise, that artifice is more contrasted than likened to fidelity and reciprocity between friends and lovers (T 521). And in the account of the origin of government Hume explicitly denies that the authority of governments derives from paternal authority (541). (It could still in theory derive from maternal authority but only via military shadow authority, which, Amazons aside, seems an unlikely story, and one there is no reason to foist on Hume.) The Humean story getting us from family cooperation to society-wide cooperation is not a story of a simple cloning of giant versions of aspects of family cooperation. Shortly I will discuss some features of that complex natural history, arguing that the generation of the artifices, that do indeed repeat and vary features of the family, is a much more "natural" history than it would have been if the family had simply reduplicated itself or its features in larger-scale copies.

Hume's account of the family, and of the causal process by which the social artifices get generated from it, is a fundamentally biological account. He sees us as a biologist does, as mammals who reproduce sexually and feed and care for our young. We are essentially family members, but the Humean concept of the family is biological, not theological. Hume sees us and our nature as continuous with the rest of animal nature. Whereas Pufendorf saw morality, including duties of obedience to fathers and husbands, to save us from "the horrid stupidity of the dumb creation,"[24] Hume goes out of his way to emphasize that we are an animal species, that our "reason" is a form of reason in animals, of animal intelligence and animal instinct; that almost all our passions have their analogues in the so-called higher animals, who outdo us in the scope of their love for others; that some cooperate instinctively and more successfully than we do. Animals are neither stupid nor horrid, in comparison with us. Our special features, for Hume, are a faculty of reflection, of turning mental processes and passions on themselves as well as their normal objects, and that inventiveness which compensates for what in the preliminaries to his account of social artifice he playfully calls nature's unnatural gifts to us in the way of "natural" equipment to survive, that is, to survive without relying on human inventions, social

24. Pufendorf, bk. 1, pt. 1, ch. 1, sec. 2, p. 2.

and other. An "unnatural conjunction" (T 485) of extreme need and infirmity typifies not merely the human infant but our species as well, if one subtracts the products of our own collective inventiveness. The fact that we do have to rely on human creations, and have to learn from each other, makes us not merely inventive but acculturated animals, and Hume would not disagree with Pufendorf about the "comeliness"[25] this introduces into our lives, nor with Pufendorf's claim that neither we ourselves, once we have acquired culture, nor any god we recognize as such, would want us to "pass our life like beasts without culture and without rule."[26] Our "natural" defects, and our compensation for them, are the source of special goods, as well as special evils when our inventions go wrong.

Grotius, who keeps telling his readers to learn from other animals, such as the storks, who are claimed to carry their infirm parents on their backs, is more Hume's predecessor here in seeing some admirable features in other animals, and some continuity between animal behavior and human moral behavior. He is also closer than Pufendorf to being in agreement with Hume's secularism.[27] But he does not really have a theory of social artifice and does not see that rights need to be invented before they can be respected. Hume's greatness lies in the way his theory of artifice is combined with and embedded in a fairly realistic account of our biologically given nature, of what features of that we can approve of and encourage when we reflect on them from a moral point of view, what other features we find it necessary to regulate by artifices. His account both of human nature and of what virtues we often have is vital to his account of artifice and artificial virtues. For without some natural virtues such as kindness to children, patience, and gratitude in family members, the family will not serve its basic biological reproductive function, let alone serve to give us the rudiments of justice.

## An Aside on Marriage and Obedience

Hume, of course, is perfectly clear that the artificial as distinct from the natural form of the family does have a "master." When he is referring to

25. Ibid.
26. Ibid., sec. 3, p. 3.
27. See Haakonssen, "Hugo Grotius and the History of Political Thought," for a discussion of the limited extent of Grotius's secularism.

family relations as they existed in marriage-initiated families, those familiar to most of his readers, he sometimes refers to the master of a family (T 487). And the artificial virtues of female chastity and modesty,
along with the legal institution or artifice of marriage that he describes
in the *Treatise* at the end of his account of the social artifices, is of course
not the natural but an artificial family. Hume describes it as socially useful and as "conspicuously" artificial. It does subordinate women's freedom and interests to men's freedom and interests, but it is not said to ·
subordinate wives to their husbands' commands. No patriarchal authority is included in the matrimonial artifice that Hume describes as serving
a socially useful purpose. Chastity, not obedience, is the artificial female
virtue he analyzes, one whose unnaturalness he takes to be "obvious"
and to need no argument (570). Where he had dignified the useful
artifices of property and its transfer by consent as "naturally" respected
artifices (533), no such claim is made for the artifice of marriage with a
double standard, even when that is not made to incorporate the addi-
tional artifice of male mastery. The most that can be said for it is that it is
*a* way to serve a vital social function, providing children with full parental care. Does Hume think that marriage, as described in *Treatise,* Book 3,
Part 2, Section 12, meets his earlier test for an acceptable social artifice,
meets the demand that it be "infinitely advantageous to the whole and
every part" of society (498)? He speaks of its acceptance by "those who
have an interest in the fidelity of women" and of others who have no
such interest as "carried along by the stream." This is tantamount to saying that not every part of society receives infinite advantages from this
artifice; it is useful only to part of society, the males intent on knowledge
of paternity.

It seems, then, that Hume is guarded in his claims about the social
benefits of a form of marriage that demands greater chastity of women
than of men and makes no claims at all for the social usefulness of any
patriarchal form of the family. Not only is patriarchy not natural, but it is
not a useful artifice either. Perhaps it should be put along with priestly
power that is exercised in the Mass, and in the laying on of hands, which
Hume mentions as being, in their artificiality, like the artifices that make
the artificial virtues possible, but unlike them in their social uselessness
or harmfulness. Hume recognizes no virtue, natural or artificial, that
consists in obedience to husbands. The only virtues of obedience in his
list are obedience to magistrates, an important artificial virtue and, by
implication, also small children's obedience to parents, both to mothers

and to fathers. Hume's ethics are radical and reformist, not merely in the demotion of the monkish virtues, and in the doubts cast on the heroic virtues, but also on the carefully limited endorsement given to obedience to any sort of human superior. His contemporary readers and reviewers saw that better than most readers today seem to: he was considered an apostle of a dangerous degree of liberty.[28] And to reject the authority systems both of churches and of patriarchal families was indeed to preach liberation.

We need then to distinguish at least three versions of the family—the natural family, the useful artifice of a family with an obligatorily chaste wife and mother, and the actual social artifice of Christian marriage in which the wife is also obligatorily obedient to her husband. It is the first of these that plays a vital role in the genesis of the useful social artifices, as Hume describes that. The second is itself an artifice that is seen to have at least sectional usefulness, and the third lurks in the background of Hume's *Treatise* account, neither endorsed nor criticized, and comes in for criticism in such essays as "Of love and marriage" (Es 557–562) and "Of polygamy and divorces" (181–190). To distinguish these three versions of the family is not to deny that vestiges of the first could remain within the second, or that the second and third could be combined. Presumably Hume's own experience of family life, with his widowed mother, older brother, and sister, was of a family of the second sort, that had been also of the third, and still retained that memory, as well as containing some vestiges of the natural family. When husbands, although seen to have superior authority, do not exert it, or when they die young, then families of the third sort will approximate more closely to the natural family. Of course, if parental cooperation is an important element in that natural family, then one-parent families will be necessarily defective. They may be free of that "real usurpation" of male sovereignty, but they will also lack that cooperation between equals which, along with cooperation between unequals (parent and child), could serve as example and paradigm. It is noteworthy that Hume, like several other enlightened Scots of the eighteenth century, not merely spent a fatherless childhood but like them also avoided both patriarchal marriage and (unless we believe Agnes Galbraith) fatherhood.[29] Avoiding male sovereignty in marriage may be essential to making fami-

28. See Mossner, *The Life of David Hume*, 120.
29. It has been noted by Charles Camic, *Experience and Enlightenment* (Edinburgh, 1983), ch. 4. On Galbraith's assertion, see Mossner, *The Life of David Hume*, ch. 7.

lies morally exemplary and nurseries of enlightenment but not sufficient to make them *serve* as example. Indeed, those interestingly fatherless nurseries of the Scottish enlightenment that produced enlightened sons generated no grandchildren (and no enlightened daughters either). Fatherless and unfathering, Hume and Adam Smith had to treat their books as their offspring; some, like the *Treatise,* deemed "stillborn," others, like Smith's *Theory of Moral Sentiments,* seen as a candidate for "immortality" (L 1.303).

But enough armchair sociology and psychology, tempting though it obviously is. To recapitulate: the point I have tried to make about the place of the family in Hume's story of the artifices and their rise and progress is that it is the natural family that is important in their rise, not departures from it in any variant of the artificial family.

## The Natural Family, Continued

My final suggestion about the centrality of the concept of the family in Hume's social theory may be found fanciful and has little direct textual support. This is the suggestion that Hume gives us a genealogy of the artifices, which are themselves seen as a family, a sequence of generations, and ones that, like human and unlike butterfly generations, overlap in a lifetime. The artifice of government, as we have seen, is found to have a "true mother," military leadership, who survives alongside her child, government. This suggestive metaphor of Hume's tempts me to extend it to his account of the "earlier" artifices, which are indeed presented by him as a sequence, later members repeating and varying features found in their ancestors but not necessarily most similar to their closest ancestors. Hume's account of how property comes about, how transfer by consent comes to accompany it, how promise gets added to the family, then government, then, to correct its abuses, a free press, is not really historical but abstruse and highly theoretical. I suggest that one key to its abstruse complexities is the root metaphor of the transmission of human life, of the family, dominating his thinking. He gives us a genealogy of obligations. Not only does he take social change seriously, but his "natural history" of civil society is also a biologist's natural history, not a chemist's, geologist's, or astronomer's. Hume's concept of the "nature" that social artifices imitate is neither the theologian's nor Newton's but more that of Darwin. It is understandable that T. H.

Huxley chose to write a book about Hume's philosophy of human nature.

Hume's story in the *Treatise* of the changes leading from natural families in a hypothetical "state of nature" to a civilized artifice-secured way of life is not, like those of his ungrateful beneficiary Rousseau and of his Scottish successors Smith and Ferguson, a stage theory, in which there is progress from food gathering to herding to agriculture to commerce. We have to *infer* from the *Treatise* account what sort of work those who invent barter are doing, what different conditions (use of measures and of money) go with reliance on contract. The story in the *Treatise* is not primarily a story of economic change (although it is incidentally that) but of change in the sorts of moral ties we have to our fellows. Hume is working at a higher level of abstraction than his fellow-Scots. Later in his economic essays and in the *History of England* he becomes very concerned to correlate the social with the economic changes, but his main interest continues to lie in the evolving network of social ties. The continuities and discontinuities he stresses in his *Treatise* presentation of these—the way, for example, promise picks up some formal features present in its immediate ancestor, transfer by consent, and foreshadows, in the conditional punitive powers it confers on promisees, the later appearance of magistrates' punitive powers, the way these latter, like specific property rights, are exclusive, or monopolies of a power—all of these recombinations of a limited number of "genetic" components in successive members of the growing family of artifices, as Hume presents them, tempt me to suggest that the concept of the natural human family, as a sociobiological reality, is the root metaphor that generates the prima facie puzzling form of Hume's social theory in the *Treatise* and inspires his genealogy of social artifices, his "natural history" of human cooperation. We should see the artifices as an ongoing sequence of family members, each dependent for coming to be on prior members, and each having traits that can be traced back through ancestors. The genealogy of Hume's theoretical guiding thread leads us to genealogy itself. But even if this claim about his metatheory is rejected as fanciful, if it is denied that the natural family provides Hume with the metaphor that dictates the form of his theory, it will be hard to deny that it has a vital place in the substance of that theory. If I am right about the biological or sociobiological tenor of Hume's social theory, of his account of our capacities and of how we overcome both the limits of our "natural" abilities and the limits of the natural family, then he was in his social theory several generations ahead of his time. His thinking has more affinities with that of Darwin and Huxley than with Pufendorf, Kant, or Mill. Nor is it clear that we today, embroiled as we are in a debate about exactly what form a coherent sociobiology of the human animal could take, have any better account than Hume's to give of how our varying cultural inheritance relates to our biological inheritance.[30] Hume's treatise of human nature treats us as an inventive species, whose cultural inventions, while they are real novelties, owe much to our non-self-invented nature. Hume's theory of social artifice recognizes the cultural component of human life, human reason, and human morality as importantly different from our more unvarying natural intelligence and "natural virtues," yet at the same time anchors these cultural variation-introducing creative capacities in the biologically given nature of those who are born into family life, who come to reflect on it and on its limits. Hume portrays us as an inventive species, as animals who by nature are cooperative, passionate, and intelligent artificers, animals whose most important inventions are the "natural artifices" that extend and transform our own powers of cooperation, creation, self-fulfillment, and self-expression.

30. See Stephen Jay Gould's endorsement of criticism of Edward O. Wilson's version of our sociobiology in "Cardboard Darwinism," *New York Review of Books* 33, 14 (September 1986): 47–54.

# 7

# Hume on Resentment

In his *Enquiry Concerning the Principles of Morals (EPM)* version of the conditions of justice, Hume adds a third modified Hobbesian condition to the two, moderate scarcity and moderate selfishness, which he had listed in the *Treatise*. The new condition is a certain measure of equality, or limit to inequality—justice is owed, he says, only if there is a society of more or less equals, and only *to* those who are members of it. The equality in question concerns the ability of candidate society-members to "make us feel the effects of their resentment" (E 190). If such ability is lacking, then, Hume says, the relationships between "us" and "them" will be those of "absolute command on the one side and servile obedience on the other. Whatever we covet, they must instantly resign: Our permission is the only tenure, by which they hold their possessions: Our compassion and kindness the only check, by which they curb our lawless will" (ibid.). This passage is interesting because Hume describes the position of such powerless "creatures intermingled with men" in terms which appear to be social—command, obedience, possession, tenure, the act of "resigning" coveted goods. But he says that "our intercourse with them could not be called society, which supposes a degree of equality" (ibid.). *True* society is, then, restricted to those who are roughly equal, whose interests help to determine the conventions which give rise to duties of justice. But intermingled with the members of such a real society there might be, were, or are "a species of creatures" who, "though rational, were possessed of such inferior strength, both of body and mind, that they were incapable of all resistance, and could never, upon the highest provocation, make us feel the effects of their resentment"

149

(ibid.). They are "rational," so can obey, can resign possessions, and can resent their inferior status. They have quasi-social relations with their masters, but not fully social ones, since they are neither parties to nor beneficiaries of the social conventions which create rights and duties. Hume seems to assume that because they are not parties to the artifice-creating conventions, those conventions will not cover relations with them, so that the convenors' "laws" are limited, and allow them a sphere of "lawless will" in their dealings with the inferior creatures. But children, for example, while not legislators, may be both right-holders and beneficiaries of the laws which adults agree on. Hume is most charitably read here to mean that the conventions which serve the interests of the superior creatures might not, cannot be, depended on, to regulate in any way the dealings of the superiors with the inferiors. The inferiors are left at the mercy of their superiors, resent that fact, and yet may be powerless to alter the situation.

It is very clear from what follows that Hume has in mind in this passage the relations of males to females, and that it is his thoughts about male-female relationships which led to his emendation of his *Treatise* account of the conditions of justice. The *Treatise* had not mentioned equality of power as a condition for justice, but had devoted a chapter to the extra obligations, of chastity and modesty, which social conventions imposed on the female sex. It was therefore a natural question to arise for Hume whether women really could be parties to conventions which imposed these obligations on them. Were *their* interests served, or did these obligations arise from "the voluntary conventions of *men*" (T 510, emphasis added) who asked themselves, "What restraint, therefore, shall we impose upon women, in order to counter-balance so strong a temptation as they have to infidelity?" (571). Hume had argued that female fidelity was needed for male paternal obligations to be properly assigned, so that it was in the interests of children, of fathers, and of society in general that fatherhood be determinable, and so that wives be chaste. Now, in *EPM*, he considers the possibility of a class of slaves whose interests, like those of animals, need not be considered in the conventions which generate duties of justice. "The great superiority of civilized Europeans above barbarous Indians, tempted us to imagine ourselves on the same footing [as to animals] with regard to them, and made us throw off all restraints of justice, and even of humanity, in our treatment of them. In many nations the female sex are reduced to like slavery" (E 191). Is female subjection like slavery in being only *imagined* to obtain? Hume has been noncommittal on slavery—Europeans are "tempted" to imagine that Indians cannot make resentment felt, and males in some nations have the same temptation in their treatment of females. What Hume goes on to say makes it clear that he believes that the conditions for excluding women from considerations of justice could be met if males were united in a "confederacy to maintain this severe tyranny" (ibid.). The chances of their remaining united, however, are slight, since women, Hume says, have such "insinuation, charm and address" that they are "commonly" able to break the male confederacy. This characterization of the power of women, as lying in their charm or refusal to charm, might not endear Hume to contemporary feminists, but he does see the issue clearly as one essentially concerning power, and what is more, he relates the power of women to break male confederacy not merely to their insinuation, address, and charm, but also to what lies behind it—the fact no human is "possessed within himself [of] every faculty, requisite both for his own preservation and for the propagation of his kind" (ibid.). Hume goes on to attribute to the natural attraction between the sexes, and the natural parental instincts, a fundamental role not merely in providing a base on which a more extensive artifice-secured society can be founded, but also in ensuring that in such a society women can qualify for membership—they can make the effects of their resentments felt.

I find Hume's treatment of the relation of resentment and power to make resentment felt to a sense of injustice interesting and provocative. If he is right, resentment may be felt by those to whom no injustice has been done, as well as by victims of injustice. Resentment becomes resentment of injustice only when accompanied by some degree of social effect. If the resentful have this ability to make trouble, then there will be some sort of recognition of their interests and their claims, even if these are not met. A sense of injustice is a sense, not of hopeless resentment, but of forceful resentment.

Resentment, as an emotion, has had a bad press. Its most recent denigrator is Robert Solomon, who in his book *The Passions* characterizes it as a passion felt by those with "utter impotence," by those whose status is "intolerable inferiority." It thrives, he says "in the dark and moist shadows of the soul away from direct confrontations with superiors, bosses, members of the 'opposite' sex, bullies and authority figures."[1] This is fine rhetoric, but is it the truth? Must resentment be concealed, must it be impotent? Hume suggests that it can be effective, that it can break confederacies, perhaps even form them. Solomon's treatment of resentment as a nasty negative emotion felt only by emotionally crippled self-haters is in what might be called the Nietzschean tradition. Nietzsche contrasts the sense of justice of the free strong man, whose own word *makes* law, and for whom justice is being true to his word, with the slave's sense of injustice, his envy of the powerful. The latter feeling is *reactive*, passive, while the superman's conscience is awareness of his own sovereign active will. The chief contrast is between the doers and the sufferers, and resentment is, like envy and pity, a feeling reserved for the passive ones, the natural victims, those who react rather than act to establish their autonomy. For all Nietzsche's talk of transformation, he gives us more a typology of emotions than an account like, say, Hegel's in the *Phenomenology of Spirit,* of how emotions might, within one individual, transform themselves. (Nietzschean transvaluation occurs across generations, not within one life.) In this respect Solomon is more Nietzschean than Hegelian, but I find in Hume the beginning of an account of how passions change direction, and of what drives the change. In this *EPM* passage on resentment, the contrast between ineffective resentment and effective resentment, the suggestion that power is acquired by confederacy, and lost by its breakup, and the linking of effective power with a role in a productive process, all foreshadow Hegelian and Marxist themes.

This Hegelian note in Hume is not confined to these pages of the *Enquiry Concerning the Principles of Morals,* but can also be detected in Books 2 and 3 of the *Treatise.* Hume gives little space to discussing resentment, but significantly he does include it in the list of basic passions, ones which "produce good and evil, and proceed not from them, like the other affections" (T 439). The root sense of resentment, that it is simply a second feeling about some matter, typically a feeling consequent upon an action prompted by the "first" sentiment, makes it an essentially reactive emotion. Samuel Johnson's first sense of "resent" is "to

---

1. Robert Solomon, *The Passions: Emotions and the Meaning of Life* (Doubleday, 1976), 354, 353.

take well or ill," and he cites Bacon's use of "well-resented" as simply meaning reacted to favorably. It was only later that Johnson's second sense of "resent," and "resentment" as "a deep sense of injury," came to predominate. That is Hume's sense. His list of basic passions sometimes has "resentment," sometimes "desire to punish our enemies,"[2] which is a more active, or less "deep," sense of injury, one which has surfaced enough to take the form of a desire to inflict a retaliatory strike. In what sense can resentment, the deep sense of injury, "create good and evil," when it does seem to "proceed from them," if it is essentially reactive? Presumably Hume means that expressing resentment, making it felt, typically in revenge, is wanted in itself, not for its hedonic promise. Just as we eat to satisfy hunger, so we make resentment felt to satisfy resentment. The pleasure of such satisfaction need not be something we recall from previous successful punitive strikes. We know a priori that we will find it good to satisfy resentment as we know that satisfying hunger is a good.

This basic desire to punish our enemies is possible only for creatures who see themselves as capable of suffering not merely pain and frustration, but also injury or wrong, and who furthermore aspire to the moral role of punisher. Resentment is not simply anger; it is the form anger takes when it is provoked by what is seen as a wrong, and when the striking back which is desired is seen as punishment. (Johnson's first sense of "injury" is "hurt without justice.") This basic passion, more than any other in Hume's list, contains the seeds of the moral sentiment—a sense of oneself as one to whom wrong can be done, and an aspiration to an active proto-moral role, that of revenger.

Hume's list of basic or nonhedonic passions is "the desire of punishment to our enemies, and of happiness to our friends; hunger, lust and a few other bodily appetites" (T 439). Earlier, at 418, he equates resentment with the desire to punish an enemy for an injury, and at 417 he lists those instinctive passions which can be calm, and this list is "benevolence and resentment, the love of life, and kindness to children." The

---

2. According to Nietzsche and Scheler, resentment is an essentially *postponed* desire to hit back, and various poisons set in due to the postponement. Hume treats it more straightforwardly as a desire to punish enemies, which may or may not be acted on by actually punishing them. Whereas for Scheler the resentful person may express resentment in lots of ways, but these ways do *not* include active revenge, Hume sees the natural expression of resentment as attempted revenge, or punishment.

resulting list of basic passions is therefore: certain appetites, resentment, the love of life, benevolence to friends, and kindness to children. It is an initially puzzling list, perhaps intended merely as a list of instincts we in fact discover in human persons, with no common factor whatever. But it is clear that Hume intends kindness to children to mean mainly kindness to one's own children, in some sense of one's "own," so this instinct, like benevolence, is an instinct which eventually gets recognized as a natural virtue, and together they may even be seen as containing the germs of that positive side to the moral sentiment, the encouragement and endorsement of good qualities in children and other loved ones. Resentment, love of offspring, and benevolence to loved persons would between them provide the seeds from which we get moral recognition of both artificial and natural virtues.[3]

Benevolence, Hume had told us, is naturally but contingently related to love, recognition of good in others. No such contingently related desire was found by Hume as the natural accompaniment to love's parallel passion, pride. It, Hume says, is unaccompanied by any desire, not immediately exciting us to any action (T 367). I want to make the admittedly bold interpretative suggestion that resentment is negatively related to pride as benevolence is to love. Pride does not immediately excite us to any action, but being prevented from having any chance of pride provokes resentment. Those masters whose permission is the only tenure which the slaves have on possessions effectively deprive them of the chance for normal forms of pride. Pride, for Hume, is essentially pride in possession, but if the slaves must instantly resign whatever the masters covet, they have no security of possession of any transferable goods. The only possessions in which they can take pride are inalienable ones. Their instinctive sense of injury, even if it begins only as resentment at cruelty or some other breach of "the law of humanity," because it is the desire to punish, to play an active role, to possess the status of punisher, will, when it becomes at all conscious of itself, become resentment at hav-

3. I am grateful to reviewers for *Hume Studies* for prompting me to reconsider my original view that all the nonhedonic passions were directly power-related. I now think we can see them all as implicitly aimed at the *continuation* of human nature in some essential aspect of it—at the self-preservation of the individual (love of life and the appetites), at the protection of the next generation (kindness to children), at the continuance of love (benevolence), and at the protection of pride (resentment). Such a will to continue could be seen as a will to power, but the power in question is power to keep ourselves going, not the power to dominate or the power to destroy.

ing no such status, or any secure possessions, at being deprived of the chance of pride. As Hume sees benevolence's natural place to be as an accompaniment to love, and one which, by conferring benefits on the loved person, increases the goods the beloved possesses and so feeds the love, so I suggest we can see resentment as the watchdog of pride, the natural response to those who injure by preventing pride. (Preventing secure possession will also be preventing humility, which for Hume is not simply feeling that one has no grounds for pride, but feeling that one's possessions are of poor quality. Humility's "subjects" are the same as pride's "subjects.")

Pride, like love, Hume says, has, as its "causes," the fine possessions of its "object." We are proud of what is ours, love another for what is hers. And what is possession? To possess something, Hume tells us in Book 3, is to be "so situated with respect to it, as to have it in our power to use . . . move, alter, or destroy it, according to our present pleasure or advantage" (T 506). Pride is essentially in possession, and possession is power. I think that, when we take Book 3's treatment of pride and of possession into account, we can see why Hume in Book 2 had cited a great variety of things in which we take pride, but had singled out virtue, riches, and power as peculiarly apt causes of pride. Pride *must* be taken in power over something, the thing possessed, and pride in generalized forms of power, such as power over others, or in riches, is pride in its paradigm form. In discussing virtuous pride, Hume says that we must recognize properly moralized pride as a virtue, since "'tis requisite on all occasions to know our own force," and pride "makes us sensible of our own merit, and gives us a confidence and assurance in all our projects and enterprises" (597). At least by the time pride is moralized, it is a sense of power, and if we take seriously Hume's definition of possession, all along it was, in all its forms, pride in what in fact is power, of less or more generalized sorts. The person proud of the climate of the country where he takes his vacations (307) is a degenerate case, since his "possession" is no more than the ability to take such vacations, no power over climate or country.

If we accept this thesis that Humean pride is essentially pride in power, and that resentment is the natural watchdog of pride, then we get the conclusion that the most proper objects of resentment are the wrongs of dispossession, expropriation, oppression, humiliation. The slave class Hume discusses, who may or may not have the power to make their resentment felt, are then ones who, because of their insecurity of possession, have none of the usual forms of limited power, who may have nothing in which to take pride except their possible power to make resentment felt, and whatever ability gives them that power.

Before looking at other essential features of pride, for Hume, and relating them to the power to make resentment felt, I want first to raise the question of the relation between this negative basic desire and the "irregular" passion of envy and the mixed passions of respect and contempt. For Hume, envy is a case of a passion dependent upon the principle of "comparison" whereby a passion in one person provokes an opposed passion in another. A passion may spread by sympathy, and produce a like passion in another, as when your grief occasions my pity, or it may spread by comparison, as when your grief occasions my malicious pleasure. The "irregular" passions (T 376) are these comparison-generated passions which are opposed in hedonic quality to the generating passion in another. Comparison is involved, since "the misery of another gives us a more lively idea of our happiness" (375). Our own feelings are enhanced or enlivened by their contrast with another's feelings. In the case of envy, another's happiness downgrades our own, especially if the other has more than one has oneself; "the enjoyment, which is the object of envy, is commonly superior to our own" (377). So far Hume is proceeding with his rather mechanical classification of passions, asking if they are self or other directed, pleasant or unpleasant, reactions to pleasure or to pain, communicated, if at all, by sympathy or by comparison. Where the account becomes interesting is always the point where qualifications, "curious" features, difficulties, are introduced into the taxonomy. Hume, immediately after defining envy in a general way as displeasure at another's pleasure, goes on to observe that the principle of comparison may work in a rather peculiar manner. He notes two things—first, that one may envy someone *inferior* in the relevant respect to oneself, if that inferior is advancing, and second, that one does not envy those who are very far above oneself, but those who are close. "A common soldier bears no such envy to his general as to his sergeant of corporal." A great disproportion, Hume says, "cuts off the relation and . . . keeps us from comparing ourselves with what is remote from us" (377–378). Envy then is felt for either superiors or inferiors who are within sight of one's hopes of rising or fears of falling. Of envy of inferiors who are advancing Hume says that it involves comparison twice repeated—we compare our present distance from the inferior unfavorably with an earlier greater distance. It is unclear from Hume's account whether this makes the object of such envy strictly oneself at a previous time, or whether, more naturally, the object of one's envy is the one who, unlike oneself, is advancing.

Hume brings the complicating factor of social distance not only into his account of envy, but also into his account of respect and contempt: "The same man may cause either respect, love, or contempt by his condition and talents, according as the person, who considers him, from his inferior becomes his equal or superior" (T 390). The passion one feels depends upon one's "distance" from the person, and whether one is above or below. Above or below in what? In whatever it is which is the "subject" of the passion, that which is deemed a pleasure- or pain-giver. Hume, in discussing envy, speaks as if it is the enjoyment itself which one covets, but surely the envied sergeant need not be actually enjoying his superior position in order to be envied. It is his *position* which the common soldier envies, perhaps assuming that it makes more pleasure possible. Respect for a superior is surely not reserved for those superior in attainment of hedonic bliss. If it were, one would respect only the expert and successful hedonists. Hume's philosophy is perhaps marred by his official hedonist line, but in many places he allows himself significant departures from it. He emphasizes that we esteem the rich and powerful whether or not they "spend" their riches and power in enjoyment: "riches and power alone, even tho' unemploy'd, naturally cause esteem and respect" (359). It is by sympathy with the "sentiment of the proprietor" (310), Hume says, that we come to esteem a person for his riches or power. We realize that whether he gets or does not get the pleasures his possessions make possible depends only on his own will. We respect his potent will.

Hume's recognition of power as a good is only intermittent. The official line of the *Treatise* is that the only ultimate good is pleasure, that power matters because it puts pleasure within the scope of one's will. But in the details of Hume's discussion of pride, respect, and esteem for the rich and powerful, as in his discussion of recognition of others as full members of a moral community, it is power, not pleasure, which seems to count. The "superiority" which is respected is not hedonic expertise or greater contentment, but superiority of rank and power.

There is another interesting passage in the section on respect and contempt where Hume deviates from his official classification of passions. According to Hume's general theory, the qualities for which one loves another are the very qualities which, if possessed by oneself, occasion pride. It is, however, a "pretty curious phenomenon" that some qualities are more fitted to inspire love than pride. Good nature, "facility," generosity, and beauty have "a peculiar aptitude to produce love in others, but not so great a tendency to create pride in ourselves" (T 392). Hume does not say that these unenvied lovable qualities are ones which confer little or no power on their possessor, but it would fit very well with the other "curious phenomena" and "difficulties" he cites to construe them this way. Pride, then, would be taken mainly in power-conferring qualities, and the recognition of such qualities in others will occasion not so much the "pure" love (ibid.) which beauty or good nature inspires, but either that love tinged with hatred which is "respect" (390), or else envy or resentment.

Resentment, envy, and respect all seem to depend upon the workings of the principle of comparison, and so to involve an evaluation of one's own position in relation to others. Envy, if Hume is right, is felt only of those whose position is not far removed from one's own, and may be felt because of another's possession of *any* good, whether that good makes the other proud or merely lovable. One *may* envy one's neighbor his car, his looks, or his influence with local government. Respect is reserved for those at a greater distance from oneself in possession of *prideworthy* qualities, that is to say, if my interpretation is correct, of power-conferring ones. What of resentment? Is it directed at the very same people who are the proper objects of Humean respect? (Hume's concept of respect allows no room for self-respect, unless one construes that as a sympathetic sharing of one's inferior's respect for one, a seeing of oneself from the inferior's lowly viewpoint.) Resentment is not merely respect gone sour, a predominance of hatred in the mixture. It is related to pride, I have claimed, in a more complex way. Respect, in Hume's account, includes humility. Resentment does not. On the contrary, it requires a certain pretension to moral status in those who feel it—it is the desire to punish (not just to strike back at) those who injure, or wrong one (not just hurt one)—it is provoked by humiliation, which is not the same as being made to feel humble. Resentment is felt not only at injustice, but at injury, at insult, at exclusion, at being ignored. But it is felt only by those who claim moral recognition, and suffer moral wrong. What all the causes of resentment—exploitation, oppression, injustice, exclusion, insult—have in common is their demeaning humiliating effect. They all are cases of refusing to treat another as someone who can have cause for pride, and resentment is felt only by those whose pretensions (implicit or explicit) to be included in the community of proud ones are somehow rejected by another.

But need pride make a claim on others? Can one not feel pride *whatever* others think about one? Hume's answer to this is not straightforward. In Book 3 he says that virtuous or due pride must be "duly concealed" (T 597), not flaunted. But it is one thing to conceal one's pride, another to base it on a self-evaluation in no way confirmed by anyone else's assessment of one. In Book 2, Hume discusses the "love of fame," and says that pride needs to be sustained and increased by the proud person's sharing, by sympathy, of others' favorable evaluation. "Our reputation, our character, our name are considerations of vast weight and importance; and even the other causes of pride; virtue, beauty and riches, have little influence, when not seconded by the opinions and sentiments of others" (316). This need to have one's own evaluation "seconded" by others, preferably by those "whom we ourselves esteem and approve of" (321), makes pride vulnerable to the contempt of others, and also to their mere refusal to "second," to their indifference or ignoring of the proud person's implicit appeal for reassurance. Hume later puts this thesis in vivid (and mixed) metaphorical terms. "The minds of men are mirrors to one another, not only because they reflect each others emotions, but also because those rays of passions, sentiments and opinions may be often reverberated" (365). Humean pride does require recognition from another for its own survival. Resentment, on my suggested reconstruction, will naturally be directed at those who refuse to mirror a person's favorable self-evaluation, who will not second one's self-evaluation.

I have elsewhere[4] explored the instabilities in a situation where Humean persons need their pride to be "seconded" by an equal or superior, yet are prone to envy of such near-equals. Hume says that "'tis necessary to know our rank or station in the world, whether it be fix'd by our birth, fortune, employments, talents, or reputation. 'Tis necessary to

4. "Hume on Heaps and Bundles," *American Philosophical Quarterly* 16, 4 (October 1979): 285–295; and "Master Passions," in *Explaining Emotions,* edited by A. O. Rorty (California, 1980).

feel the sentiment of pride in conformity to it, and to regulate our actions accordingly" (T 599). This conservatism, this faith that within each "rank" a person will find a mirror for pride, is belied by other insights of Hume into the instability of such passions and the way they can correct themselves. He gives a long intricate account of avidity's self-transformation. He does not do the same for meekness and resentment, but he has given us all the needed elements. "'Tis requisite on all occasions to know our own force" (597). If pride is, at base, a sense of one's own adequate power or force, and if resentment is felt at the refusal of others not merely to allow it, but to recognize it, to second it, then, if there really is power there to be recognized, there will be power to make resentment felt. If the resenters are, as they are in Hume's example of women, essential co-workers with those who refuse them recognition, a dynamic force for change is provided. Hume, when he discusses the pride of masters, says that there is a special satisfaction in the control of other persons. "The vanity of power, or shame of slavery, are much augmented by the consideration of the persons, over whom we exercise authority, or who exercise it over us" (315). And again, "there is a peculiar advantage in power, by the contrast, which is, in a manner, presented to us, betwixt ourselves and the person we command" (316). The master *needs* the "consideration" of the slave yet cannot return a like consideration. Resentment is thereby fomented. As Hegel pointed out, the need of the master for the slave's respect, for confirmation of his superiority, as well as his need to have his pride seconded by someone *he* respects, puts the slave in a position of unrecognized but real power. The resentment which is the proper response to this situation is *not* impotent, and its emergence from Solomon's "dark shadows of the soul" into the light of recognized power can be blocked, as Hume recognized, only by a temporary and self-defeating confederacy of masters. Cooperation between equals is the only stable solution to the problem facing vain and needy masters and competent resentful slaves. Hume's account of the moral sentiment describes such a cooperative equilibrium, but in his social and political philosophy he fails to finish the story of how the instabilities of unequal power can correct both reactive resentment and equally reactive "vanity of power," transforming both into active principles which are "common and universal," the principles of action of the "party of humankind against vice and disorder" (E 275).

I have tried to show that the role Hume gives to resentment suggests an interesting relation between that passion and pride, one's perception of one's own power and one's claim to have that perception reinforced. I have claimed that Hume's emphasis on the difference made to various passions by perception of social power and status, along with his theory that persons need their self-assessments "seconded" by a noninferior, implies instabilities which he only partially recognized. I believe, but cannot here show, that his account of the moral sentiment does give us a general sketch of the dynamic by which pride in individuals who are socially interdependent can produce equilibrium out of disequilibrium. It is one of the great interests of Hume's moral philosophy that he gives two accounts of this process, one leading to the recognition of the natural virtues, another to the creation of artifices and the concomitant recoqnition of justice. It is partly for this reason that he can distinguish true society, secured by artifices or conventions which involve a "sense of common interest" (T 490), from quasi-social relations governed only by the "law of humanity." His definiton of the conventions which give rise to justice has two separable components—the requirement that "the actions of each of us have in reference to those of the other, and are perform'd upon the supposition, that something is to be perform'd on the other part" (ibid.), and the requirement of "like interest" (ibid.) The first requirement guarantees cooperation, and the second secures a fair cooperative scheme. Hume's "species of creatures intermingled with men" are cooperating with their masters, the actions of the slave make reference to the actions of the master, but what is lacking is a sense of like interest. The relations, therefore, are quasi-social but not justice-rules. Hume's correct perception of this possibility, in *EPM,* amounts to a recognition that not *all* conventions are rules of justice, and his brief diagnosis of when resentment can be effective suggests a scenario whereby conventions can be changed so as to become rules of justice. Once those who are cooperating in the workings of a convention in which they do not have a "like interest" not merely feel resentment at the nonrecognition of their interests, but realize that by withholding cooperation they can make their resentment effectively felt, then the conventions can be expected to change so as to serve their interests. Their resentment, which may begin as resentment at, say, cruelty, can grow into resentment at lacking a remedy against cruel treatment, into an awareness that not merely do they lack this right to redress but that they lack *any* security of alienable possessions, and from that to both resentment at this exclusion from the group of those to whom the conventions give any security of possession, and so any chance of pride in such possessions, and also to a pretension to full moral status and an awareness of the dependence of the oppressive conventions on their own cooperation. They then have, and know they have, the power to make resentment felt, the power to get the conventions changed into ones serving the interests of all those whose cooperative activities the convention coordinates.

Even if Hume is correct in supposing that constraining artifices will always be needed, that we will never achieve a society "where every man . . . being a second self to another, would trust all his interests to the discretion of every man; without jealousy, without partition, without distinction" (E 185), nevertheless his definition of a truly social convention requires a sense of like interest and a willingness to trust that interest to another's cooperative action. Even if all one's interests will never be safely trusted to every "man," it may not be too much to expect that one vital interest we all have, the interest in "knowing our own force" (T 597), in having due pride sustained, can be trusted to every person, without jealousy, partition, or distinction. Unless it is a reasonable hope that resentment can achieve its own overcoming, its transformation into due pride in recognized power, then social conventions can never be backed by a sense of like interest, or ever therefore be "stedfast and immutable" (620), or even be "as immutable as human nature" (ibid.).

# 8

# Promises, Promises, Promises

## Various Views about Promises

A promise, according to Hume, Austin, Searle, and Anscombe, is a speech act whereby one alters the moral situation.[1] One does not merely represent some possible state of affairs; one brings it about—makes it the case that, from being free in some respect, one is thereafter unfree, until the obligation taken on in the promise is discharged.

This is surely correct, as far as it goes. To give a promise is to alter one's moral position, to take on a new responsibility. But, as Stanley Cavell has objected,[2] one does not need anything as elaborate as a special ritual act, with well-defined roles or offices, the "promisor" and "promisee," to do that—we are continually altering our moral situation by what we do, committing ourselves or extricating ourselves from commitments, and it seems absurd to suppose that we need a special "institution" or "convention" to do this. It is the norm in human life that our actions change the moral state of play, as it were. I injure someone, either knowingly or unknowingly, and so owe that person at least an apol-

Versions of this chapter were given at the Oberlin Philosophy Colloquium in 1981, where David Falk disagreed constructively with it, and at CUNY Graduate Center in 1981, where several people, in particular Arthur Collins, made helpful comments. I am also indebted to Robert and Carolyn Birmingham for their legal as well as philosophical advice on an earlier attempt to relate Hume's account of promise to what he might have learned while a law student.

1. *A Treatise of Human Nature*, Book 3, Part 2, Sections 4, 5, and 8; J. L. Austin, *How to Do Things with Words* (Harvard, 1975); J. R. Searle, "How to Derive an 'Ought' from an 'Is'," *Philosophical Review* 73 (1964), and *Speech Acts* (Cambridge, 1969), ch. 8.; G. E. M. Anscombe, "Rules, Rights and Promises," in *Midwest Studies in Philosophy*, vol. 3, *Studies in Ethical Theory* (Minnesota, 1980).

2. Stanley Cavell, *The Claim of Reason* (Clarendon, 1979), ch. 9, and also chs. 5 and 11.

ogy and perhaps reparation. I bring a new person into being, intentionally or unintentionally, so incur parental responsibility. I oppose some plan of a colleague, so owe the colleague an explanation of my opposition. I allow someone to come to depend upon me, so owe the one who depends upon me the gentlest of abandonings, if I leave him. Almost everything we do or say alters the moral situation between ourselves and some other, so we either distort the nature of moral responsibility if we suppose we need a special form of words to incur it, or we have not yet found what is special about the form of responsibility incurred by saying "I promise."

Cavell tries to show us that promising is not "the golden road to commitment" by drawing attention to all the other roads.[3] A different sort of challenge to the standard philosopher's account of promising, as taking on the obligation to do a particular specified thing, has been posed recently by Atiyah,who charges the philosophers with "an apparent or overt belief in the sanctity of promises and contracts which is no longer to be found in the value systems of modern England at least."[4] The charge here is not that promising and contracting do not alter the moral and legal situation, but that they do not make the *sort* of difference the philosophers have claimed. To oversimplify Atiyah's view, what one must do, if one has given a promise, is nothing at all unless one has also received some consideration from the promisee, and, if that condition is satisfied, then one must either do what one promised or pay damages. For Atiyah (and, he claims, the common law) promises are merely fragments of an agreement to an exchange and admission of that agreement. What one is committed to by a promise is the same as what one would be committed to without one, namely, to do one's part in some reciprocal transaction, to complete some exchange. "The English common law has never treated the mere fact that a promise has been made as even prima facie a sufficient condition for the creation of a legal obligation. . . . To them [the common lawyers], it was of vital consideration to ask *why a* promise had been given. A promise made for a good reason—a good consideration as it came to be said, was prima facie enforceable. Very roughly, it could be said that a promise was only legally actionable if the

<hr>

3. Ibid., 298.
4. P. S. Atiyah, *Promises, Morals and the Law* (Clarendon, 1981), 7.

promise was to do something which the promisor should have done anyway."[5]

Do promises create new obligations? Is there anything special and unique about promising—is it the golden road to anything of special moral interest? Does a promise create an obligation only if there is some intended *exchange*, and is it a matter of moral indifference whether one keeps one's promise or breaks it and pays fair damages? I shall address these questions, and I shall claim that the correct answers to them are to be found most perspicuously not in any of the recent discussions but rather in the account given two and a half centuries ago by David Hume.

Atiyah cites Hume's account as a "utilitarian" one, which sees promising as a useful artifice. I find Hume's account of all the artificial virtues (of which "fidelity to promises" is one) to commit him not to utilitarianism but more to a sort of enlightened egoism,[6] since he requires that for any social convention to give rise to an obligation each person must find himself (or herself?) "a gainer, on ballancing the account" (T 497). He does also say of promises that they are "an invention for the interest of society" (524), but this general social interest will not give rise to any individual obligation, for Hume, unless "the whole system of actions, concurr'd in by the whole society, is infinitely advantageous to the whole *and every part*" (498, my emphasis). This is a particularly strong egoist constraint on any supposed requirement to promote the interest of society. Hence my defense of Hume's version of what a promise is, what it obligates us to do, and how it does that, is not intended to be a defense of a utilitarian account of promising.

It is, however, an account which, like that of Austin, Searle, Cavell, and Atiyah, rejects the Natural Law account of promissory obligations. In its usual religious version, this view held that all obligations are obligations to obey God's laws, one of which forbids promise-breaking. On such a view, obligations are all of the same sort, dependent on a divine law somehow promulgated through natural human reason. One is obli-

5. Ibid., 3. Atiyah's final account of a promise as admission, a form of consent that there is already an agreement to reciprocal transfer, is given later, in ch. 7.

6. See David Gauthier, "David Hume, Contractarian," *Philosophical Review* 88 (1979): 3–38, for a persuasive account of Hume's nonutilitarianism. (I do not, however, think that Gauthier succeeds in showing that Hume in his account of obligation is a contractarian. Not all enlightened egoists who believe in cooperation are contractarians.)

gated to do what God requires of one, and that includes whatever (not otherwise forbidden act) one has promised another that one will do. Anscombe may perhaps have a way of seeing the sort of non-natural "logos"-discerning "reason" she recognizes as the vehicle for a divine law, but she does not see divine law in the way Hume's main opponents in ethics did. When Hume denies that justice and promise-keeping are natural virtues, because their virtue is not "naturally intelligible," and when he nevertheless calls the obligations they give rise to "natural obligations," the human artifices they depend upon "natural artifices," and their content the three "laws of nature," he is arguing with and to some extent mocking the Natural Law tradition in ethics. He is keeping the terminology of this tradition but emptying it both of its theological implications and of its rationalist implications.

Today, in our post-Wittgensteinian philosophical times, both "reason" and "God" can appear in guises Hume would not have recognized. His battles both with old-style rationalists and supernaturalists in ethics seem largely won, and the issues today are ones which arise within an area of agreement that morality is a human cultural phenomenon, that discerning its content is not much like using reason to discern order in nature. The starry heavens above and the moral law within have drifted further apart than they were to Hume's opponents, despite Kant's efforts to bring them together as both recognized by human reason. If they come together today, it is not through Kant's or Aquinas's notion of reason or of law, not because we think that, as the heavens can be charted by law-recognizing reason, so too can morality. It is rather because we see in any law-discovery (or law-following) that norm-recognizing, correction-sensitive participation in a form of life, or practice, which is also needed for morality and its understanding. The fact-establishing, fact-connecting, law-discovering work of science requires and presupposes both rule-following and the more primitive social capacities that involves. When Hume opposed rationalism in ethics, it was reason as nature-representer that he dethroned, in favor of corrected sentiments and reflectively approved customs and conventions. Today's version of reason, whether it be Anscombe's or Cavell's, is not the reason Hume tried to dethrone. It is much more like that capacity to acquire what Hume called "habit," to learn and operate with "customs," "conventions," and social "artifices." This was a capacity Hume usually contrasted with "reason." Custom is the great guide to human life, and has "equal weight and authority" (E 41) with reason. Among the customs Hume analyzed were those which, unlike the habit of ordinary causal inference, required a certain "agreement" between those following the custom, an agreement "changeable by human laws" (T 528). One such agreement-based custom, or convention, is that recognizing the special force of the words "I promise."

## Representation and Commitment

Hume's discussion has been cited by writers like Anscombe as recognizing the important fact that the words "I promise to help you with your harvest" change the moral situation and do not merely represent such a change, or represent the future help that is promised. They create the obligation to help, and represent that obligation. Hume clearly recognizes the situation-altering power of promising, and what is more, he also makes clearer than recent accounts just how, in a promise, the act of representing is linked to the act of binding oneself. He shows us what commitment it is to which explicit promises are indeed the golden road.

   Promising, like articulating one's intentions, seems both to describe or represent an action, and also to do something to ensure that the described action becomes actual.[7] It also declares itself, the verbal act, for what it is, and simultaneously makes it that. "I promise" makes it a promise, and in a different way from the way in which "I am speaking" makes that statement a true one. Promising, therefore, is one of those verbal actions J. L. Austin called performatives, a species of illocutionary act. It is one of the things we can do with words, and it is a particularly interesting case of an illocutionary act. Unlike congratulating or greeting, promising must be promising something, and what is promised must be represented or signified. Hume has an interesting account both of how the signifying in a promise differs from that in an intention-avowal, or even in such "symbolic delivery" as may attend barter and gift, and of what it is that a promise does which gives an important job both to the verbal representation of what is promised, and to the words "I promise." He says:

---

7. I discuss the way intention-formation does this in "Mixing Memory and Desire," in *Postures of the Mind* (Minnesota, 1985), 8–21, and also in "The Intentionality of Intentions," *Review of Metaphysics* 30, 3 (1977): 389–414.

When a man says he promises any thing he in effect expresses a resolution of performing it; and along with that subjects himself to the penalty of never being trusted again in case of failure. A resolution is a natural act of the mind, which promises express: But were there no more than a resolution in the case, promises would only declare our former motives, and would not create any new motive or obligation. They are the conventions of men, which create a new motive, when experience has taught us, that human affairs would be conducted much more for mutual advantage, were there certain *symbols or signs* instituted, by which we might give each other security of our conduct in any particular incident. (T 522)

The key elements in this Humean account, ones I shall be alluding to in what follows, are the promisor's explicit expression of *what* she resolves and binds herself to do; subjection to the penalty of distrust, should she not perform just that; the "new" self-interested motive to avoid this penalty; and the community's conventions recognizing the force of those "symbols or signs," the words "I promise," and so recognizing the promisor's obligation and also empowering the promisee to initiate the withdrawal of trust, should the promise be broken. This account makes both the words "I promise . . . ," and the exact words completing the utterance begun thus, of significant moral importance. Is Hume right about this?

Cavell and Anscombe both say that we do not need to use the form of words Hume attributes such force to, nor to perform any other particular ritual act, to make a promise. Cavell believes that, in any case, a promise, however given, gets its moral force from being a case of "commitment," and commitments require neither ritual acts, nor the sort of explicitness about what one is committed to which promises usually involve, nor any constitutive rules. Promising, he says, is not a social "institution" that defines roles with rights and obligations attached to them. Indeed, he suggests an indicator of a real institutional role involving obligations, namely, that one can take an oath of office on assuming it.[8] The implication is that we take no such oath when we become promisors. As Hume noted, "We are not surely bound to keep our word because we have given our word to keep it" (E 306). For Cavell, to give a promise is to spell out a commitment, but what binds is the commitment. Spelling it out may make it more easily ascertained, later, whether the commit-

8. Cavell, 297.

ment has been kept or not, but the commitment itself does not depend upon the spelling out or on any implicit oath. "There is nothing sacred about the act of promising which is not sacred about expressing an intention, or any other way of committing oneself. . . . If it is important to be explicit then you may engage either in the 'rituals' of saying 'I really want to . . . ,' 'I certainly intend, will try to . . . ,' or the ritual of saying 'I promise.' It is this importance which makes explicit promises important. But to take them more seriously than that, as the golden path to commitment, is to take our ordinary nonexplicit commitments too lightly."[9] This makes the crucial act commitment, and promising becomes just one form of it. Cavell says, "The appeal [to rules] is an attempt to explain why such an action as promising is *binding* upon us, but if you *need* an explanation for that, if there is a sense that something more than personal commitment is necessary, then the appeal to rules comes too late. For rules themselves are binding only subject to our commitment."[10]

Has Cavell a disagreement with Hume? Hume can agree with Cavell that unless we already understand what it is to be bound (for example, by one's consent), or to be under obligation (for example, to respect the property rights of others), the question of how promises can bind can never be answered, since in Hume's view the force of promises presupposes prior convention-generated obligations, those of property and consent to its transfer. But Cavell's point is *not* that promising is one of a mutually referential family of conventional acts, all of them rule- or convention-dependent. That is Hume's position. Cavell's point seems rather to be that we must understand how individual commitment can bind to be able to understand how any rules or conventions bind, since they bind only if accepted by individuals, only if individuals *commit themselves* to those rules. Here, too, we can find partial agreement between Cavell and Hume, since Hume, of course, supposes that the conventions of property, its transfer by consent, and by promise or contract, must be somehow accepted before they can generate obligations. Hume calls this acceptance "agreement," not "commitment," and this may not be merely a terminological difference from Cavell.

The "agreement" on the first rules, namely, property rules, Hume says, is a matter of an expressed sense of common interest and of mutually

9. Ibid., 298.
10. Ibid., 307.

referential intentions, but it "arises gradually and acquires force by a slow progression, and by our repeated experience of the inconveniences of trespassing it" (T 490). There is no datable occurrence when all persons commit themselves to all the rest, nor any occasion on which each new member of a society commits her or himself. Agreement and acceptance can arise gradually, but it is less easy to see how individual commitment can arise except by some definite acts of the committed person. I can find myself in "agreement" with my fellows, in Hume's sense, if I find myself willingly doing something, like rowing, or talking, or using money, which presupposes "that something is to be perform'd on the other part." It would take a deliberate act of disengagement to avoid being caught up in the general cooperative practices of the community into which I am born. How could I show that I was not in agreement with others in accepting the current language, monetary system, or set of property rules? By a deliberate proclamation, or public act of disrespect? If I take no such measures, then I am presumed to be in agreement, and to have an obligation to respect the currently recognized rights. I am born into obligations. I do not need to take any initiative, or do anything to *commit myself*. Indeed, if Hume is right, the very possibility of an individual act of commitment, consent, or refusal to consent depends upon general acceptance of some recognized ways of making individual adjustments. Once there *is* the general practice of property recognition, it takes new general practices to enable individuals to make individual adjustments, to relinquish or exchange property. The binding general practice precedes the binding conventional acts by single individuals. Cavell asks how a general rule can bind unless individuals bind themselves to respect it. Hume's (implicit) answer is that individuals can *agree,* and express agreement, by something less individualized, and less definite than is needed for an individual commitment. Hume describes a bootstrap operation whereby from an informal general agreement on a convention that invents rights, namely, property rights, his convenors move on to another informal general agreement to recognize the force of a more formal and more individual act, consent to transfer property, and from that to another informal agreement to recognize a more explicit and more formal individual act, namely, promise. The issue between Hume and Cavell is not whether rules bind only if accepted, but rather what counts as acceptance; what the relation is between acceptance and commitment; what moral difference is made by different degrees of initiative, formality, and explicitness in acceptance; and what the relation is between acceptance of a general practice and acceptance of a particular understanding with specific persons.

Only if one saw all obligations as incurred by avoidable commitments on the part of the obligated persons would it be necessary to reduce the obligations engendered by generally accepted rules to a series of acts of individual acceptance or commitment by individual persons. Does Cavell believe that about obligations? I do not think so. The existence of an established practice, cooperative scheme, or form of life establishes a presumption of acceptance by new members of the society. They may do things that rebut this presumption, but there is no need for any oath of allegiance to established customs or any acts of commitment before persons can acquire the obligations of participants. This is part of Cavell's own point—that obligations are not something one can avoid simply by avoiding certain ritual acts or oaths. They are the normal accompaniments of normal relationships with others, relations that do lead to gradual acceptance of accustomed ways of acting to one another. One can agree with Cavell about this yet still see a place for *special* obligation-assuming acts, and for oaths to solemnize those acts, be they ones of commitment to individual persons or commitments to uphold laws or rules.

Hume sees promise as a special sort of act whereby a new obligation to a specific person or persons is taken on, where this sort of individual act is possible only because people in general recognize the force of such a verbal act. To agree with him one need not claim that all special obligations to particular individuals arise from promises (he believes that subjects have special obligations to sovereigns, with or without an oath of allegiance), or that without promise there could be no commitment-dependent special obligation to particular people (he believes that parents owe a "fidelity" to one another that is distinct from "fidelity to promises"), or that obligations arising directly or indirectly from an acceptance of a general convention such as that making promises possible have any greater moral seriousness than a two-person nonpromissory and informal agreement, such as that between friends or lovers whose "intercourse" is "more generous and noble" (T 521) than that of the parties to a promise. Hume believed that there must have been limited cooperation and trust between persons, in the family, before any conventions could arise (490), and he insisted that promise, a convention-dependent explicit agreement between private individuals, "does not entirely abolish the more generous and noble intercourse of friendship and good offices" (521). There is the natural duty of parents to care for children, of friends to be true friends, and so on, independently of all the artifices. So Hume certainly does not treat promise as the golden road to commitment. But he does treat it as a rule-dependent or convention-dependent road to commitments beyond family and friends, to those for whom we bear no "real kindness."

## Symbolical Delivery of the Absent and General

Hume sees promise as an obligation-creating device that is useful between strangers and especially when they wish to transfer either *future* goods or services, or *distant* goods, or a certain definite *measure* of goods. Without promise, with only the artifice of transfer by consent, even when that is embellished by the lawyers' superstition of the symbolical delivery (T 515) of what is present but too bulky to literally hand over, "one cannot transfer the property of a particular house, twenty leagues distant, because consent cannot be attended by delivery, which is a requisite circumstance. Nor can one transfer the property of ten bushels of corn, or five hogsheads of wine, by the mere expression and consent; because these are only general terms and have no direct relation to any particular heap of corn or bushel of wine" (520). Hume sees a need for promise, with both the penalty it involves and the verbal representation of what is to be transferred that it involves, for transfers, between strangers, of absent (distant or future) goods, and of precise amounts of some general type of goods. This limited rationale does make Humean promises "mere contrivances for the convenience and advantage of society" (525), clarifying as it does both the convenience and the fact that what provides it is described by Hume not, like the artifice of property, as "infinitely advantageous" (498), but as a *mere* contrivance, albeit a useful one for limited purposes. The rationale also explains the special features Hume finds and emphasizes in the artifice of promise, and in particular that of penalty, and of explicit statement of what the promisor must do to avoid that penalty. To see exactly how the explicitness of promises connects with the obligation to perform them, it will be helpful to consider Anscombe's treatment of Hume's account of promising.

Anscombe praises Hume for seeing that there were two problems, "one, what sort of beast a promise is; and the other, concerning how, given that there is such a thing, it can generate an obligation."[11] She goes on: "One may fail to note that there are two problems, because a promise signifies the creation or willing of an obligation. It might be thought that if you could show that there were a sign with that signification, you would be home and dry: the obligation is generated by giving the sign which has that signification! Hume's clarity of mind perceived that this is not so."[12] Anscombe regards Hume's thesis of the "natural unintelligibility" of promissory obligations as a great discovery. She also says that this thesis has wider application than Hume gave it. But he in fact gave the thesis a fairly wide application—to all agreement-based or "convention"-based obligations (including the obligation to keep rowing in stroke). To be not naturally intelligible, in Hume's sense, is to be intelligible only once we understand what a convention or "artifice" is. He discusses a limited number of social artifices—property, its transference by consent, government, some forms of marriage. But he makes it quite clear that he regards money as another case of something not naturally intelligible, and he also regards words as cultural and convention-dependent things, to be understood only by reference to human artifice. "In like manner [i.e., to property conventions] are languages gradually established by human conventions. . . . In like manner do gold and silver become the common measures of exchange" (T 490). So the application of his thesis of natural unintelligibility is fairly extensive, and Hume is in explicit agreement with Anscombe that "no language is in Hume's sense naturally intelligible."[13]

Anscombe sees what is peculiarly puzzling about promises, among what she calls the naturally unintelligible things, to be the fact that "a promise is essentially a sign, and the necessitation arises from the giving of the sign."[14] Social or "artificial" necessitation can arise, say within a game, without any sign-giving by the party under the necessity or by other parties. In the children's hand-piling game Anscombe discusses, one must lift one's hand from the bottom to the top of the pile when it is on the bottom, and musn't lift it before then. No signs are given by the

11. Anscombe, 318.
12. Ibid., 319.
13. Ibid., 318.
14. Ibid., 322.

players, and their moves in the game are determined without the need for signs. But in a promise words are used, and used to signify both a future action and the non-natural necessity to perform it. Because the giving of a promise simultaneously creates an obligation, and signifies the precise obligation it creates, it is easy, Anscombe thinks, to suppose oneself home and dry if one can account for the feat of signification, and so miss the deeper problem of the very possibility of what is signified, a non-natural necessity. She credits Hume with seeing the deeper issue.

So, I think, he did. But he addressed this "deep" issue of how it comes about that one must repay a loan, or keep one's promise, why one can't take another's property without the other's permission, in his general account of "convention," and of the sort of "agreement" involved in that. His thesis of the natural unintelligibility of promises is simply an application, to this case, of his general thesis about all the "laws of nature" and the "natural" obligations they engendered. They are, all of them, intelligible only when we see that conventions or general agreements are involved. Property is unintelligible until its conventional character is acknowledged, consent cannot alter rights unless it is recognized to do so, and promises cannot bind unless a convention enables them to bind. Hume continues to call these convention-dependent obligations "natural" obligations partly because of their link with the "laws of nature," and his usage is ironical. Natural obligations, for him, are precisely the obligations that are naturally law-dependent. Since the only natural laws are human customs, they are *not* naturally intelligible, and no rational motive to perform them can exist until there is an agreed custom or convention. When Hume gets to the third artifice he discusses, namely, promise, he does make some puzzling departures in his terminology, claiming that because there is no convention-independent motive to keep promises, there is therefore *no* "natural obligation" (T 525), as if he had forgotten that in his ironical usage (at, for example, 498) a natural obligation just *is* a convention-dependent one.[15] This may have misled

15. A "natural obligation" at T 498 is one that is not yet a moral obligation, since not yet approved or disapproved by the moral sentiment. But it *is* one done from a motive that is "not naturally intelligible," since we must refer to an artifice or convention, as well as natural self-interest, to spell out that premoral motive. Hume had warned us, at T 474–475, that no word is more ambiguous and equivocal than "nature," and his own usage in what follows displays this ambiguity. Although he officially opposes "natural" to "artificial," he also opposes it both to "moral" and to "civil." "Natural motives" and the "naturally intelligible" are what involve no necessary references to any artifice. "Natural obligations" at T 498 are those which involve no

Anscombe into thinking that, for Hume, promises are more "naturally unintelligible" than is property or consent to its transfer. But Hume in the next section resumes his ironical usage and speaks of the three "laws of nature," or pre-government sources of obligation, as "that of the stability of possession, its transference by consent, and of the performance of promises" (526). He does admittedly go out of his way to emphasize the "contradictions" in promise, if we try to treat it as a natural phenomenon, and to emphasize its family resemblance to religious practices such as baptism, the Mass, and the laying on of hands, which he characterizes as superstitious artifices. He had earlier (515–516) likened symbolic delivery in transfer by consent to religious ceremonies. It may well be that he did wish to make some special point about promises, and all cases of symbolic delivery, over and above his general point that all the "natural obligations" of justice arise from artifices: "Unless we will allow that nature has establish'd a sophistry, and render'd it necessary and universal, we must allow that the sense of justice and injustice is not natural, but arises artificially, tho' necessarily, from education, and human conventions" (483). Hume may be emphasizing the oddities of promise, as an artifice, and its link with the lawyers' superstition of symbolical delivery, in order to combat the tendency to see it as the fundamental source of obligation. A few sections later, in "Of the source of allegiance," he argues against Hobbes, Locke, and all contractarians, that there is no good reason to assimilate other obligations to that of promise.

Because Anscombe sees Hume's achievement as the recognition of the natural unintelligibility of promises, she misses his more detailed thesis about how *this* naturally unintelligible thing differs from its close rela-

---

necessary reference to the deliverances of the moral sentiment, but may refer to artifice. "Laws of nature" are rules of pre-government artifices, contrasting with laws. But Hume seems to speak not merely ambiguously but equivocally when he says that "where an action is not requir'd by any natural passion, it cannot be requir'd by any natural obligation" (T 518, repeated at 523). Natural obligations here seem to exclude artifice-dependent ones, whereas at 498 they include them. As for the *moral* component in promises, Hume also says some puzzling things. At 516 he says, "If we thought that promises had no moral obligation we shou'd never feel any obligation to observe them." This seems to contradict both his later spelling out of the "new" motive that subjection to threat of penalty brings, and also his statement at 523 that "afterwards a sentiment of morality concurs with interest, and becomes a new obligation on mankind. This sentiment of morality, in the performance of promises, arises from the same principles as that in the abstinence from the property of others." It is hard to save all these textual phenomena, but I think that the interpretation I am offering involves minimal reconstruction.

tive, "mere expression and consent" (T 520). Both consent and promise are artifices,[16] but to understand what promise adds to consent Hume has to give a fairly detailed account of how representation enters into these two artifices. Both the common elements linking promises to other grounds of non-natural obligation, and those special to it, are fairly clearly laid out by Hume, but we do not see these clearly unless we read his section on promises in its context within his total account of human social conventions and the natural order in which they develop. If one reads only the section on promises, and not the preceding section on transfer by consent, one may not understand the emphasis given by Hume to the role of the verbal signs in promising. If one reads the account in that one section of the unintelligibility of the idea of willing an obligation, without the more general earlier account of the unintelligibility of any obligations of justice, until we invoke the existence of conventions, we may be misled into thinking that promises are more "unnatural," or more naturally unintelligible, than is property, or than is permission to take or borrow. To see what Hume is saying about promissory obligations, one must see it in the context of what he is saying about property rights, rights transferred by owner's consent, and about magistrates' rights. None of these are naturally intelligible; all of them depend on general social "agreements" or customs. Some but not all of these, as I shall shortly go on to emphasize, involve provisions for sanctions against those who fail in their obligations. Some but not all of these

---

16. Like Atiyah (see note 5), Hume sees consent as more "basic" than promise. Unlike Atiyah, he does not reduce promise to a form of consent. Atiyah sees it as irrevocable consent to the existence of some other obligation owed by the promisor (see Atiyah, 184). The explicit promise has merely an evidentiary function—it is an irrevocable and conclusive admission that there is an obligation. "A promise is an admission concerning the existence and extent of other obligations which either pre-exist the making of a promise, or which anyway would arise before, or at the same time as, the promise becomes obligatory" (ibid., 193). This view seems to conflate consenting into *assenting* to a fait accompli, and Hume's question of what obligation it is to which our will supposedly assents in a promise arises. Atiyah has an answer to that—namely, a whole range of obligations arising out of receipt of benefits and a basic moral requirement of reciprocity, but he has to strain hard to find one of these prior obligations in every case of an apparently binding promise; and he has to dismiss some gratuitous unilateral promises as "senseless act(s), not capable in a rational world of creating an obligation at all" (ibid., 214). Hume remarked that, in the view he rejects, in which the assent of the will is what binds in a promise, this will "must be express'd by words or signs, in order to impose a tye on any man. The expression being once brought in as subservient to the will, soon becomes the principal part of the promise" (T 523). In Atiyah's view, the subservient *evidentiary* function of the representation of an obligation in a promise becomes the principal part of a promise.

involve the power of individuals to alter rights and obligations. Some but not all of these, like both consent and promise, involve the giving of signs. Some, like promise and some forms of transfer by consent, involve symbols or representations.

Hume, unlike both Anscombe and Cavell, sees what makes promises puzzling and to some extent suspect as the element of symbolism they involve, and what makes them distinctive and distinctively useful as the element of *verbal* representation or signification they involve. Whereas contemporary philosophers, accustomed to attending to language and particularly to the representational function of language, had a sense of puzzlement and of "deep" discovery when they saw that a verbal act could create an obligation and not merely represent one, Hume came to the matter the other way around. Having satisfied himself that what he called "conventions" create obligations, he then went on to look at how conventions governing the use of sign and symbols extended the scope of non-natural obligations, and how words came to play a vital role. He began his discussion of promising already clear that there could be what Anscombe calls non-natural necessitation (indeed, in a sense, it is for Hume the only kind of necessitation there is),[17] and that it could come into being by an individual's voluntary act within a context of social customs (as the giver is necessitated, by his act of giving, not to later attack the recipient of the gift to regain what was once his property). The only puzzling issue facing Hume when he came to discuss promising was how its being a ritual *verbal* act made a difference, and what difference it made. Whereas later philosophers, thinking they understood the phenomenon of language, hit on non-natural necessitation or obligation, and found it a deep, puzzling phenomenon, Hume, having understood artifice-based obligation, then hit on the role of signs and language, and had to account for their special contribution there. It was part of his genius to be puzzled by the role of representation, not to take it for granted. His account of promising, taken with his earlier account of the role of symbols in transfer by consent, gives representation in language a vital role, and shows how there are some things we can do with words only by acts of representation, by using words to represent what is not present. For Hume representation in language was more, not less, of

17. I think that Hume's treatment of the "fiction" of causal and of logical necessity (T 166) in Book 1 should be linked to his account of the distinctive sort of "inflexibility" (531–533) that the social artifices introduce into morality.

a mystery than was obligation-creation. That linguistic representation could be given an intelligible role in obligation-creation demystified it, gave it its place among other useful artifices.

Hume begins his discussion of sign-giving in his account of transfer by consent, the artifice that enables persons to acquire wanted property of others with the owner's "consent," often in exchange for something they want. His first artifice is property, whereby possession becomes stable. His second artifice is consent to transfer, whereby it becomes less stable again, but is transferred voluntarily and to mutual advantage. Barter, gift, and loan are now possible because the owner can signify consent to transfer of his property. The first complication to arise is what is to happen when you give me, say, gold in exchange for my land or my herd of cattle. I cannot literally hand over my land as you can your gold. What do I do to give you any security? Unless you want to make a gift, you would be a fool to relinquish your gold without getting something more than the hope that I will vacate my land for good, or not reclaim my cattle. Hume says that, once there is the convention of property, we should be able to see that what you get is the *right* to the land or cattle, but since rights are abstract entities, we don't easily understand how they are transferred when nothing perceivable is transferred. So we, or the lawyers, invent symbols that can be literally transferred. "Men have invented a symbolical delivery, to satisfy the fancy, where the real one is impracticable" (T 515). I hand you a lump of soil or stone from my land, and it symbolizes the land itself, the right to which I relinquish by handing over the stone. Or I give you the key of my granary, when the wheat that is in it is too bulky for me to literally hand over to you. Hume describes as "a kind of superstitious practice in civil laws and in the laws of nature, resembling the Roman Catholic superstitions in religion" (ibid.) all these symbolic transfers, these ritual acts with their sometimes elaborate rules. (For land transfers in Scotland, the stone had to be handed over in daylight, on the land to be transferred, in the presence of the workmen who had worked on that land.) All they do is mimic the important thing, the transfer of rights, by a physical delivery of something. The whole act symbolizes the transfer of rights, and the stone symbolizes the transferred property. "The suppos'd resemblance of the actions and the presence of this sensible delivery deceive the mind and make it fancy that it conceives the mysterious transition of the property" (ibid.). This description is of what happens once law and lawyers get into the act, and it is unclear if Hume thinks that there were prelegal precursors of such symbolical delivery not yet amounting to giving a promise.

When Hume turns to promising, he already has an account of how consent creates or transfers rights, and of how a superstitious practice of symbol-giving can accompany the transfer of rights. The first question he raises is whether a mere act of mind, a willing to be bound, could make one bound, and he dismisses this as impossible. What he had called "consent," in the previous section was no mere mental act, but a public, social one—transfer by consent is a new artifice, a second "law of nature." "The translation of property by consent is founded on a law of nature as well as is its stability without such a consent" (T 514). Consenting is not mere willing. As Hume puts it in a footnote (517–518), the individual will would merely return on itself *in infinitum,* would never find its own object, what it willed, in trying to will a right or an obligation. Only within a social practice and by a social act can a new obligation be created. Only then can one effectively will to assume a new obligation. But there is another reason why the individual will cannot produce the obligation of a promise, one that Hume puts in the main text, not merely in a footnote. This is that "a promise always regards some future time and the will has an influence only on present actions" (516). Humean will, like Hobbesian will, is the transition from deliberation to action. I can now will to say "I promise," and do so, but that doesn't explain how promising now makes me bound later, how I get a grip now on a "remote" future time, the time when I must do what I now promise to do.

At this point, I think, someone like Cavell might object and say that our language does refer to future time in many of its uses, and so do we in our commitments, nonverbal and verbal, nonpromissory as well as promissory. A commitment must include some future, however brief, in its scope. Has Hume any problem with deciding to promise that is not also present when we decide to utter a prediction, or a generality, or even when we decide without words to go on a journey and so knowingly prevent ourselves from being here tomorrow? Isn't every willing, for an intelligent creature, a plunge into the future, a ruling out of possibilities for tomorrow? Isn't every use of language a use of a language with future and continuous tenses, so that claims about the future and commitments concerning it are given and implied constantly?

I think we see where promises involve future time in a way other agreements or commitments need not when we remember what, in Hume's view, promising enables a person to do, and look at his implied account of how the community as a whole is involved in making that power possible for individuals. A promise, Hume says, enables a person to transfer not merely particular goods in his possession at the time of transfer, but "absent and general" possessions. Tomorrow's labor, or next year's corn, or the cargo in ships still at sea, can be transferred to someone who accepts one's word when "consent *cannot* be attended with delivery" (T 520, my emphasis) of those goods. The rights are transferred, but what they are rights to cannot be delivered now if they do not yet exist, or are too far away. A promise is something that must *later* be performed, and then the promissory obligation is discharged. When one makes a gift, or barters something, immediate delivery obviates the need for any later "performance," and such obligations as the giver takes on, in virtue of having made the transfer, are never "discharged," since they stem from the standing obligation to recognize the altered property rights. But a promise provides, as it were, the script for its own future performance, and that performance can fully discharge one's obligation. The future time a promise regards is the time of a performance that terminates the obligation the promise created. A promise creates a limited obligation for a limited time. The obligation ceases to exist once the promise is performed, or once one is released from one's promise by the person to whom it was given.

## Threats and Promises

This bond for a limited future, for "*some* future time" (T 516, my emphasis) contrasts with the obligations created by the general agreement which constitutes the convention of property, or of consent as a way of transferring property, or indeed of the convention which gives the words "I promise" their special force and so enables anyone to make a promise. In all these cases of Humean conventions everyone in a society agrees to recognize certain rights—of ownership, of transfer with owner's consent, to performance of promises. This recognition of rights, in Hume's first two conventions, brought with it only negative correlative standing obligations—the obligation not to steal, or to interfere with voluntary transfers, or to reclaim the property one consented to be transferred. But to recognize the rights of someone to whom a promise has been given, noninterference is not enough. The promisor must perform, and everyone else must demand that he does, on pain of "never being trusted again in case of failure" (522). This introduces an element of threat into the basis of an obligation to perform according to one's promise, a threat that the promisee alone could not convincingly make. That I won't trust you again if you break your promise to me is fairly easy for me to ensure, unless you disguise yourself when you return with tempting offers, but is no great threat to you, if you do not need me to trust you again. But if I can have you as it were stigmatized, so that others recognize you as someone not to be trusted, then you have a fairly strong self-interested reason not to break your promise to me. Can I do this? If we are talkers, as we must be to give or receive promises, then I can harm your reputation; I can spread the word that you are not to be trusted.

Without promises, on Hume's account of them, trust would be more restricted—one might trust one's family, friends, or neighbors to do what they know one expects them to do, either from their established habits and customs or from their statements of intention, but one will have no such reason to depend upon some stranger's future action, even if he expresses an intention. He may change his mind, or forget, or have intended to deceive one. But if he promises, gives his word, one has some hold over him. Promises are "the *sanction* of the interested commerce of mankind" (T 522, my emphasis). What one "holds" in one's power is his reputation as a reliable person of his word. Should he break his promise, his reputation, at least among those one can communicate with, can be ruined. Thereafter others will not accept his promise, and so his dealings with them will be restricted to simultaneous, direct exchange, if indeed they will be willing to have any dealings with him. He will have lost what Nietzsche called the permission to make a promise.[18]

Hume sees promise as an "invention" which comes about after consent and before government, and which by its "sanction" facilitates, in fairly small communities, cooperation between nonintimates. What makes government necessary is the growth of wealth and of community size, which makes it possible both for thieves to escape proprietorial vigilance, and for promise-breakers to move on to new victims, to move away from their bad reputations. Only when magistrates are invented to

18. Nietzsche discusses promising in the second part of the *Genealogy of Morals*. See the quotation with which I begin in "Mind and Change of Mind," in *Postures of the Mind*, 51–73.

receive complaints and to keep official track of a person's record can persons in a large society count on a promise-breaker being generally known as such, and/or effectively punished. Hume says that it is "possible for men to maintain a small uncultivated society without government" (T 541), that is, without any official whose job it is to detect, declare, and punish those who break the generally accepted rules. In such an uncultivated society, he says, there will, before government, be justice, "and the observation of those three fundamental laws concerning the stability of possession, its translation by consent, and the performance of promises" (ibid.). What induces people to institute government, to divide off the task of stigmatizing and punishing the untrustworthy, is the increase of successful theft and fraud; and this comes with the change from small to large societies, and with the change to more cultivated societies in which individuals achieve such "encrease of riches and possessions" (ibid.) that their transfers typically are transfers of "absent and general" goods, requiring contract, and where these same absent goods provide both targets for easy theft and opportunities for lying promises. The informal enforcement of promises by withdrawal of community trust from the word of a known promise-breaker works only as long as the community is small enough for word to get around when anyone proves not to be a reliable person, not a "man of his word."

Thus, in the story Hume gives us, threat is an essential element in promise, and it takes community cooperation in the relevant convention or practice to pose that threat of destruction of one's power to ever have one's promises accepted. "They are conventions of men which create a new motive, when . . . certain symbols or signs [were] instituted by which we might give each other security of our conduct in any particular incident. After these signs are instituted, whoever uses them is immediately bound by his interest to execute his engagements and must never expect to be trusted any more if he refuse to perform what he promis'd" (T 522). Hume here quite clearly refers both to the community interest in giving each other security by "instituting" these signs, with backup penalty of withdrawal of trust from those who take them lightly, and to the individual promisor's interest in performing what he promised, so as to remain in good standing, to keep his reputation as a trustworthy person. The conventions of men give the promisor "a new motive" to perform according to his promise. Hume slightly obfuscates his account of exactly what sanction and what new motive a promise introduces, when in the next paragraph he describes the practice of a promise-recognizing society as based on an obvious interest in the "institution and observance of promises" (ibid.), but then seems to confuse the interest all have in the institution with the interest a given promisor has in observance.

> When each individual discovers them [the advantages of the institution and observance of promises] to every mortal, and when each individual perceives the same sense of interest in all his fellows, he immediately performs his part of any contract, as being assur'd that they will not be wanting in their part. All of them, by concert, enter into a scheme of actions for common benefit, and agree to be true to their word, nor is anything requisite to form this concert or convention, but that everyone have a sense of interest in the faithful fulfilling of engagements, and express that sense to other members of society. (Ibid.)

This seems to say that the interest each person has both in the institution *and in the performance* of promises is simply the common benefit, and that the only threat or worry on the horizon is that others might be "wanting in their part" of any contract or mutual promise. It would have been better if Hume had separated out the motive each has for the institution of the whole scheme of action that sets up promise as "the interested sanction of mankind," and the motive each *then* has for performing anything he may go on to promise, once he uses the instituted practice. The interest in the institution is an interest in the common benefit, and this interest is conditional on general conformity to the rules of the institution. Penalty helps ensure this conformity.

The interested motive to perform one's part in any contract one has made includes a wish to avoid the sanction that has been instituted, but of course it need not be the whole of the motive. As Hume emphasizes, one condition on one's willingness to fulfill engagements is the expectation that others will do likewise, as well as one's belief that the whole scheme of actions is for common benefit. Whether or not one can expect others to conform depends not just on the expected common benefit of "correspondence of good offices" (T 251), but on the penalty for promise-breaking, and the assurance that it will be levied. So for the expectation that others fulfill their engagements one needs also one's own and their willingness to exact the penalty for nonfulfillment. Once the penalty ceases to be effective, and violations of equity become frequent, then "your example both pushes me forward in this way by imitation, and also affords me a new reason for any breach of equity, by showing me, that I should be the cully of my integrity, if I alone shou'd impose on myself a severe restraint admidst the licentiousness of others" (535). This is Hume's description of what happens when riches and population have increased, and a need for magistrates as official rule-declarers, rule-appliers, and rule-enforcers becomes evident. At the earlier stage, when the artificial custom of promising "arises gradually and acquires force by a slow progression" (490), there is no reason not to expect the informal victim-initiated penalty of withdrawal of trust to be workable and efficacious, so that there can be assurance that others will fulfill their engagements. Their interest in so doing, like one's own, can be threefold: to help keep a useful custom going, not to disappoint the other party, and to avoid the penalty for promise-breaking.

Hume's account of promise-keeping is like Hobbes's account of obedience to any of his "laws of nature"—one needs assurance of others' conformity, for obedience to have point, and one needs not just conditional reciprocity but the institution of a penalty to get that assurance. But unlike Hobbes, Hume saw that promises themselves had to be "invented," along with their penalty, and unlike Hobbes he seems to think that this need for penalty is special to promises. We need to keep the threatened *penalty*, withdrawal of trust from individual promise-breakers, distinct from the equally important foreseeable danger that promise-breaking brings, namely, collapse of the climate of trust, as promise-breaking spreads by imitation. The interests everyone has in "the faithful fulfilling of engagement" are interests in three distinguishable connected policies:

1. In principle being willing to accept the mere word of another, unless that one is known to be a promise-breaker. (Of course, whether or not one actually accepts a promise will depend not just on one's confidence in the promisor, but in whether one wants what that one offers.)
2. Providing an interested motive for all promise-givers to keep their promises, by participating in the practice of making a public record of a person's performances, letting each have a reputation that can be ruined by failure to keep promises.
3. Being faithful to one's own word, as long as others can be expected to do so, and giving weight to the interest one now has in main-

taining one's status as a trustworthy person. (This interest is among those Hume later describes as real but "remote" ones, which in some conditions are outbalanced by the more immediate advantages of "violations of equity" [T 535].)

One might perhaps think that the element of community-levied penalty for disregard of obligations is not a special element in promise but is involved in all convention-based obligations, even if one does not agree with Hobbes in thinking it a necessary backing for every moral requirement. Will we not communicate to our fellows our knowledge that Jones is a thief, as well as that Jones is not a man of his word? Surely we will, and surely the threat of withdrawal of trust provides some motive for refraining from stealing. In Hume's account of acceptance of the convention of property, and of transfer by consent, there is no mention at all of penalty, or any reliance on the existence of it to motivate the convenors to conform to the convention. Their self-interested reason for conforming is not fear of penalty, but the "infinite advantages" of the whole "system of actions" whereby stability of possessions is achieved. When Hume considers how "a man may impoverish himself by a signal instance of integrity" (T 497), he does not cite fear of penalty as the self-interested reason why such a one should accept impoverishment—the threat is not of a contrived cost to the individual thief, but merely his share in the loss, or diminishing, of "peace and order," and of the infinite advantages that brings. When this loser by integrity balances his account, fear of reprisals need not go into the balance on the side of conformity.

This may seem just a mistake on Hume's part—why should threat of penalty be needed to motivate promise-keeping, but not needed to motivate honesty? Here we must remember that the question is not whether, in some conditions, the threat of penalty is necessary to motivate honesty—Hume grants that when societies become large, and individual holdings also large, the "artifices of politicians" (T 523) will be needed to bolster both the motive to be honest and the motive to keep promises. The question is whether Hume is right in thinking that promises require some penalty, in all conditions, before and after magistrates, whereas property does not. Why should one think there is a real difference? Is the difference just an accident of Hume's expository fiction of a step-by-step development from a hypothetical state of nature, or is it one of the truths that fiction is intended to reveal? I think that there is reason in Hume's order of exposition, which places property before promise, and promise before government, and there is also reason in his introduction of penalty only when he gets to promise. This new element of penalty comes in along with two other new elements—the essential reliance on linguistic representation, for incurring the obligation and transferring the right, and the inclusion of particular remote and general goods within the scope of voluntary transfer. I suggest that the full utilization of language, by the promisor and his fellows, makes possible the sort of penalty Hume makes part of the interested obligation to keep a promise, and that the special reference to the future a promise involves makes the threat of that possible penalty necessary to provide self-interested motivation to keep a promise to a stranger (and strangers will be the ones Humeans reserve their promises for).

Do not the trusting always need protection from those who might exploit their trust? Do not property owners, who trust their neighbors not to steal, need protection? Is protection by the contrivance of a penalty not needed wherever persons risk something by trusting others? Hume seems to be saying "no," that protection by penalty is needed when what we trust someone to do is not merely what we trust all our fellows to do, namely, to refrain for the indefinite future from stealing, or in other ways violating our property rights, but is some special individual "performance," in "some future" that he and only he owes us. In virtue of his promise, we expect more of him than of others, and we expect a definite "performance," not merely a refraining. We need protection because we are at special definite risk from a special definite person. The existence of the penalty of victim-initiated general withdrawal of trust, made possible by the ancillary linguistic invention of "reputation," gives us this protection.

What would it be to withdraw trust from a person who had proved a thief, as Hume supposes we withdraw trust from the promise-breaker? If someone steals some object while in my home and if I know this, I can try to keep this person out of it in the future, and warn others to do likewise, but I surely cannot, short of banishing or deporting the thief, remove him from all opportunity to steal again. The promise-breaker can be prevented from having a promise accepted again, but no such "suitable" penalty exists for the thief. Promise-breaking presupposes both a prior promise-giving and a prior acceptance of one's promise, but theft has no parallel presupposed prior actions on the thief's or his victim's part. We cannot deprive him of the opportunity for further thieving by the sort of relevantly specific incapacitation we inflict on the promise-breaker when we refuse to accept further promises from him.

## Acceptance

Accepting and rejecting are actions that are of vital importance to all agreements and all agreed transfers. For Humean conventions there must be general acceptance, and a theoretical option of rejecting disadvantageous or exploitative schemes of action. His second convention, instituting transfer by consent, enabled persons to make gifts, loans, and to engage in barter. The "consent" whose force is thereby recognized is the consent of the one who gives up what was hers, so that the relevant actions seem to be requesting, consenting, and refusing. Must something be offered before anything can be refused? Once we see gift and barter as made possible by this second convention, then we will find offer and acceptance of individual transfers as well as request and consent to transfer as made possible by it. The right of refusal by someone to whom one wants to make a gift or loan, or with whom one hopes to engage in barter, could in theory provide a way in which one's fellows could relevantly incapacitate those who had broken the rules of giving, loaning, and bartering, but only the barterer and the recipient of a loan, not the giver or the lender, is likely to have any motive to break these rules. It is much more likely that the costs of bad behavior as a party to gift, loan, and barter will be a drying up of offers to one, than of refusal of the offers one might make. Only with promise does the right to refuse an offer give one any significant power in dealings with one's fellows.

Of course, a penalty, even a "fitting" one, can always be contrived, if one wants to contrive one. One might cut the hand off the thief, and some communities do just this (but usually only by means of magistrates' powers). Had Hume's initial convention of property included a right of the victims of theft to attempt such retribution as dispossession or maiming, then it is certainly not clear that either private or public interest would be furthered by such an agreement. It simply would not qualify as a scheme that would arouse "a sense of common interest," especially as the levying of the penalty would re-create the very violence and disorder the convention is supposed to end. "To . . . allow every man to seize directly what he judges to be fit for him wou'd destroy society" (T 514). Hume speaks here of acts of redistribution of property, but the claim holds good as much when the reason for my judging it fit that I have your goods or your hand is that I reasonably believe that you took my goods, as when the reason is simply that I would like your possessions. Revenge by victims simply cannot be made a part of an acceptable convention of property. But some form of revenge by victims might be made part of an acceptable convention of barter, or exchange by consent, and must be made a part of any acceptable convention whereby strangers are induced to rely on another individual's performing a specified future act that is not obligatory on other grounds. The cluster of special features Hume associates with promise—namely, linguistic representation, acceptance, acknowledged threat of victim-initiated penalty for nonperformance, trust in future or delayed delivery—are an interdependent group of features. Language makes the penalty possible, as well as making possible both that exact (possibly conditional) undertaking a promise typically involves, and the sign that it is solemnly undertaken. The penalty and the solemnity and the precise spelling out of the obligation (which facilitates later determination of whether or not it has been discharged) are needed because someone, the accepter of the promise, is relying on that performance or "delayed delivery," is trusting the promisor, and so needs protection.

There are three features promissory obligations have, which make penalty both something it is safe to allow victims to inflict or initiate, and also something it is advisable to institute. First, there can be no doubt who the promise-breaker is, as there can be doubt who the thief is. With promise-breaking there can be no detection problem. Second, since promises must be accepted before any obligation arises, there can be such a thing as the power to make a promise, and threat of forfeiture of that power. Suitable incapacitation is therefore possible for promise-breakers but not, for example, for thieves. Third, there is the fact that promissory obligations are each of particular content, owed by a particular person to some particular other, and are dischargeable within some limited time. This means that, especially when they are not part of a contract or mutual promise, they put the accepter of a promise in a position where some more security is needed than one needs where one relies on others "doing their part" in some open-ended scheme of reciprocal services. I can expect my neighbor to continue not blocking my driveway if I don't block his because this is a private "scheme of action" we have for an open-ended future, one in which "I foresee that he will return my service in expectation of another of the same kind" (T 521). It is not an obligation dischargeable once and for all, like that which a promise typically creates. Just because an individual promise need *not* be part of a mutually advantageous reciprocal transfer, and because even when it is part of a mutual promise it is possible for one party, before he does his part, to have already *obtained* all the "goods" that the other is to transfer, that other *needs* the security which penalty provides.

## Deposits, Penalties, and Oaths

Hume studied law and practiced commerce before writing the *Treatise,* and his discussion of promise shows both an appreciation of the importance of this device for commerce and trade and also a familiarity with lawyers' inventions, both superstitious and fanciful ones and useful ones. One concept he would have encountered in his law studies was the canon law notion of *interpositio fidei,*[19] the doctrine that a promise is binding because the promisor puts his Christian faith and salvation at risk, since in promising he invites the promisee to call down damnation upon him should he fail to perform his promise. This interposition of a threat of divine punishment, cued by a human accusation, turns promise into a case not only of delayed delivery but also of simultaneous delivery of something, namely, the promisor's status as a Christian in good standing, into the power of the other party, the receiver of the promise. This amounts to a pawn or deposit, recovered when the promissory obligation is fulfilled, and the threat of losing one's deposit operates as an interested motive. A penalty for nonperformance is created by this handing over, by the promisor, of his moral status. Hume's version of promise includes a secular version of *interpositio fidei*—the promisor, in promising, "subjects himself to the penalty of never being trusted again in case of failure" (T 252). It is not merely that the community will thus react to

19. My information about this and other facts about Scottish law comes from James Dalrymple, Viscount of Stair, *The Institution of the Laws of Scotland,* edited by David M. Walker (Yale, 1981), and from Richard Keith and George Clark, *A Guide to Scots Law* (Johnson and Bacon, 1978).

his failure, but that he acknowledges that fact, he "subjects" himself to the penalty as he himself takes on the obligation it enforces. Were there no such penalty, why should anyone accept and rely on any promise?

This subjection to acknowledged conditional penalty, levied by some higher power, is exactly what an oath is. Hobbes says that an oath is "a form of words, added to promise, by which he that promiseth signifieth that unless he perform he renounceth the mercy of his God, or calleth to him for vengeance on himself."[20] Hobbes believes that "oath adds nothing to the obligation," but that may be because "there are no oaths but of God," and Hobbes has the sovereign's sword to make promises more than mere words, so needs no invocations of *divine* punishment. Hume, like the canon lawyers, makes oath (or secular oath-equivalent) a necessary part of promise, not a superadded extra. Of course, an oath can be added to solemnize any obligation, and so once there *is* a power of penalty, it can be conditionally invoked to solemnize standing obligations as well as dischargeable ones. If Hume is right, however, it *must* be present in promises. The threat of the penalty of loss of reputation as a reliable promise-keeper, to which the promisor knowingly subjects himself, provides that "new motive" without which promises would not differ from "mere expression and consent." And without the community's practices of promise-receiving only from those not known to be promise-breakers, and of reputation-giving, the threatened penalty would be nonexistent. So Cavell's *reductio* of promising to entering an "office," and so taking an *oath* of office, turns out to be, for Hume, no *reductio* at all. To promise *is* to take an oath of performance. Hume finds a third alternative between the punitive power of God and the punitive power of magistrates—the punitive power of one's fellows, the keepers of one's reputation. The "word" without the sword is enough to bind, when words are available and used not only to undertake and to solemnize undertakings, but also to communicate a person's positive or negative record as a "man of his word." Truth or fidelity as the virtue of those who are true to their word needs the assistance of truth-telling about persons, of truth in reputation-giving, and this requires the practice of keeping track of a person's moral performance. Representation in language is not only needed in the very act of promising, to specify a future act that becomes obligatory, but is also necessary to provide the motive for keeping prom-

20. Hobbes, *Leviathan*, ch. 14.

ises. Past performance or nonperformance must be represented and conveyed in reputation for it to be possible for the giving of a solemn representation of a future action to bind a person to perform that action. J. L. Austin, arguing for the binding force of the word "I promise that . . . ," said, "Accuracy and morality alike are on the side of the plain saying that *our word is our bond.*"[21] We can now say, not so plainly, that the bond is our word, given the background uses of other words to keep and destroy reputations.

Cavell claims that a promise does not bind one any more than does an expression of one's intentions. We need to see how the representation of a future action, in a Humean promise, binds in the way the representation of a future action, in a statement of intention, does not. In a community where reputation is kept track of, one may get the reputation for fickleness as well as for infidelity, for being a person whose plans and intentions change rapidly and inconsiderately. Cavell is surely correct in saying that one can commit oneself to another by saying "I intend to. . . ." Austin too lists "I intend," with "I promise," among the speech acts he calls "corn-missives."[22] But the commitment of a serious avowal of intention to another is not that of a promise, as can be seen if we look at what discharges the obligation in the two cases. If having said to you that I intend to attend the meeting and support your proposal, I find it very difficult to do this, I am at moral liberty to change my mind, but I surely should let you know and apologize. Had I promised to attend, letting you know I will not attend and saying "sorry" may be better than breaking my promise without warning, but certainly does not discharge the obligation I took on. A statement of intention made seriously to another *limits* my freedom to change my mind. I need good reason, but not necessarily in the form of another overriding obligation, to change my mind, and I owe it to you to keep you informed, so that your plans, where they depended on mine, can also change. I may even owe you some help in your efforts to make compensatory changes of plan, so that a serious statement of intention attaches *costs* to any subsequent change of mind. But if I *promise* you to attend, I have no freedom to change my mind. A more important moral necessity or a physical necessity may prevent me doing what I fixedly had a mind to do, and so excuse me, or

21. Austin, 10.
22. Austin, 156.

you may release me; but if I simply decide that on second thought I won't go, I must acknowledge that I fail in my obligation, whatever I do to let you know or to help you to find other support for your cause. I have no excuse, and must accept the penalty of being "branded" as unfaithful, of having others in future refuse to accept my promises. I changed my mind after renouncing my liberty to do so, after giving you both the go-ahead to count on me and the connected right to penalize me by withdrawal of trust if I change my mind. In a promise, *what* is promised is what is obligatory. Change of mind is not allowed.[23] In an intention-avowal, what is obligatory is to either fulfill the stated intention or to let the other know of one's change of mind. The obligation is explicit in a promise, not fully explicit in an intention-avowal. Of course, in both various possible excuses for nonperformance of one's obligation are tacitly understood—that inability excuses, that some moral emergencies may override the obligation. But these are standard excuses in moral matters, not special to obligations originating in acts of individual commitment, so they can go without saying. Hume points out some invalidating conditions special to verbal obligation-incurring acts like promises—for example, that one did not understand what one was saying; or that the words, although spoken with understanding, were spoken in obvious jest, that is, with "contrary signs." The best contrary sign is "That's not a promise." Since promises can be given without saying "I promise," we can cancel the apparent commissive force of a serious "I intend to be there" by adding "but that's not a promise."

Hume is quite clear that the conditions invalidating apparent promises do not include deceit or insincerity, even when they are detected or suspected. "Withdrawing one's intention" while apparently expressing it in words does not invalidate a promise, as long as it is accepted by the other party. One is bound by it whether or not one intended to keep it when giving it. Hume takes this as an indicator of its being contrived for social convenience, unlike those other less useful ceremonial acts like baptism, the mass, or holy orders, where the priest's "withdrawal of intention" destroys the force of the act, takes the magic out of it. The magic of a promise is carefully contrived for the convenience of a trading society, and its purpose explains its intricacies, even what Hume calls

---

23. I discuss change of mind, and treat promise as a renunciation of the right to change one's mind, in "Mind and Change of Mind."

"all these contradictions" (T 523)—that for a valid promise one must understand what one says, but need not mean what one says, that withdrawal of intention by "evident signs," but not secret withdrawal of intention, invalidates the act.

A promise, then, on this slightly reconstructed Humean account, is a convention-dependent, two-party verbal act, in which several things happen at once. The promisor expresses a serious intention to perform a particular future action that the second party wants her to perform. She makes that very action obligatory, one she is no longer free to decide not to perform. She does this by introducing the verbal representation by a special ritual act or "sign," the words "I promise," which get their force from community recognition and enforcement of the obligation thereby created, once the promise is accepted. By this act, or oath-equivalent, the promisor acknowledges the other party's right and power to destroy her good standing as a promise-giver, should she fail to perform as promised. She ritually hands over her reputation to the other party, as a pawn or security, to be redeemed by her performance of her promise. There is both representation and what Anscombe calls "the giving of a sign." The latter makes obligatory what the former represents. The non-natural necessitation is done by the giving and receiving of the sign, and what is necessitated is elaborated in the representation. But the sign gets its power to bind from other acts of representation—from the public representation of a person's moral record and character, and from the general agreed intention to receive promises only from those not known to be promise-breakers. These background representations of character and conditional intentions to withdraw trust make it possible for the promisor to *have* a reputation to pawn, and for the promisee to ruin it should the promisor not perform.

The penalty for nonperformance of a promise might therefore be seen as forfeiture of one's deposit, what one gave as security. Once one has not merely the social practice of promising, and of mutual promises, but also the legal institution of contract, with magistrates to enforce contract, then a failure to honor one's contractual commitments may be responded to in several ways:

1. Forfeiture of whatever security one gave
2. Enforced performance according to the contract (an edict *ad factum praestandum*)

3. Payment of damages (reliance or expectation damages)
4. Penalty (fine, imprisonment, deportation, disablement from future contracting)

The last three depend upon the victim's initiating some legal action, but (1) is more automatic. In promise, (1) and (4) are fused, since the deposit forfeited is one's good name as a promise-keeper, and one's ability to give promises in future. This disablement is the form penalty takes, before there are magistrates, and in some cases after there are magistrates. Because of the special nature *of what* is "deposited" in a promise, forfeiture of deposit is also social disablement. No pre-legal forerunners of enforced performance or of damages are present, unless the promise included a penalty clause that the promisor observes in order to retain reputation, to recover deposit.

## Promises and Exchanges

This way of looking at promise, as essentially involving not merely the representation and simultaneous creation of an obligation, but also subjecting oneself to a penalty that the victim can initiate, makes the apparent one-way transfer of rights to what is to be delivered later into a case of two-way transfer of something, and of immediate delivery of something, namely, power to harm. The promisor delivers her good name into the power of the promisee; the promisee receives it. The promisee puts the success of his future plans into the power of the promisor; he gives her his trust. There is an immediate exchange of powers to harm, but not of the same sort of power to the same sort of harm. The promisor gives her "word," and that word both spells out her obligation and subjects her to a penalty made possible by the power of words the other party has, the power to accuse, to brand, to disable. But all these social powers are dependent on the nonpromissory "agreement," or as Cavell might call it, "commitment," of the community to cooperate in giving persons "repute" and in refusing to accept promises from those with a bad repute in this respect.

Atiyah says that "gratuitous" unilateral promises do not bind at all, especially if not relied on.[24] The two-way voluntary transfer is a natural place to start when thinking about what makes a transaction between

24. See Atiyah, 212ff.

persons just, and the simplest case is a simultaneous immediate transfer. There are no outstanding obligations if you and I swap, say, pens, each getting what we want and giving what the other wants. Commitments and obligations arise, or seem to arise, only when there is *delay* in delivery, or when only one party receives something (or one receives more than the other). "Artifices" are needed to make possible transfers *other* than simultaneous immediate two-way transfer, and in Hume's account, which *does* make unilateral promises binding, this is done by inventing a "fiction" of immediate delivery when there is not immediate delivery, a fiction of simultaneous transfer when there is not simultaneous transfer, and a fiction of receiving something when one party does not receive anything, or anything of the same sort. The handshake, the mutual giving and receiving of hands, symbolizes all these fictions. For them to be useful fictions they must be backed by socially conferred powers, and recognized obligations. The obligations "tie," as it were, the fictions to the real thing; they enable cooperative transfers to stretch to include the nonsimultaneous transfers, the delayed delivery, and the one-sided delivery. Hume derides the "lawyer's superstitions" which demand immediate delivery of some physical token, and which insist on some *causa* or "consideration" to make a deal seem to be two-way immediate transfer, but his account of the obligations of promises retains a "spiritualized" version of what the lawyers wanted. "Words" are given to effect immediate delivery, and powers are exchanged to make a promise a mutual transfer. But Hume shows how the words "I promise" can do their magic, what makes these exchanged powers real powers.

He locates the convention of promise-receiving within a family of other obligation-generating conventions or agreed forms of life. He distinguishes the cooperation through contrived vulnerability of promisor and promisee from the more generous cooperative practices of friends and loved intimates, who need no conventions to help them become mutually trusting and so mutually vulnerable, who, as he says, "do services" without "any prospect of advantage," and "make return in the same manner, without any view but that of recompensing past services" (T 521). The friends' and lovers' reciprocity is not a penalty-backed exchange of definitely specified future-including services, but a natural response to love and kindness. It creates its own vulnerabilities, but Hume neither confuses them with those of the parties to a promise nor confuses the latter contrived trust and concomitant vulnerability with other contrived dependencies on others, those produced by the conventions of property, consent, and authority. He shows how, in promise, our word is our bond—how there we use the powers language gives us to represent the future, the general, the conditional, to keep and make known an individual's moral record, to explicitly commit ourselves, subject ourselves, denounce others. This enables him, I think, to account for all the features of promissory obligations, both those shared with other obligations and those peculiar to promises. He can agree with Cavell that we should not construe all ties between persons on the model of promise, let alone on the model of bargain.[25] Some personal ties are natural, and depend upon no general rules or any contrived penalties. Neither all the natural ties nor all the contrived ones are voluntarily assumed or taken on by those who are tied, and not all the voluntary assumed ones are penalty-backed, nor all the penalty-backed ones contracts or bargains. Hume can agree with Anscombe that the non-natural necessity to keep one's promise is like the non-natural necessity to obey rules, such as property rules or rules of a language, but he can show how in this special case of promise language must *both* do what other rituals might do, change the moral situation, and *also* do what only language can do, represent the precise conditions under which the ritually invoked penalty will be avoided, if promises are to play their special and limited role. Hume shows us what sort of beast promise is by putting it in its natural habitat—trust-requiring cooperation, on a limited matter, within a limited time, between particular strangers, who need no greater cooperation with each other, and need the presence of penalty to make possible even such limited trust.

Such individual binding agreements occur not only when labor is contracted for harvests, before magistrates are invented, but in commerce, after their invention. Hume's year in Bristol must have made clear to him both the extent to which commerce depends upon the convenient contrivance of legal contract, and also how frequent breach of contract is in that sphere, breach which is *not* always followed by exclusion of the contract-breaker from the community of traders. For, as Atiyah

---

25. Cavell, 299, says that utilitarian accounts of promising, such as that offered by John Rawls in "Two Concepts of Rules," *Philosophical Review* 64 (1955): 3–32, not only make commitments more like explicit promises than they are but also make promises more like legal contracts than they are, adding that the central idea underlying the English law of contract is that of a bargain.

has emphasized, as long as one collects enough reliance damages when the other party breaks his contract with one, one may have no occasion to shun further equally profitable deals with that contract-breaker. Does this mean that the preceding account makes no sense of the very commercial activities in which promise and contract are such convenient contrivances that without them the activity would be scarcely possible? Atiyah's charge that philosophers in their treatment of promising have shown more belief in the force of "bare" promises than does English law appears to apply to Hume, as I have understood him. Hume must have become familiar with English law of contract, as it was in the eighteenth century while he was in Bristol, if he had not earlier become familiar with it as a law student in Edinburgh. That he was reacting to the Natural Law tradition in his account of all the artifices is quite obvious, and I have claimed that he puts to his own secular uses the canon law concept of *interpositio fidei*. But the influence of the English common law must also be presumed present, given Hume's legal studies and apprenticeship in commerce. Atiyah has helpfully traced the changes that the concept of contract underwent, and Hume lived during one of the periods of fairly dramatic change. According to Atiyah, before 1600 the common law treated as legally binding only such promises as were given in return for a "consideration," and only such as had in fact been relied upon. But by 1800 "the common lawyers had largely come round to the modern viewpoint that promises *per se* are morally binding."[26] By "modern," Atiyah here seems to mean the "classic," not the contemporary lawyer's view. Atiyah sees the later legal development, in the nineteenth and twentieth century, as a return to the earlier view. Hume lived and wrote after the rise and before the fall of freedom of contract, and so one must expect in his account of promising to find "the modern viewpoint that promises *per se* are morally binding," that concept which, if Atiyah is right, contemporary philosophers but not contemporary lawyers still hold. And, if the preceding interpretation is right, we do indeed find that in Hume. Does this mean that Hume's account cannot explain the fact that sometimes a tradesman accepts a promise that he will happily see not performed, as long as he collects enough in damages? Is he pleased at the "immorality" of the contract-breaker, from which he may reap good profits? There is no need at all for Hume to have to say this about the

---

26. Atiyah, 4.

sort of commercial exploitation of the device of promise with which it is reasonable to suppose him familiar. The account he gives us in the *Treatise* is not an account of what becomes of promise once there are magistrates, but of what it can be without them. Once the full panoply of the law is there, everything is changed by its presence. Only when there are magistrates can damages be assessed or awarded, so contract-making with an eye to the other party's expected contract-breaking, followed by one's own receipt of reliance damages, is a form of life made possible by Hume's fourth artifice, the invention of magistrates who declare and administer the rules, as much as by his third artifice, promise.

What is good about his account, however, is that it does contain the germs of all these later developments, and of the various possibilities that Atiyah sees realized at different times in the history of the English common law's attitude to promise and contract. A promise is given in return for receipt of something, namely, trust, which the promisor is presumed to want, so there is an element of "consideration." The promisor receives this and in return she gives her word, thereby giving the promisee a right to future goods or services, as well as putting her reputation in the promisee's safekeeping, giving him power to initiate the penalty of harm to reputation resulting in a general refusal to accept her promises, should the promise not be performed. The promisee relies on the promise being performed, if he really gives his trust. He may, if he is as scheming as some later tradesmen, rely not on the main performance but on the performance of a penalty clause or even on his power to blackball the promisor when she fails to perform. He cannot rely on performance-or-damages, before there are magistrates, but he may rely on performance-or-ruin of the nonperformer's chances of trading again. Since this penalty, of "never being trusted again in case of failure," is a very drastic one, which it may not always suit the interests of the promisee to inflict—he may after all *need* to make deals again with the promise-breaker—it is to be expected that a community of wise Humeans will go on, once they invent magistrates, to include, among their powers, power to substitute a less drastic and more generally beneficial contrived consequence of nonperformance, namely, monetary damages. The law of contract, unlike the natural artifice of promise, enables us to cooperate with those who are known to be untrustworthy, known *not* to be "men of their word." Hume's account is of the convention of promise, not of the legal institution of contract, but the account he gives us shows how the latter could develop from the former, as well as making it understandable that promise survives as a convention alongside legal contract. After all, there are spheres of life where we do not want to cooperate with the untrustworthy. Promise helps us cooperate with strangers, on a limited basis, and the penalty it incorporates helps us limit that cooperation to strangers not known to be untrustworthy in the relevant respects.

Like Atiyah's account, Hume's is a historical account of how a certain contrivance comes to be invented and used because of its usefulness. Promise takes varying forms in different societies, and has changed in ours. But I think we nonlawyers and nonbusinesswomen do still, sometimes, give and accept promises that are still recognizably Humean.[27] To be recognizably Humean, a promise must not be the golden road to commitment, must not be as basic as contractarians must make it, but must be what we can resort to for some of our dealings with strangers, and it must differ from a serious statement of intention. It need have no more "sanctity," to use Atiyah's phrase, than any other useful artifice. But to see it as the artifice it is, we need to see the traces in it of the older sanctity of oath, as well as of the eternal apparent sanctity of mutually profitable exchange. Better, I think, than any more recent account, Hume's helps us put promises in their proper and properly restricted place.

27. Charles Fried, in *Contract as Promise* (Harvard, 1981), accepts much of Hume's account of what a promise is, but differs from Hume on why it binds. Fried's account of that appeals to "basic Kantian principles of respect and trust" (17). As his title indicates, Fried holds that the law of contracts is rooted in promise.

# 9

# Good Men's Women:
# Hume on Chastity and Trust

At the very heart of Hume's philosophy in the *Treatise,* namely, between his discussion of the artificial and the natural virtues, he places a short chapter entitled "Of chastity and modesty." Its central position is appropriate, since these supposed virtues present something of a test case for Hume's account of the relation between nature and artifice, and, more generally, beyond his moral philosophy, for his views on regularity and constancy in and out of individual lives. For these theoretical reasons, as well as for the calm realism of his treatment of sexual inequality, the chapter warrants more attention than it has received.

I am indebted to William Charron for extremely helpful comments on the first version of this chapter, read at the Seventh Hume Conference, Banff Springs, September 1978. In particular, I was helped by his comments to see how a male *virtue* depends on an artificial female one, in Hume's account. I was also provoked, by his emphasis on Hume's definition of a convention as re-requiring a "sense of common interest," to consider whether the artifice Hume describes does serve female interests as well as male ones. Clearly it does serve the interests females have in shared care of "their" children, and serves the atemporal interest they have in institutions ensuring that children (and so themselves when children) be cared for. But just as clearly it also goes against an interest of theirs insofar as it subjects them to male sovereignty, and is against everyone's interests insofar as it subverts true love and friendship. None of Hume's artifices serve the interests of all those involved equally well, despite his claim (E 190) that conventions arise only between those roughly equal in power to make their resentments felt. Just as he believes that it is better for *all* people, including younger sons, and the poor, that there be rules of inheritance and property, although some benefit much more than others from the details of these rules, so he believes that both men and women have a common, if unequal, interest in the institution of monogamous marriage between the chaste woman and a less chaste man. Charron's questions also led me to look more closely at the central place Hume assigns to friendship in marriage, and to the rationale which that might generate for fidelity even in childless marriages.

Perhaps Hume's most important contribution to moral philosophy is his account of the difference between natural virtues, displayed in actions which do good one by one, each act having value independently of whether similar acts are performed by oneself and others on other occasions, and artificial virtues displayed in acts in essential conformity to established socially useful conventions, which do good only insofar as they are supported by general conformity. Hume does not, like Kant, insist that we always see morally good action as obedience to law, nor does he neglect the importance of those areas where good can be done only if acts are correctly seen as conforming to general laws, general conformity to which is not only willed by the agent but also assumed by him to be in effect. Hume gives a subtle and elaborate account of when we do and when we do not need moral and social conformity, of which virtues are and which virtues are not mediated by changeable public will or convention. Conventions must operate before any act can count as property-respecting, but there is no need to ask, "Can I will this as universal law?" before soothing a frightened child. Whatever the conventions, whatever others do, such an act does some good, and is the sort of act which displays the natural virtue of kindness.

Hume requires of a virtuous act not merely that it be helpful or agreeable to someone (or some public) but also that it display a durable character trait in the agent. An uncharacteristic act of kindness to a child may do good without displaying a virtue or a good character. Approval is given, according to Hume, to persons on account of their durable character traits, as displayed in their actions and reactions. The natural response to virtue is to welcome its possessor—"His company is a satisfaction to me" (T 588)—and virtue in rags will be the exception in a smoothly functioning society. The fact that Hume's ethics is an agent ethics, and that the concept of welcome virtue is more fundamental to it than that of a useful action, commits Hume, throughout his moral philosophy and especially in his treatment of the natural virtues, to an emphasis on consistency or integrity of character, to a search for durable character traits and so for characteristic actions.

Now a person might be characteristically kind, yet on occasion, under stress, give expression to unaccustomed malice. The uncharacteristic malicious act may weaken but not destroy the virtue of kindness which kind acts have both expressed and *infixed* (T 411). When the malicious act is known, the person's reputation for benevolence may be slightly sullied, but certainly not ruined. Both within one person's life, and within one population, there will be reason to encourage consistently virtuous action, but no reason to feel that all is lost or spoiled if lapses from the natural virtues occur. Even when cruelty is the norm, the rare kind act may be appreciated, if not rewarded, and the rare kind person may be welcome, if also exploited and victimized.

With the artificial virtues there is a stronger demand and need for uniformity in a population, since the value of any one just act, or one person's character trait, depends upon the support received from the similar acts and traits of others. "Every single act is performed in the expectation that others are to perform the like" (T 498). To display artificial virtues, actions must be seen as rule-governed, and the rule must be "inflexible either by spite or favour" (502). The generality required for the utility of an artifice is impersonal and interpersonal. It would seem to matter little whether the few lapses, the inevitable small cracks in the "vault" (E 305) of justice, be spread across many lives or concentrated in the lives of a few unjust individuals. Does it matter, to the victims of theft, if the thieves be many or a few very busy ones?

Where it surely *does* matter not only how many lapses occur but also how many nonvirtuous persons there are is where reputation is affected and relied on, since the more dishonest people there are known to be, the more restricted are the opportunities for cooperation. As Hume's account of them makes clear, all the artificial virtues are displayed in *cooperative* action, requiring trust, which is protected by the fact that reputations are at stake in such action. Where we count on others, we also keep account of their performance. It is more important to know others' reputation for the artificial virtues than for the natural virtues, since in cooperating with others we make ourselves vulnerable to their lapses from artificial virtue, as an animal bears its throat to inhibit fatal attack. Both natural goods and reputation are deliberately put in jeopardy in the cooperative ventures which alone provide opportunity for display of artificial virtues and vices. To display kindness or cruelty, I need not first be trusted by another, but to show fidelity or infidelity to promises I must first have been included in the circle of trusted ones with whom another will have "any commerce" (T 521, 583). A bad reputation will effectively exclude me from the society of those who have opportunity to display artificial virtues or vices. Lapses from artificial virtues, unlike lapses from natural virtue, are always breaches of trust. If I show myself untrustworthy, I will "never be trusted any more" (522).

All the artifices extend or create a climate of trust in a variety of areas by altering presumptions concerning trustworthiness. Before the artifice of property, the presumption would be that transferable possessions cannot be left in another's safekeeping. Once there are rules of property, this presumption is reversed. Before the artifice, a person might be trusted because of his special position to one, say, parent or lover, or might earn trust by proven conspicuous trustworthiness; after the adoption of the artifice, trust on some matters is extended to all, on credit, and it is distrust which must be individually earned. In a society where trust is extensively eroded, it is perhaps difficult to realize how social conventions do make trustworthiness the normal expectation. But even in a distrustful society like the United States, where gunsmiths and locksmiths prosper, most of us still walk abroad unarmed, trust our property to tenants and repair workers, and trust our lives and health to airplane pilots, bus drivers, doctors, and suppliers of food and water. No doubt we do so with increasing risk, but the alternative, increasing distrust, brings an evil worse than risk of individual loss, namely, that pervasive climate of distrust which Hobbes correctly called "Warre, and such a warre as is of everyman against everyman."[1] Better to be trusting fools than distrusting war-makers.[2]

The fact that existing societies differ in their climate of trust shows an important fact about the artificial virtues which Hume's account does not point up, namely, that a reputation for honesty is quite compatible with known limitations on the scope of that honesty. In the United States, but not in New Zealand, a person may count as honest who observes the maxim "finders keepers." Standards of honesty vary, and awareness of this fact introduces the concept of degrees of honesty into our assessment of our fellows. In writing testimonials we will describe some as scrupulously honest, others merely as honest. A person may have a reputation for being more or less honest, honest in all matters except turning in money found in public places, or except in income tax returns. A person does not lose a reputation for honesty because of ac-

1. *Leviathan,* ch. 13.
2. I have discussed this in "Secular Faith," *Postures of the Mind* (Minnesota, 1985), 292–308.

knowledged limits to it. Some limits are built into the convention itself, and it may be that in this society careless owners and internal revenue departments are by tacit agreement accepted as fair game for takers. But there are always areas of uncertainty and room for discretion, and a person's character will be judged by behavior in this gray zone.

There is, of course, a difference between acknowledged limits to the field within which a person's, or a population's, honesty operates, and acknowledged lapses within this field. In practice, however, it is difficult to decide whether, for instance, a person's failure to correct a mistakenly high insurance claim submitted on her behalf shows that insurance companies are beyond the pale, for her, or whether, due to unusual temptation, there was a lapse from standards usually applied "inflexibly by either spite or favor" (T 502). I think we can grant Hume's claim that artificially virtuous acts do depend, for their worth, on dependable consistency of behavior not only within a life but also within a population more than do naturally virtuous acts, without denying that the artificial virtues can admit of degrees, of limitation of range, and of occasional lapses. A formal feature of all the artificial virtues, as Hume presents them, is that one lapse destroys the virtue. This fragility of an artificial virtue links with the role of the artifices in securing trust and enabling cooperation. I have so far argued that, granted that the artifices have this vital role of altering presumptions concerning the trustworthiness of persons in particular matters (can I trust my possessions to him, can I trust his word, can I count on his allegiance?) and granted that the artificial virtues are more fragile than the natural virtues, nevertheless they are not so fragile that one lapse is fatal to their survival in a person. They may not survive unharmed, but survive they may, and their reflection in reputation may register both the limits of a person's virtue's reach and any recorded lapses within that field. One blot on one's copybook need not destroy reputation nor condemn one to social ostracism.

The artificial virtues, then, are more like chastity, as it is normally understood, than like virginity—they are not so fragile as to be destroyed by one lapse. But when Hume, after considering the special freedom granted to princes, turns to the special restriction placed on women, when he turns to consider chastity, he treats it as conceptually analogous to virginity, an all-or-nothing affair, an inviolate state of a person not yet seduced into ruin. This is because the trust he associates with the virtue is trust concerned with guarantee of paternity. The vital determination of which children are one's own cannot be made by the male parent unless he trusts the female, and trusts her exclusive attachment to him, by Hume's account. Strictly speaking, the exclusive attachment is needed only during a limited period, if the rationale is the one Hume gives. There is no conceptual reason why chastity should not be merely monthlong exclusive sexual fidelity, and the reputation for it lost only by known switches of sexual partner within any one period of possible conception. Hume does not consider this, but had he done so, he could have explained the exaggeration of the demand for chastity, in relation to its rationale, in the same way he does for modesty, namely, the human tendency to carry general rules beyond the "original principle" (T 573), especially when that principle goes against a natural tendency. We must shoot beyond the target to hit the target. A more general restriction may be less likely to be critically examined by its victims than one of such baroque complexity that they are encouraged to probe for a rationale. Practicality demands a simple rule, where there is any case for a restriction. Hume says that if the rule made an exception for women past the age of childbearing, "the example of the old would be pernicious to the young and . . . women, continually foreseeing that a certain age would bring them the liberty of indulgence, would naturally advance that period, and think more lightly of this whole duty, so requisite to society" (E 208).

In determining which children are one's own, there is inequality of need for trust, since no mother need depend on another person to determine which child is her child. "From this trivial and anatomical observation is deriv'd that vast difference betwixt the education and duties of the two sexes" (T 571). By Hume's account the male *needs* to know which children are his children more than does the female, since he is expected not merely to "give a loose to love and tenderness" but also to "undergo cheerfully all the fatigues and expences" (570, emphasis added) of child care. He also wants to ensure that his property is not passed on to a wrong "object" (ibid.), by Hume's earlier account of the "natural" right of succession (510ff). The female parent may trust the male to share the "fatigues" of child care, but by Hume's account it is the males who are most vulnerable to breach of trust, who are forced into trust, by that lack of "security" concerning which "objects are their own, due to the fact that since, in the copulation of the sexes, the principle of generation goes from the man to the woman, an error may easily take place on the side of the former, tho' it be utterly impossible with regard to the latter" (571).

Hume's account of the demand for female chastity depends upon his psychological premises that men will be unwilling to care for children not believed to be biologically their own, as well as on his epistemological and "anatomical" premises concerning the natural uncertainty of paternity. It also depends upon an assumption made but not stated, namely, that a society be both patriarchal, so that control of "expences" is in male hands, and patrilineal, so that property passes through the male line. In a matriarchal and matrilineal society the question of true paternity would become as "trivial" as the anatomical facts which make error there so easy.

Another suppressed premise in Hume's account is that a double standard operate not only between the sexes, but also within the female sex. Although Hume says that special restrictions are imposed "over the whole sex" (T 573), his account requires that there be some women available as partners for those "debauch'd bachelors" (572) and straying husbands who are granted a greater "liberty of indulging their appetites in venereal enjoyment" (573). As Hume knew very well, neither the servant women at Ninewells nor the royal mistresses of Paris aspired to be mothers of children of recognized lineage and title to property, so could afford to risk "bad fame" (571) by their "lewdness and impudence" (572). His contemporary, Bernard Mandevilie, is very clear on this point: "If courtezans and strumpets were to be prosecuted with as much vigour as some silly people would have it, what locks and bars would be sufficient to preserve the honour of our wives and daughters. . . . [I]t is manifest that there is a necessity of sacrificing one part of womankind to preserve the other, and prevent a filthiness of a more heinous nature."[3] Hume knows and by implication recognizes these simple truths, but his emphasis in the chapter "Of chastity and modesty" is on the role of the artificial virtue of chastity in persuading males to share responsibility for child rearing, and the preparation of all women for their childbearing role. He sees clearly that the heart of the problem concerns the role of childbearing, the responsibility for child rearing, the unalterable division of the labor for the former, the socially contrived division of respon-

---

3. Bernard Mandeville, *The Fable of the Bees,* Remark H.

sibility for the latter, and the complicating thread of trust tying the sexual parties together in different sorts of dependency.

Hume's chapter is sometimes perceived, and was earlier perceived by me, as sexist in tone and content, but now I find it remarkable for its devastating clarity, its exposure of the double standard as a "useful" means of indulging the vanity of socially powerful males, and as a response to their reluctance to share the costs of childbearing, their stinginess or "confin'd generosity" (T 495) in assumption of responsibility for new members of society. Hume does not minimize the costs of the artifice to women. Unlike Mandeville, he does not see the drive for sexual pleasure as originating only in the males. "The principle of generation" may go from the man to the woman, but the pleasure principle is seen as operating as strongly or more strongly in females than in males: "All human creatures, especially of the female sex, are apt to overlook remote motives in favour of any present temptation: the temptation is here the strongest imaginable" (571). Some readers of Hume may find these words evidence *for* rather than against his sexism, but it ought to be noted that Hume's ideal for human beings is not a preference for remote interest over contiguous agreeable pleasure, but an alignment of the two. Hedonistic indulgence is no worse a fault, in his account, than cold calculation of interest, neglect of the agreeable for the useful. Throughout the *Treatise,* in Book 2 in the section on "the amorous passion" and in Book 3 in his account of sexual union as "the original principle" (486) of human society, of the natural family as the forerunner of artifice-secured societies, in the nice reverse sexism of his account of the natural virtue of being what "we call good women's men" (614), as well as in the section on chastity and modesty, Hume shows himself in his writings, as he did in his life, remarkably free of discriminatory sexism. Even his failure to note the socially contrived condition of patrilineal succession as a needed background for the virtue of female chastity is only a local failure. Elsewhere[4] he shows considerable awareness of and interest in that convention, an awareness helped by his high esteem for his mother, and by the fact that her sex prevented her from inheriting the Falconer family title.

Hume considers the demand for female chastity so unnatural, the difficulty of combating natural desire so great, that the artifice of chastity

4. See E. C. Mossner, *Life of David Hume* (Oxford, 1980), and Hume, *My Own Life,* Es xxxii.

needs the supplementation of the sister virtue of modesty. Fear of "bad fame" for lapses from chastity is insufficient as a motive; a woman may still "flatter herself she shall find certain means of securing her reputation and preventing all the pernicious consequences of her pleasure. 'Tis necessary, therefore, that besides the infamy attending such licenses, there shou'd be some preceding backwardness or dread" (T 571–572). Modesty prepares the way for chastity, and Hume presents it as a socially approved deformation, like Chinese foot-binding. Here Mandeville is more explicit than Hume: "Miss is scarce three years old but she is spoke to every day to hide her leg, and rebuked in good earnest if she shows it, while little master at the same age is bid to take up his coats and piss like a man."[5] Hume emphasizes the exaggeration of the demand for modesty in relation to its rationale: "Men have undoubtedly an implicit notion that all those ideas of modesty and chastity have a regard to generation . . . yet the general rule carries us beyond the original principle and makes us extend the notion of modesty over the whole sex, from their earliest infancy to their extremest old age and infirmity" (573).

Hume regards it as "so obvious" (T 570) that female chastity and "exterior modesty" have "no foundation in nature" (ibid.) that he says any doubts his reader may have concerning his general thesis that some virtues depend upon useful artifices will be removed by a consideration of modesty and chastity. These, he says, are "still more conspicuous instances of the operation of those principles which I have insisted on" (ibid.). Here Hume is in error. Conspicuous instances of artificial contrivance though they may be, they are also counterinstances to three important ingredients in the principles Hume insisted on in his treatment of the main artificial virtues: honesty, fidelity to promises, and loyalty. First, they were claimed to be dependent on "obvious and absolutely necessary" artifices (484), and so to be "as natural as anything which proceeds immediately from original principles, without the intervention of thought or reflexion" (ibid.). No such claim is made for chastity and modesty, which are presented as useful but dependent upon highly unnatural, not natural, social contrivances. Chastity is vaguely related by Hume to "fidelity to the marriage bed" (E 206) and so to fidelity to promises, but it is not reducible to a special case of that, since the obligation of chastity is supposed to lie on all women, regardless of the partic-

5. Mandeville, Remark C.

ular content of promises they have made. This inflexible,[6] unvarying requirement leaves room for choice only with respect to which male shall be the one sexual partner, and so contrasts with the adaptability of promise, which is "warp'd into as many different forms as that (social) interest requires" (T 524). Voluntary binding of oneself by a promise is a natural artifice; but the nonvoluntary other-imposed obligations of modesty and chastity are portrayed by Hume as contrary to nature, as the forced "backwardness to the approaches of a pleasure, to which nature has inspir'd so strong a propensity; and a propensity that 'tis absolutely necessary in the end to comply with, for the support of the species" (572). There may be a "sense of common interest" (490) lying behind recognition of this virtue, but it is not a sense of equal interest.

The second difference between chastity and other artificial virtues is that they involve a motive, avidity, which corrects itself by artifices,[7] since "there is no passion . . . capable of controlling the interested affection, but the very affection itself by an alteration of its direction" (T 492). By contrast, the sexual appetite is not a self-correcting passion, but is corrected, in Hume's account, by *independent* motives, concern that one's children receive paternal recognition and inheritance. Concern for the "support of the species" is not what corrects sexual desire. What corrects it is male vanity and lack of generosity, female concern for reputation, and the concern of both sexes for the recognition and privilege of those *individual* members of the species who are biologically "their own." The whole reproductive process in the species may correct itself, but in individuals sexual appetite and parental concern are separate passions.

Third, the artificial virtues of chastity and modesty are unlike the others, in Hume's treatment of them, in the emphasis given to the importance of *individual* constancy of behavior, as distinct from constancy in a population. Up until this point in Part 2 of Book 3 Hume had emphasized the need for general consistency of behavior within a population if artificial virtues are to merit recognition, and so, since their existence,

6. Hume, in his essay "Of polygamy and divorces," notes that marriage takes different forms in different cultures and conditions, and that "in Tonquin it is usual for sailors, when the ship comes in to harbour, to marry for the season and, notwithstanding this precarious engagement, they are assumed, it is said, of the strictest fidelity to their bed, as well as in the whole management of their affairs, from those temporary spouses" (Es 107).

7. I have discussed the details of Hume's account of this self-correction in "Hume on Heaps and Bundles," *American Philosophical Quarterly* (October 1979).

unlike that of the natural virtues, depends upon recognition, if they are to exist at all. Related to this demand for general consistency, but not very clearly or persuasively related, is his emphasis on individual reputation for *intralife consistency,* or *virtue,* and on the risk of losing it by a single theft, breach of contract, or treacherous act. When he turns to chastity, the spotlight *is* on *individual* spotless lifelong reputation, not on consistency within a population. Indeed, as I have shown, for Hume's account of the rationale for a *special* demand for chastity imposed on women but not men to work at all, he assumes that a convenient number of the female population will be immodest and unchaste. The modesty and chastity of mothers of sons of wealthy males may be useful to those males but are conspicuous *counterinstances* to the claim that I "should be the cully of my integrity if I alone shou'd impose upon myself a severe restraint amidst the licentiousness of others" (T 535). The licentiousness of other women will not only not diminish the point of the virtuous wife's "fidelity to the marriage bed," if that point is assurance for the husband of his paternity of her children, but will also be depended upon to relieve her from the importunities of those "debauch'd bachelors" and straying husbands who make up the male population, by Hume's account. It is not consistency in a population which is emphasized in the "rationale" Hume gives of chastity, but consistency within an individual life. If the point of the virtue is assurance of true paternity, then "fidelity to the marriage bed" can be as decisively destroyed by one lapse as can virginity. Hume shows some uneasiness over the correct classification of these virtues by his inclusion of "fidelity" in a list of natural virtues at T 603. This cannot be fidelity to promises, which is definitely an artificial virtue, nor surely is it chastity. Some more primitive and nondiscriminatory virtue, fidelity to an informal understanding between lovers which "unites them and preserves their union" (486), may be the *natural* virtue which has one formal feature Hume requires of chastity, namely, that one lapse destroys it by destroying trust.

That some such mutual fidelity is a Humean virtue is clear from his references to the virtue of constancy in friendship, along with the fact that his opposition to divorce, in his later essay "Of polygamy and divorces," is grounded in part on his belief that friendship is the chief element in marriage. He opposes divorce not merely because of its supposed ill effects on children and on the birthrate, but also because "the marriage knot . . . chiefly subsists by friendship" (Es 107), and friend-

ship thrives under constraint and requires an expectation of perma-
nence. If there is to be this great good of friendship between husband
and wife, some sort of fidelity will be essential, whether or not it be that
exclusive sexual fidelity Hume thought necessary "for rendering the
union entire and total" (ibid.). It is conceivable that exclusive sexual
fidelity is one of those pseudo-virtues which "stupify the understanding
and harden the heart, obscure the fancy and sour the temper" (270).
Such fidelity as is involved in marriage must be mutual, if the friendship
is to be between equals, as Hume implies that it must be. Earlier in the
same essay he opposes polygamy because "this sovereignty of the male is
a real usurpation, and destroys that nearness of rank, not to say equality, which nature has established between the sexes. we are by nature
their lovers, their friends, their patrons: would we willingly exchange
such endearing appellations for the barbarous title of master and tyrant?" (109).

But even in monogamous marriage, in Hume's account of it, the males
have, regretfully, made such an exchange, since they demand more chastity than they give—perhaps because they give that monetary "patronage" which Hume sees as the male's province. Hume is not explicit concerning the standards of chastity applicable to males, but is content to
say that their obligations "bear nearly the same proportion to the obligations of women as the obligations of the law of nations do to the law of
nature" (T 573). This is a dangerous comparison, if Hume believes a
friendship between equals to be the basis of a marriage. He says that "the
morality of princes has the same extent, yet it has not the same force as
that of private persons, and may lawfully be transgressed for a more trivial motive" (568). Males then have an obligation to be as chaste as
women, but are, like princes, more readily *forgiven*, excused for lapses.
This accords badly with Hume's proper evaluation of the importance of
friendship in marriage, and its incompatibility with male sovereignty.
That "entire and total union" which he takes as the *telos* of marriage
would seem to be possible only if whatever restrictions there are on sexual freedom are mutual.

I think Hume was aware of these tensions in his account of what
marriage demands. He himself never risked it, preferring close, nonty-
rannical (if also sometimes patronizing) relations with women, where
the requirements of love and friendship could take precedence over the
eugenic and social considerations which provide the rationale for mar-

riage between chaste females and less chaste males. His reference to
fidelity, in his treatment of the "natural" virtues, at T 603, occurs in a list
of valuable things, and what precedes fidelity on that list is friendship.
He himself seems to have opted for a version of that, forgoing the satisfactions and costs of "the appetite for generation."

The artifice of marriage with acceptance of a double standard is, then,
not a case where artifice completes nature, but one where there is a direct conflict between the asymmetric sexual fidelity it requires and that
more natural mutual fidelity of lovers and friends on which marriage
supposedly subsists. Had Hume followed out the implications of his account, he might have seen that the passions which need correction are
*not* the sexual inclinations of either the female or the male but the pro-
prietary passions of parents, especially those of the male parent. The
need for female chastity arises, in Hume's account, only because of the
male's greater willingness to care for children who are thought to be biologically his own. Friendship between husband and wife is sacrificed to
cater to that. For the cautious jealous natural virtue of male "kindness
to children" to get expression, females must cultivate the counter-to-
natural virtue of chastity. Yet in Hume's own account of "mine and
thine," it is a purely conventional matter, changeable at public will, what
counts as "mine," for anything not an internal quality of mind or "advantage of body" (T 487). One's own children then ought to be those society deems to be one's own special responsibility. Hume does not see
this, but in effect assumes that only *one* of his five ways of determining
ownership, namely, accession, is to be used for deciding which children
are "one's own." (Accession is the principle which gives us "the fruits of
our gardens and the offspring of our cattle" [509].) There is no reason,
in principle, why first possession, occupation, prescription, or succession should not determine which children are treated as "belonging to" a
particular adult. If the eugenic considerations Hume cites (E 208) support a prohibition on incest, then it may be socially useful or economical
to allocate the care of a given child to adults within the prohibited degree of affinity, but this still would not select as "father" the biological
male parent rather than, say, the mother's brother. There *may* be ways of
determining which child is one's own which allow the virtue of care of
one's "own" children to coexist with the great good of friendship between a man and woman, and with the virtue of mutual fidelity to such

friendship and love. Hume, if he did not draw these implications,[8] at least laid out the important considerations with unequaled clarity. His failure to suggest any reforms may stem from his pessimism, from a conviction that the best care for children cannot be combined with the best form of love between men and women. Until we have a case of their being so combined, in some proven superior artifice, we cannot say that Hume was wrong.

I have argued that Hume's account of chastity shows it to be a highly atypical artificial virtue, not a "conspicuous instance" (T 570) of the principles he insisted on in his account of the main artificial virtues. It is atypical in that it *conflicts* with natural tendencies, and is not shown to be "absolutely necessary." It is also atypical in that not only does its presence give new occasion for the display of natural virtues, but also it is needed for Hume's version of the male virtue of kindness to children to find its proper objects. Unless females have the artificial virtue of chastity, males cannot have the natural virtue of being "indulgent fathers" (606). It is atypical in that it involves not a self-correcting passion, but the correction of the sexual appetite by other passions. It is also atypical in that its possession and value in some women depend not on its possession by all women, but on the nonpossession of it by some of them. This last point of difference, and lack of clarity in Hume's account, are also of importance for more of Hume's philosophy than his ethics. It points to a pervasive lack of clarity concerning constancy in one life, in action and experience, and constancy in the general "course of nature in human action" (403). Both in his account of the custom on which causal inference is based and in his account of the particular constancies of motivation on which the punisher relies (410–412), unanswered questions arise concerning the relation of constancy in one life to constancy at the interpersonal level, within a population, where one person's experiences may supplement another's, one person's strengths compensate for another's failings. For these theoretical reasons, as well as for its demonstration of Hume's remarkable degree of social self-consciousness, of his recognition of the hard core of sexism, the brief chapter "Of chastity and modesty" deserves our close attention, and our admiration.

8. The centrality to Hume's philosophy of the natural family, namely, children and their common biological parents, is explored in my "Helping Hume to Compleat the Union," *Philosophy and Phenomenological Research* (September–December 1980).

# 10

# Incomparably the Best?

Hume, in his brief and somewhat disingenuous autobiography, found his *Enquiry Concerning the Principles of Morals (EPM)* to be, "of all my writings, historical, philosophical or literary, incomparably the best" (Es xxxvi). (He presumably meant the best of those published in his lifetime—no comparison or, strictly speaking, impossibility of comparison, with his *Dialogues Concerning Natural Religion* is implied.) Nor can this be dismissed as a bit of farewell irony, to be put with his claim later in *My Own Life* that he had been untouched by the baleful tooth of calumny. Twenty years earlier he had told a correspondent, Le Blanc, that *EPM* was his "favorite Performance" (L 1.227). So his preference for this work seems to have been considered and stable. It challenges us to try to understand what it was about *EPM* that so particularly pleased its author. He wrote, in that same remarkable little memoir, that it was more the manner than the matter of "the unfortunate *Treatise*" that he believed to have led to its initial lack of success. He had therefore decided to "cast anew" the matter of its three books in his two *Enquiries,* and the *Dissertation on the Passions. EPM* is definitely a "performance," and has fairly obvious literary as well as philosophical pretensions (not to mention a fairly stiff dose of history in its examples). It is the mark of a fine literary

The study of Hume is gradually converting me to his sort of skepticism, and the history of this essay about him has given me plenty of cause for diffidence. Generous critics have alerted me to some places needing adjustment, as well as making helpful suggestions at the start. For both sorts of aid I am greatly indebted to James Moore and M. A. Stewart. For adjustments along the way I also thank Donald Ainslie, Tom Beauchamp, Stephen Buckle, Stephen Darwall, David Gauthier, Maurice Goldsmith, James Harris, James King, Elizabeth Radcliffe, and Robert Shaver.

214

performance to suit the manner to the matter. I think Hume set himself, in *EPM,* to do just that. In what follows, I shall largely be concerned with its ostensible "matter," but matter and manner cannot be kept entirely separate. I begin with some remarks about *EPM*'s structure, and I will end with some questions about the relation of that to the work's matter and its chosen manner.

*EPM*'s nine main sections are followed by a series of appendices, in the first edition two (the first and what became the third), four by the 1777 edition. In the first edition, and in all later ones until Selby-Bigge's in 1894, a final dialogue, which had been written separately, and may have been inspired by Montesquieu's *Persian Letters,* was included, as a final touch. Possibly it is an afterthought, but the appendices to *EPM,* unlike the appendix to the *Treatise,* are not second thoughts. If *EPM* is seen as a grand villa, then they are its workrooms, its kitchen, scullery, laundry, and cellars, lying behind, or under, the nine grandly furnished reception rooms with their many portraits, while off to one side is a more frivolous independent little building, a summerhouse or gazebo. Some of the materials for the main building, especially for its workrooms, are taken from one of the three wings of an earlier, condemned building, and the summerhouse may be partially modeled on a French one, but the main effect is of a fresh start, not an adaptation.

In *A Treatise of Human Nature,* Book 3, Hume had invoked facts about our moral capacity in support of a general and abstruse thesis about the limits of "reason," the derivative status of all "ideas," their association, and their subordinate role in motivation. It, after all, is the third book in the *Treatise.* The concern of *EPM* is to understand morality in its own right, and it is not so much moral motivation, as human recognition of human merit, that is now under scrutiny. Its avowed aim is to reveal "the true origin of morals"; its method, "to analyze that complication of mental qualities, which form what, in common life, we call Personal Merit" (E 173). Shaftesbury had undertaken a project of this sort, half a century earlier, in his *Inquiry into Virtue or Merit* (first published in 1699), and not just Hume's preference for the term "merit," but many other choices of words (dresses for morality, the interested obligation to virtue, a character with oneself and others, what it is to wear a human heart, etc.), echo Shaftesbury. He is the first philosopher to be named in *EPM,* on its second page, and it is not only his predecessor's possible confusion over the roles of reason and sentiment (mentioned there), nor his interest in the relation of religion to morality (clearly shared by Hume), nor his thesis about reflex affections (which seemed so important in the *Treatise*), that are now on Hume's mind. It is also Shaftesbury's concern about how reflections on manners of life are best presented to a general, well-educated readership. *EPM* is no more a compendium for students than is Shaftesbury's *Characteristics of Men, Manners, Opinions, Times*, in which, in 1711, a revised version of his *Inquiry* was imbedded. Both Shaftesbury's and Hume's mature writings about morality are more like Theophrastus's amusing portrayal of unwelcome "characters," than like Aristotle's (or, for that matter, Hutcheson's) lecture notes. *EPM* is a book for well-read adults with a sense of humor, not a solemn moral manual for the young. It is definitely no *Whole Duty of Man, Laid Down in a Plain and Familiar Way . . . Necessary for All Families, with Private Devotions for Several Occasions*;[1] indeed, it continues the case against religion that Hume had begun in his *Enquiry Concerning Human Understanding (EHU)*, Sections 10 and 11.[2]

Despite its impressive display of learning ("so much ingenious knowledge so genteelly delivered" [E 269]), *EPM* is a genuine inquiry. It has a "Conclusion," but that is by no means its last word. This inquiry, unlike *EHU*, is left fairly open-ended and inconclusive. A firm finding is reached about the "true origin" of morals, but the morals with this human origin are not so firmly set in stone. *EPM* is in its main sections an empirical investigation into what human judges have recognized as human merit, in a variety of conditions of life, and, as such, it must be left unfinished, just as a history of Britain has to be left off, "to be continued." As long as conditions of human life continue to change, the perceived value of some particular mental traits can be expected also to change. Hume gives the example of good memory as one that, in eighteenth-century Europe, had lost the special value it once had, and he mentions some fearsome skills that had been understandably prized in "barbaric" conditions of life. He makes it quite clear which traits he himself esteems, but he is also engaged in a sort of moral anthropology, which includes some comparative anthropology. His own selective index

1. Anonymous, *The Whole Duty of Man* (London: R. Norton for Robert Pawley, at the Sign of the Bible in Chancery Lane, near Fleetstreet, 1684), title page.

2. See J. C. A. Gaskin, "Religion: The Useless Hypothesis," in *Reading Hume on Human Understanding*, edited by P. Millican (Oxford, 2002), and Stephen Buckle, *Hume's Enlightenment Tract* (Oxford, 2001).

to *EPM* includes entries on the Athenian, the French, and the Irish conceptions of merit, and the Spanish conception of politeness. Facts about what has been praised in human persons are assembled, and the terms in which the praising has been done are examined.[3] *EPM*'s wealth of examples, mostly historical, contrasts strikingly with *Treatise,* Book 3. There we were offered only Marcus Brutus, Alexander, Caesar, and Cato. Now they are joined by a host of others, and in almost every case, Hume quotes someone else's assessment of their character, before endorsing or disagreeing with that judgment. He is not just giving exemplars of the virtues; he is giving empirical evidence about what traits have in fact been praised and condemned, and by whom. So we have Diodorus Siculus on Epaminondas, Plutarch on Phocian, Demosthenes on Philip of Macedon, Livy on Hannibal, Sallust on Pompey, Tacitus on Vitellius, St. Evremont on Turenne, and so on, down to Hume's own assessment of the fictional Cleanthes, the perfect son-in-law. All these panegyrics and censures show as much about the one praising or censuring as about the character of the one assessed, but this is precisely what Hume's bootstraps method involves. Just as Samuel Johnson compiled his *Dictionary* by citing evidence from "the best writers," so Hume cites the best historians, orators, and satirists to show what has been praised and criticized in human persons. (Must we agree on who the good historians, orators, and satirists are, before we can agree on what makes a good person? And to what critics shall we turn, for assessing historians, orators, and satirists?)

In Books 1 and 2 of the *Treatise* Hume had attempted to analyze persons, their motivation, and the mechanics of their mutual sympathy, before giving, in Book 3, any analysis of how they correct the bias of natural sympathy in order to assess each other's merit. In *EPM* we have to do without any such "metaphysics" or mechanics of morals. Sympathy still plays a major role, and there is some moral epistemology, mostly in the first appendix, where Hume gives a very judicious settlement to "a controversy started of late," the one that had been at the forefront of his attention in *Treatise,* Book 3, Part 1, Section 1. Neither this debate, about the roles of reason and sentiment in discerning virtues, nor any other ab-

---

3. See John Valdimir Price, *David Hume* (Twayne, 1969; updated ed., 1991), 82; James T. King, "The Place of the Language of Morals in Hume's Second *Enquiry,"* in *Hume: A Re-evaluation,* edited by Donald W. Livingston and James T. King (Fordham, 1976), 343–361; and Jacqueline Taylor, "Hume on the Standard of Virtue," *Journal of Ethics* 6 (2002): 56.

struse topic, is the main business of the nine sections. Their task is to analyze personal merit, and so to compile a richly illustrated "catalogue of laudable qualities" (E 243), in every case suggesting the reasons why that particular trait in a person is welcomed, and identifying the principles or sources from which that welcome springs. All more intricate matters are discussed in the appendices, the workrooms, and Hume a month before his death was still busy revising his decisions about what should be transferred to them. Because they link *EPM* most closely with the most famous theses of *Treatise*, Book 3, and because I do not see what Hume put in them to have been "relegated to a subordinate place,"[4] I shall look first at them. But we should note that one change Hume made from the *Treatise* was to let any conclusions he drew about how we recognize virtues, and what this shows about our nature, wait until after considerable virtue-recognition has been conducted.

## The Appendices

It is in the first appendix that we find Hume's reconsideration of the famous *Treatise* claim about the "impotence" of "reason alone" to motivate us, or serve as a basis for morals. He repeats that it is the "sentiments and affections of mankind, without any dependence on the intellectual faculties," that determine "the ultimate ends of human actions" (E 293), but it is no longer as certain as it seemed in *Treatise*, Book 3, Part 1, Section 1 that moral considerations do provide an independent source of motivation, for most of us, most of the time. And for discerning which natural motives and mental abilities should count as virtues, he finds that our intellectual faculties have a very important role to play. In place of the master-slave pair, lively passion and inert reason, we now have the cooperating partners, warm sentiment and cool reason. The "distinct boundaries" of reason and taste are still firmly drawn, and we get the famous metaphor of the "gilding and staining" by sentiment of "objects, as they really stand in nature" (294). Morality may well be "a new creation," the creation of human sentiment, but before we, the creators, can select which natural mental traits to "gild," making them into virtues, many facts must be assembled, and many utilities weighed. "One principal foundation of moral praise being supposed to lie in the usefulness of

---

4. David Daiches Raphael, *Concepts of Justice* (Clarendon, 2001), 91.

any quality or action; it is evident, that *reason* must enter for a considerable share in all decisions of this kind; since nothing but that faculty can instruct us in the tendency of qualities and actions, and point out their beneficial consequences to society and to their possessor" (285). Reason in the form of tracing consequences and weighing utilities seems, in *EPM*, to have acquired considerable potency. The contrast between lively "impressions," without representational content, and "inert" ideas, with such content, which was essential to the *Treatise* argument for reason's limited moral role, in *EPM* is not even drawn. Reason is still "cool and disengaged," but taste and sentiment must secure its "concurrence" before there can be any moral outcome. Hume has not really altered the substance of his position, which all along was that both reason and sentiment are vital to discernment of moral merit, but there is, in Selby-Bigge's words, "a very remarkable change of tone or temper" (xxiii).[5] Gone are the provocative antirationalist pronouncements, and master-slave reversals. Logicians will search in vain here for any reissuing of "Hume's Law," supposedly forbidding inferences from "is" premises to "ought" conclusions; the most they will find is the distinction between mistake of fact and mistake of right.

The fourth appendix, with its dismissal of the importance of the distinction between what is and what is not voluntary, its rejection of a punitive or pre-punitive role for disapprobation, and its consequent disdain for the question of whether the vicious person could have helped having the vices he has, is the one which, along with the third (which elaborated on the already controversial theses of Section 3), gave most offense to Hume's contemporaries, and still upsets some readers.[6] The theses are familiar from the *Treatise* section "Of natural abilities," but now Hume compounds the offense by associating the sharp distinction between virtues and abilities, which he is rejecting, with religious doctrines of divine retribution for vice. The offended eighteenth-century "philosophers, or rather divines under that disguise" (E 322), included not only James Balfour, Thomas Reid, and James Beattie, but also Adam Smith, a believer in natural and divine justice and in moral responsibility in a stronger sense than Hume can accommodate. Smith complains that, by his refusal to restrict moral assessment to those traits showing

---

5. But see also John Laird, *Hume's Philosophy of Human Nature* (Methuen, 1932), 236ff.
6. Terence Penelhum, *Themes in Hume: The Self, the Will, Religion* (Oxford, 2000), 173ff.

proper "self-command," and by his emphasis on utility, Hume makes moral beauty of character not essentially different from the beauty of a chest of drawers.[7] Hume, in a footnote which was apparently added in reply to his upright friend, significantly does not say that the reason why we respond to beautiful human characters differently from the way we respond to beautiful furniture is that the former, through their self-command, are responsible for their own moral beauty. What he says is that we have a special interest in "rational thinking" beings like ourselves, the objects of our love and hate, while we cannot be in love with a chest of drawers (213n). The fourth appendix was originally part of Section 6, where some other factors influencing whom we fall in love with are discussed, to Balfour's at least pretended embarrassment.[8] Beattie too speaks bitterly of those, like Hume, whose corrupted morals "seduce others to vice and perdition."[9]

Hume put his restatement of his views, not only on providence, but also on "liberty and necessity," into *EHU*, not *EPM*. The morals of the latter are, however, definitely designed for determinists. (For lapsed Calvinists? Within two years of its publication, a move was afoot in Edinburgh to have Hume charged by the General Assembly of the Church of Scotland with infidelity and immorality.) Like Spinoza, Hume contents himself with listing and commenting on the character traits we have reason to welcome, and pointing out the consequences, such as loss of trust, that usually follow if the worst vices are displayed. There is occasional talk of what we "ought" to do, and there is talk of "blame," especially when the rules of "justice" have been broken, but the language of morals that Hume invokes in *EPM*'s conclusion is not a deontology. It is a descriptive-cum-evaluative language ascribing the character traits that make a person "amiable or odious" to other human beings. As for moral responsibility, the only overt ascription of that in *EPM* is to "the Supreme Will," which, in a mischievous aside at the end of the first appendix, which echoes the line of thought expressed in the last paragraphs of *EHU*, Section 8, is credited with control over all human sentiments and

7. Adam Smith, *The Theory of Moral Sentiments,* edited by D. D. Raphael and A. L. Macfie (Liberty, 1982), 188.

8. James Balfour, *A Delineation of the Nature and Obligation* of Morality (Hamilton, Balfour and Neill, 1753; reprint, Thoemmes Antiquarian, 1989), 118.

9. James Beattie, *An Essay on the Nature and Immutability of Truth, in Opposition to Sophistry and Scepticism,* 10th ed. (Lackington, Allen, 1810), 204.

reactions, presumably including human choices. Hume, while casting off most of his paternal Calvinist heritage, retains the belief that our given natures, together with the culture and institutions into which we are born, "predestine" our adult characters.[10]

Morals without any mention of a moral law, or much concern with moral responsibility, are not morals as most of Hume's British contemporaries knew them. By 1753 Balfour was publishing his alternative "delineation" of morality and its divinely sanctioned obligations, cold-shouldering Hume's invitation to a civilized discussion of their differences, and trying, in his later lectures, to protect his Edinburgh students from Hume's dangerous influence (L 1.172).[11] Balfour's version of our obligations is certainly more suitable "for families" than is Hume's, but prudery is not all that is at issue. More fundamental differences are at stake—the relation of religion to morality, and the free will question. Since Hume's time, morality without God has become fairly standard, but a determinist version of morals is still controversial.[12] Hume does, of course, include intentional action in the scope of moral assessment, and he does talk of "duty," of "a rule of right," and of the "obligations" not to steal, break promises, or disobey magistrates. But moral assessment goes beyond and behind the will. Even the virtue of self-command is, he notes, not within our will's command (E 313). The normative-sounding idioms Hume sometimes uses are easily translated into factual claims about community expectations, and about what will be found "odious," "contemptible," or punishable by magistrates. Hume "defines virtue to be *whatever mental action or quality gives to a spectator the pleasing sentiment of approbation;* and vice the contrary. We then proceed to examine a plain matter of fact, to wit, what actions have this influence" (E 289). If it is a fact that we cannot but be displeased by extreme stupidity, as well as by malice, since both can do great harm, then both go into the de-merit column, in Hume's moral ledger.

Hume's least controversial appendix, and the last that he gave that sta-

10. See Roger L. Emerson, "Science and Moral Philosophy in the Scottish Enlightenment," in *Studies in the Philosophy of the Scottish Enlightenment,* edited by M. A. Stewart (Clarendon, 1990), 34; and Paul Russell, *Freedom and Moral Sentiment: Hume's Way of Naturalizing Responsibility* (Oxford, 1995), ch. 9.

11. Richard B. Sher, "Professors of Virtue: The Social History of the Moral Philosophy Chair in the Eighteenth Century," in *Studies in the Philosophy of the Scottish Enlightenment,* edited by M. A. Stewart (Clarendon, 1990), 110–112.

12. See Haji Ishtiyaque, *Deontic Morality and Control* (Cambridge, 2003).

tus, is the second, on self-love, originally the first part of the section on benevolence. It is probably its abstruseness, its indulgence of a speculative curiosity about human nature, rather than anything very controversial in the position taken, that led Hume to move it to an appendix. If it "may be esteemed, perhaps, a superfluous task to prove, that the benevolent or softer affections are ESTIMABLE" (E 176), it will seem even more superfluous to prove that there are any such affections. But since writers of the stature of Epicurus, Horace, Hobbes, and Locke, who were no strangers to these affections, had taken them all to be (possibly unconscious) modifications of self-love, a philosopher engaged in "the speculative science of human nature" will want to examine "the selfish system" (298). Hume says that the question is not very material to "morality and practice," since "I esteem the man whose self-love, by whatever means, is so directed to give him a concern for others, and render him serviceable to society" (297). As a speculative scientist of human nature, he suggests that it has been an exaggerated love of simplicity that has led thinkers to try to reduce the apparently disinterested affections to self-love, and that, where human passions are concerned, the obvious cause is probably the true one. In the end, he thinks, there is "really more simplicity" in the hypothesis that allows disinterested benevolence to exist than in the selfish hypothesis.

Like Butler before him, and Balfour after him, Hume distinguishes self-interest or "cool self-love" from particular propensities or passions, such as the desire for power, for fame, or for vengeance, and finds in human nature plenty evidence of disinterested, sometimes even self-sacrificial, benevolence. Butler, however, might not have appreciated one of Hume's arguments for its existence—that "the rules of analogy" require us, if we allow that "inferior species" of animal exhibit some benevolence, to grant that it is also to be found in "superior species" of animal, namely, us human animals (E 300). This was not quite "the analogy of nature" Butler wanted us to draw (even though, in his *Analogy of Religion,* he was open-minded about the prospects of "the brutes" for possible progress and immortality). Maybe the second appendix is not so inoffensive.

One way to read all four appendices is to see them as saying "If you think I have, in the nine main sections, taken back the substance of what offended the reviewers and readers of *Treatise,* Book 3, think again." There are some concessions to rationalists, and some bad arguments against them are gone, but readers like Balfour were not misled about the main message, nor about the challenge it presented to a religious and puritan culture.

## The Analysis of Personal Merit

Postponing comment on the third appendix, which differs only in degree of detail from Section 3, I turn now to the nine sections. Their main task is to compile the catalogue of virtues, with illustrations and annotations. The list itself does not differ from what could be compiled from *Treatise*, Book 3, and there are the same significant absentees— namely, piety, humility, self-denial, and obedience—but we are now offered a more extensive gallery of dubious characters. To the *Treatise*'s province-devastating military heroes, insipid conversationalists, and debauched bachelors shocked at any lewdness in a woman, are added effeminate men and rough-mannered women, pompous declaimers, sloth-encouraging alms-givers, pernicious inquisitors, splenetic misanthropes, griping misers, indiscreet gossips, drinking companions with too good a memory, serious melancholics, egregious blockheads, harmless liars, ferociously coiffed Swabians, scalp-collecting Scythians, harebrained enthusiasts, sour-tempered monks, and sensible knaves. This gallery is instructive as well as entertaining—the Swabians, for example, who dress their hair more to make themselves hateful to enemies than attractive to friends, are for this very reason deemed laudable by as esteemed a historian as Tacitus (E 255). To martially minded historians, the odious as well as the amiable can be found laudable. (Does this mean that their esteem should be discounted?)

The first section begins by raising the question of the roles of reason and sentiment in morals, and, while postponing the final decision on that until the catalogue has been compiled, correctly predicts what it likely will be. Hume then raises the question of how a cataloguer of virtues is to proceed. He says that, to frame the catalogue, all that we need do is ask ourselves which traits we would be pleased to have ascribed to us. He optimistically thinks we cannot be mistaken in this, and that language will guide us, since "every tongue possesses one set of words that are taken in a good sense, and another in the opposite" (E 174). It is interesting that the acid test is not "would I want to have this trait?" (or even "would I want my child, or my son-in-law, to have it?") but rather "would I want to be taken to have it?" In the fourth appendix, Hume draws a distinction between what he most wants for himself (to have a friendly humane heart), and how he wants the world to see him ("one endowed with extensive genius and intrepid courage" [316]). "Character," for Hume, is close to reputation and name; it is a person's mental characteristics as shown to others. So to frame the catalogue of meritorious character traits, one asks how one would like others to see one. This means that the knave, although proud of his successful secret knavery, can put honesty on his version of the catalogue, and a person who would feel damned with faint praise if described as "very good-natured" should have doubts about its presence on Hume's list. It may not be as easy as Hume here makes out to compile this catalogue, and in Section 2 he allows that reflection and "sounder reasoning" often lead us "to retract our first sentiment, and adjust anew the boundaries of moral good and evil" (180).

In the second section Hume begins his disentangling of the different strands that, in his judgment, make up personal merit. (There are sixty-seven named ones, by my count, although only a select seventeen get onto Hume's own brief index. That short list is: benevolence, chastity, cheerfulness, cleanliness, courage, decency, delicacy of taste, discretion, frugality, honesty, justice, memory, modesty, politeness, tranquillity of mind, wisdom, wit.) First to be examined are the two main "social virtues," or rather groups of virtues: benevolence (which includes "beneficence and humanity, friendship and gratitude, natural affection and public spirit" [E 178]) and the conformity to various conventions that constitute Hume's "justice." He predicts that explicating these will "probably give us an opening by which the others may be accounted for" (175). He reverses the *Treatise* order, by dealing first with benevolence, which Hutcheson had made practically the whole of virtue. Justice had been the first virtue to be examined in *Treatise*, Book 3, giving the title of the lengthy Part 2, which detailed a series of "artifices or contrivances," those presupposed by the approbation we give to respect for property, promises, magistrates, marriage vows, and treaties. Some commentators have found that the early placement of a discussion of social artifice, and the coordination of attitudes it requires, were important for Hume's later specification of the shared point of view from which any virtue, including benevolence, is discerned, but Hume now seems to see no need for such a tactic. He is first assembling all the traits admired by reflective people, before making any generalization about why they are all admired, or drawing any conclusion about the point of view needed for their recognition. And he looks first, and more carefully than in the *Treatise*, at forms of benevolence that deserve admiration. Whereas, for the other virtues that Hume lists on his index, we get entries of the form "Chastity, its merit, whence," for benevolence the entry has to be much more complicated, and to include "its kinds."

His finding is that benevolence has many kinds, not all of them admirable. The virtue he endorses, whose merit comes both from its immediate agreeableness and from its social usefulness, is humane, thoughtful beneficence, not mere goodwill, nor impulsive charity. "Giving alms to common beggars is naturally praised because it seems to carry relief to the distressed and indigent: but when we observe the encouragement thence arising to idleness and debauchery, we regard that species of charity rather as a weakness than a virtue" (E 180). This observation about giving to beggars is the first intimation that the Christian virtues, not only Knox's stern ones but also Hutcheson's gentler ones, are in for a hard time, in Hume's analysis. From the "humane beneficent man" the hungry will indeed receive food, and the naked clothing. But not necessarily from handouts, since the humane beneficent man will also give "the ignorant and slothful skill and industry" (178). Utility, and utility of the sort Hume was attending to in his essays on economics, is a constraint on the merit of benevolent intentions. It is merchants and manufacturers, the makers of machines, the planters of trees, and the cultivators of fields, not the members of charitable religious orders, who show the meritorious thoughtful benevolence that Hume wants us to appreciate. Any "heedless praises" we might be tempted to give to the ostentatious liberality of princes are to be retracted. (Replaced by praises of Caxton, Arkwright, and some of Hume's own relatives who were improving farming practices in the Scottish lowlands?) Hume's pretense that all he is doing is recording agreed approbations, rather than educating and "adjusting" them, is fairly hollow, right from the start. His treatment of benevolence is as distinctly revisionary as his later treatment of the "monkish virtues." Hutcheson is not mentioned, but his shade is surely a background presence, subjected to polite correction. Cicero is quoted twice, and it is his views, not those of Christian writers, that

Hume is largely following. Even when he disagrees, as he does on ty-rannicide, it is Cicero's questions that are being addressed.[13] For Hume, a well-disposed will is not the only thing we should want in each other; indeed, benevolence without wisdom can do more harm than good. In a human community we also need wisdom and knowledge, enterprise and industry. Some people, indeed, Hume says at a later point, may be "too good." But to say that of someone is to praise as well as to criticize. He concludes this second section: "Upon the whole, then, it seems undeni-able, *that* nothing can bestow more merit on any human creature than the sentiment of benevolence in an eminent degree; and *that* a *part*, at least, of its merit arises from its tendency to promote the interests of our species, and bestow happiness on human society" (181). This sentence incorporates the last small correction Hume sent to his publisher, two weeks before his death, namely, the deletion of the clause "that there is such a sentiment in human nature as benevolence," which came after "undeniable." (I presume Hume deleted the clause since the defense of the claim it makes had been transferred to Appendix 2.)

Having established the importance of "public utility" in the valuing of benevolence, and in the selection of which forms of benevolence are re-ally to be welcomed, Hume moves on, in the third section, to explicate an equally essential virtue, this time one whose "*sole* origin" is public utility. This is the complex virtue Hume calls "justice," the virtue of re-spect for recognized rights and entitlements. This is a "curiously nar-row" sense to give the word,[14] omitting the traditional elements of con-cern for equality and for desert. (Is this just a "verbal dispute"?) Hume reiterates the *Treatise* thesis that it is scarcity, and the need for coopera-tive schemes to prevent a disorderly scramble for the scarce goods, that make room for what he arguably misnames "justice." He characterizes it as the "cautious, jealous virtue." Frugality too is a virtue that depends on scarcity, but not on social measures to distribute the scarce goods peaceably, and it is these distributive schemes that give Hume's justice its special features. Justice has been famously declared, by John Rawls, to be the first virtue of social institutions. Hume takes the virtue he calls "justice" to be closely linked with—indeed, inseparable from—social in-stitutions, but what he means by it is not the fairness that institutions

13. See James Moore, "Utility and Humanity: The Quest for the *Honestum* in Cicero, Hutcheson, and Hume," *Utilitas* 14 (2002): 356–386.
    14. Raphael, 87ff.

can have, or lack. (Like Aristotle, he lists equity as a separate virtue, one he never calls "artificial.") Hume's "justice" is not any sort of virtue of institutions, but is rather an individual person's acceptance of the need for them, and willingness to conform to their rules as long as others are doing the same. (A sort of unfairness or inequity would be involved in exempting oneself, while counting on others' conformity, and Hume does speak of justice as requiring "equitable conduct.") Justice, or what might better be called "conformity to cooperative schemes," is cautious, compared with generosity and benevolence. In our "necessitous condition," it restrains immediate self-interest, and we accept that restraint cautiously, only on the understanding that others are doing the same. And justice is "jealous," because its rules determine what each can count as exclusively "mine," what is each person's "due," or "*ius.*"

The point of inventing property and other rights depends on general scarcity. "Why call this object *mine,* when upon the seizing of it by another, I need but stretch out my hand to possess myself of what is equally valuable?" (E 184). What had not been said in the *Treatise,* and is now said, to Balfour's and Broad's outrage, is that just as "profuse abundance" would make justice pointless, so extreme scarcity, say, in a shipwreck or a famine, would suspend its rules.[15] Whatever might lead Broad to share the last biscuit with his starving wrecked shipmates, and so starve "decently, and in order," it would not be a sense of Humean justice. Balfour cites Cicero and Lactantius against Hume on the "injustice" of seizing a plank to which another survivor had been clinging, in order to save one's own life. Hume could easily allow that humanity or equity, or even Broad's "decency," might stop one from being so ruthless in extreme conditions, but for him justice will have nothing (except possibly rowing in stroke) to contribute to lifeboat ethics. By balancing the psychological condition, moderate selfishness, with the external circumstance, moderate scarcity, Hume completes his account of "the circumstances of justice" (an account admired by Rawls).[16] He goes on to face and answer a very important question left unasked in the *Treatise,* that of who exactly are parties to these cooperative schemes, the ones who get to have rights. The answer is "all those who can make resentment felt," and Hume makes it clear that this excludes other animals, but includes

15. Balfour, 80–81; C. D. Broad, *Five Types of Ethical Theory* (Kegan Paul, Trench, Trubner, 1944), 98.

16. John Rawls, *A Theory of Justice* (Harvard, 1971), 127–128; (rev. ed., 1999), 110.

all human beings. It definitely includes women, on whom men depend, not merely for charming company, but for "the propagation of [their] kind," and, most importantly, the knowledge that they have done so. (Hobbes, who said that it was our mutual vulnerability that makes acceptance of moral rules rational for us, and who took women to be strong enough, in the "state of nature," to rear their children without help from the children's fathers, would certainly have approved.) These are important clarifications of the *Treatise* account of justice. Despite the brevity of the section, compared with *Treatise,* Book 3, Part 2, it is more theoretically complete.

Another clarification, given in the second part of the section, concerns inequality of material possessions. Just as Hume's version of the virtue of benevolence/beneficence is a proto-capitalist version, so too is his version of what sort of inequality of wealth has to be tolerated. Although the cooperative schemes in which we are required to do our part were supposed to be adopted because they were "infinitely advantageous to the whole, and to every part" (T 498), and although they presuppose "some measure of equality" in all human persons, some end up doing a lot better than others from the adoption of property rights and from particular ways of transferring them. Hume expresses some sympathy with the "Levellers," but believes that egalitarian measures, such as redistributive taxation, would be too socially costly. If there were insufficient incentive to enterprise and hard work, we would soon have general indigence. And "rigorous inspection" by official redistributors of property would be offensive, even bringing the risk of "tyranny." Inequality of material possessions has to be accepted, as the price of liberty. Should the wealthy have the virtues of generosity and public beneficence, this inequality may be slightly mitigated, but only slightly. And after all, the poor, to make up for having to go without "the feverish empty amusements of luxury and expence" (E 283–284), may have the consolation of "the unbought satisfaction of conversation, society, study, even health and the common beauties of nature" (ibid.). Their conversation, however, may have to be with the equally poor, since their "dirty furniture, coarse and ragged cloaths, nauseous meat and distasteful liquor" will, Hume believes, be off-putting to the more fortunate (248).

Are there corrections, as well as clarifications, in the revised version of Humean justice that we find in Section 3, supplemented by Appendix 3? (The "further considerations" advanced in the latter are said to give "a more particular explication of the origin and nature of justice, and . . . mark some differences between it and the other virtues" [E 303].) We no longer get the puzzle about what the motive to honesty can be, a puzzle Hume used, in the *Treatise,* to show how "artifice" must be invoked to understand justice and honesty. We still get the *Treatise* contrast between a virtue like beneficence, which does good act by act, and does some good even if it is rarely shown, and justice, where the benefit "arises from the whole scheme or system concurred in by the whole, or the greater part of the society" (304). We are now offered the simile of the "wall" of benevolence, built stone by useful stone, versus the more contrived "vault" of justice, where "each individual stone would, of itself, fall to the ground" unless it had the support of the others. Since these schemes and systems are of collective human making, we are still given an account of a *human* "origin of justice," but, and not merely because of the compression of the account, we are no longer given the *Treatise's* sequential story. In that story, property rights were first fixed, and then various ways of exchanging and transferring property and services were invented, before magistrates were given authority to give the "*execution and decision* of justice" (T 538). In *EPM* he invokes laws and statutes in his discussion of property; it is almost as if magistrates are there from the start. By the time Hume completed his *History,* he had come to acknowledge, in that work's first appendix, that rights to command might, as in the Germanic tribes, precede property rights in land. Here, in *EPM,* we find him noting that rights of inheritance can be recognized in a pre-agricultural society, and that rights to water are mentioned in the biblical book of Genesis before rights to land (E 184). It was a nice touch on Hume's part to invoke the Bible to show the human origin and culturally varying content of justice, as, in Appendix 4, he quotes Psalm 49 on the praiseworthiness of doing well to oneself. He was clearly pleased with himself about this, since both passages are included in his own selective index, under the entry for "Scriptures, holy, quoted" (291). Different sorts of scarcity in different places will determine the sequence in which different sorts of property right come to be recognized, and there is no particular reason why promissory rights, and rights to inherit from relatives, should not be established in a pre-agricultural society. Promissory rights, however, will become of central importance in a commercial society, with various forms of "paper money" used in exchanges.

Hume speaks throughout of justice and fidelity (to promises) as if they arise together, and at times brings in, not only equity, which he takes to be a "natural virtue" (T 578), but also veracity and integrity (E 204), whose status as natural or artificial is less clear. (The offense-giving adjective "artificial," kept out of Section 3, is allowed back in, in a footnote to Appendix 3.) He has not given up what may be his most original thesis in ethics, the thesis that promises have to be humanly invented before they can be used to bind. (Hobbes, whose "artificial man," Leviathan, lurks in the background to Hume's discussion, had said that neither property rights nor rights to allegiance existed in a "state of nature," but he seemed to take the force of "covenant" to be natural and unproblematic.) Hume makes it clear, in Appendix 3, that the sort of "agreement" that sets up these convention-dependent rights and obligations is an informal one, arising out of a sense of common interest, like that of rowers who coordinate their strokes. It cannot itself be a contract or promise. "The observance of promises is itself one of the principal parts of justice, and we are not surely bound to keep our word because we have given our word to keep it" (E 306). But nothing in the account now given rules out the possibility that the invention of some sort of promise, say, between co-parents, might precede the invention of property rights. Hume had all along supposed property conventions to be adopted by people who already know the benefits of cooperation in the natural family, and now he is less dogmatic about what the first, most urgent convention will be. In some conditions, the first convention will create rights to command, in some rights to wells, in others rights to land, in others rights to navigation on rivers and seas. In almost all conditions there will very soon be rights arising from some sort of binding agreement between individuals, be it a form of marriage, of employment, or of tutelage and apprenticeship.

Existent customs and institutions can, of course, be subject to criticism, and Hume occasionally talks of what laws and customs ought to allow, as well as what they do. He was already writing his political and economic essays at this time, and he has firm views about such matters. "Who sees not . . . that whatever is produced or improved by a man's art or industry ought, for ever, to be secured to him, in order to give encouragement to such *useful* habits and accomplishments?" (E 195). However, most of the "ought's" in Hume's version of morals arise within existent artifices of "justice"; that is, they are "deduced" from the fact of a particular social institution, along with a general sense of its public utility, and the consequent moral approbation of conformity to its rules. "By the laws of society, this horse, this coat is mine, and *ought* to remain perpetually in my possession: I reckon on the secure enjoyment of it: By depriving me of it, you disappoint my expectations, and doubly displease me, and offend every bystander" (310–311). Without customary rules, "the distinction between *mine* and *thine* would be unknown in society" (ibid.), but once it is known, then, if anyone takes Hume's splendid coat, he will be doubly displeased: displeased to lose what he reckoned on securely enjoying, and displeased, as any honest bystander would be, on the public's behalf, that its laws are being flouted. Hume in this passage calls these rules "the rules of equity," since equity demands that we not excuse ourselves from rules we want others to keep. If we do, we must expect "universal blame," and, if found out, loss of trust. Hume takes equity and impartiality very seriously, and the one unequivocally endorsed "ought" in *EPM* outside the scope of "justice" occurs when Hume agrees with Polybius that a historian ought to list the strengths as well as the weaknesses of those whose deeds he relates (321). Hume himself certainly showed this basic virtue when he turned historian, and it brought him to the attention of Hippolyte de Saujon, who in her first letter to him praised his account of the Stuarts for its "divine impartiality."

The short fourth section, "Of political society," looks only in a cursory fashion at government, to which so much of *Treatise,* Book 3, Part 2, was devoted, and which provides the topic for many of the essays that Hume was writing at this time. Section 4 quickly moves on from the state to the great variety of other convention-governed circles we move in, from marriages, friendships, and leagues to loose communities of road-users, drinking clubs, and boxing fraternities. Some interesting virtues are recognized, such as selective and considerate forgetting, and some unwelcome characters are sketched—the gossip, the person who opens and reads others' mail, the nosy person who "plays the spy" upon his neighbor's "words and looks and actions," the person who presumes upon casual acquaintance. The background presence of Theophrastus and La Bruyère, in Hume's library, can now be felt, lightening the Ciceronian *gravitas* of Sections 2 and 3, and their influence will continue, when Hume gets to the "agreeable" virtues.

In the central fifth section, Hume pauses and reflects on where his analysis of the virtues is taking him. So far it has led him to an emphasis on utility. But since a virtue, by Hume's definition, is a quality we are *pleased* to find in others, and pleased to have found in ourselves, utility must please, to have any moral importance. The last virtues Hume will go on to survey, in Sections 7 and 8, are those that are directly pleasing, rather than pleasing for their utility. The question now arises of what the relation is, for Hume, between what pleases and what has utility, between Theophrastus's properly salted soup, and the Ciceronian prudence and enterprise of those who make salt available.

For Bentham, utility is simply stock of pleasure, although he has nice and possibly Hume-derived distinctions between what has hedonic "fertility" and what yields pleasure more directly. For him, the question of why utility pleases could not arise. As Sidgwick noted,[17] Hume does not use "utility" in this "utilitarian" way, but restricts it to "what advances some *ulterior* good." For Hume, utility is what advances someone's interest (E 218), and one's "interest" is not the same as one's pleasure. It is a fact that most of us are concerned for our futures, and so pleased when our interests are advanced. Utility usually pleases, but voluptuaries who live for the day may not care much about their interests, nor always welcome what advances them. It is also a fact, important for the refutation of "the selfish hypothesis," that most of us care about others' interests, as well as our own, so are pleased about public benefits, even when we personally will not profit from them. There may be occasional people with "affected spleens" who welcome public catastrophe, just as there are a few misers who get no pleasure except from what advances their own pecuniary interests, but most of us get pleasure from many sources, including what advances our own and other people's interests. What is in our interest matters, in Hume's version of morals, but so do "play, frolic and gaiety" (279).

Hume's look at the role of utility in explaining what we value in the social virtues has, as he had predicted, given him an opening for accounting for other virtues. These include those, such as enterprise, economy, perseverance, and common sense, that are discussed in the sixth section as "useful to ourselves" (as well as being, very often, useful to others), and also the directly "agreeable" virtues, those discussed in Sections 7 and 8. These three sections, like the fourth, contain some pro-

17. Henry Sidgwick, Outline of the History of Ethics, for English Readers (Macmillan, 1902), 209, note 2.

vocative inclusions in Hume's catalogue of endorsed virtues, and he deliberately rubs in the fact that many of them, such as quickness of conception and facility of expression, are no less "involuntary" than are the breadth of shoulders, taper legs, and sexual potency that are listed as "bodily endowments" in T 615. His ostensible reason for discussing these last, nonmoral endowments is to confirm the link between beauty and utility, but he surely knows he is asking for trouble when he reduces moral merit to a "beauty" of character that is as much a gift of fortune as is physical beauty, or sexual attractiveness. Moral charm and moral potency were new and offensive notions to many of his contemporary readers, and many, including several professors of moral philosophy in eighteenth-century Scotland, and some in other universities since, duly took offense. However mischievous, this second part of Section 6 of *EPM* does mediate nicely between the mainly "useful" virtues, discussed in Sections 2 through 6, and the mainly agreeable ones, discussed in Sections 7 and 8.

The directly agreeable traits are important since "something must be desirable on its own account, and because of its immediate accord or agreement with human sentiment and affection" (E 293). Health, wealth, and our other important interests point us to the "ultimate ends" of pleasure and absence of pain. Once something, such as money, has been shown to be an instrument of pleasure, "it is an absurdity" to keep asking for a reason why it should be wanted. Hume is unabashedly Epicurean on this point. Some virtues please because of their means-value, or utility; others, such as wit and delicacy of taste, please directly, before the special pleasure of approbation gets added on. And since all of them must give this special pleasure, to be accounted virtues, then "virtue is an ultimate end, and is desirable on its own account, without fee or reward, merely for the immediate satisfaction it conveys" (ibid.). A useful virtue, such as justice or frugality, may have its costs, but no contrived "fee," and the benefits and satisfaction that virtues bring their possessors are not "rewards," in the sense of contrived recompense. Like Shaftesbury, Hume believes that belief in specially arranged rewards for virtue and punishment for vice, including divine arrangements, tend to corrupt virtue. "The steady attention to so important an interest as eternal salvation is apt to extinguish the benevolent affections, and beget a narrow, contracted selfishness" (D 222). The only dependable human

response to perceived virtue is the harmless uncorrupting one of approbation, and that is a natural and inevitable reaction, not a contrived "reward."

Hume says that a virtue, such as benevolence, can be valued mainly
for the utility of its results, yet also be "sweet, smooth, tender and agreeable" to its possessor, and agreeably contagious. This immediate agreeableness will presumably be independent of the extra pleasure the virtue
brings by occasioning "the pleasing sentiment of approbation" (E 289).
Virtues can be both useful and immediately agreeable, and "qualities
often derive their merit from complicated sources." A virtue, such as
"fidelity to promises," may be first valued for its usefulness to society,
making transactions secure, and trust in future delivery of goods and
services a possibility, but it soon, by a "progress of sentiments," also becomes something a person wants for himself, if he is not to be "contemptible, no less than odious" (238). Is this not only because we need a
reputation for honesty, but also because we like being approved of? Certainly such a shift in valuation is assisted by our supposed need to share
our self-evaluations, and have them confirmed by others. What begins
by being valued for its utility can become valued for the approbation it
occasions, and can end by being taken to be intrinsically valuable. (Bernard Williams has recently given a Hume-inspired account of a similar
"progress of sentiments" with respect to the virtue of truthfulness.)[18]

## The True Origin of Morals

Hume does not claim to have completed his catalogue of virtues; it is
left open-ended. (In the sixth section, after listing twenty-four qualities
"useful to ourselves," he waves his hand toward "a thousand more of the
same kind.") But everything he has surveyed that is "admitted to the
honourable denomination of virtue or merit" has been found to be "useful or agreeable to the person himself or to others" (E 268) (where these
"or's" are definitely not exclusive). He is now in a position, in the "Conclusion," to turn (or rather, to return, since the fifth section prepared the
ground for the ninth) to the question of "the true origin" of the morals
he has outlined, and to specify the point of view from which recognition

18. Bernard Williams, *Truth and Truthfulness: An Essay on Genealogy* (Princeton, 2002), chs.
2 and 3.

of moral merit is made. For theological moralists, God's will is the "true origin" of morals. For Hume, its origin is entirely human. Despite slight differences in terminology, *EPM's* finding is pretty much the same as that of the *Treatise,* that virtues are discerned from a general human point of view, requiring extensive but regulated sympathy in those who manage to take it up. It cannot be the viewpoint of self-love, which, however strong, has not "a proper direction for that purpose" (271).

> The notion of morals implies some sentiment common to all mankind, which recommends the same object to general approbation, and makes every man, or most men, agree in the same opinion or decision concerning it. It also implies some sentiment, so universal and comprehensive as to extend to all mankind, and render the actions and conduct, even of the persons the most remote, an object of applause or censure, according as they agree or disagree with that rule of right which is established. These two requisite circumstances belong alone to the sentiment of humanity here insisted upon. (271–272)

The "sentiment of humanity," as a name for the virtue-recognizing moral sentiment, is new, and underlines what Hume had written in a famous letter to Hutcheson in 1740, that morality "regards only human nature and human life" (L 1.40).

The double requirement, that the moral sentiment be shared by almost all human beings, and that all be subject to its findings, is similar to the requirement that Hume's later friend/enemy, Rousseau, made for his authoritative "general will," which governs all and only those who go to comprise it. It is just as stringent, and just as unlikely to be met with in the real world, where moral judges do not always agree, and are not always judged by the same standards that they impose on others. It makes "the rule of right" (not to be confused with the culturally varying rules of "justice") cosmopolitan, rather than local, and makes it democratically arrived at. Taken seriously, it means that the most we usually do when we judge actions and character is aspire to the point of view from which truly moral judgments would be made, make judgments that we hope but cannot be sure have the requisite commonality and universality. James Beattie found Hume's ethics elitist, a concession to the tastes and views of the fashionable French circles that Hume went on to move in, and this is ironical, if the official theory is radically democratic. Hume, in an intemperate moment, called Beattie "that bigotted silly Fellow" (L 2.301), but his theory seems to require him to get Beattie's and Balfour's agreement, as much as that of Shaftesbury, Cicero, or the judicious Polybius.

Or can Hume properly dismiss the disagreement of those he has reason to think bigots or silly fellows? His theory does require that moral judges rid themselves of "the deceptive glosses of superstition and false religion," and does allow that reason needs to be "fully assisted and improved" if it is to "instruct us in the pernicious or useful tendency of qualities and actions," so that we can, where necessary, "adjust anew the boundaries of moral good and evil" (E 285). Ignorant or silly persons, who do not discern these tendencies, or splenetic misanthropes who do not care about them, or hidebound traditionalists who are unwilling to do any adjusting, are, in Hume's theory, disqualified as moral judges. Beattie is, I think, right to judge that Hume's morals are elitist, but the elitism is more intellectual than social, more a matter of having the right education and caste of mind than of wearing the right waistcoat. Hume's list of virtues is likely to prove acceptable only to peaceable, sociable, intelligent, reflective, not zealously religious persons (and it will help if they like reading history).

Hume, of course, speaks of "false religion" as the enemy of his humane and human version of morals, not of religion as such, and always disclaimed being an atheist. It is pretty clear that neither Pascal's nor Knox's religion is his "true" acceptable one. It was the grandfather of "the elegant Lord Shaftesbury" who set the fashion for avoiding being Bacon's double fool (D 139) by claiming to be an adherent of the religion of all sensible men, and then, when asked what that religion was, responding: "Sensible men never say." Hume, in *EPM*, as elsewhere, preserves a truly Shaftesburian reticence on the true religion. In this, as in so much else, he is also following the prudent Cicero. Certainly the Christian virtues, not just "celibacy, fasting, penance, mortification, self-denial, humility, silence, solitude" (E 270), but also charity in the form of handouts to beggars, are judged to be "rejected by men of sense." Hume, as most of his contemporaries realized, as Leslie Stephen saw very clearly,[19] and as J. B. Schneewind, Isabel Rivers, and J. C. A Gaskin

19. Sir Leslie Stephen, *History of English Thought in the Eighteenth Century* (Smith Elder, 1902), vol. 1, ch. 6.

have more recently emphasized,[20] is fairly openly defying the officially Christian culture in which he was writing. Gerhard Streminger even finds *EPM* to be blasphemous, for its implicit denial of original sin, and dismissal of the possibility of an afterlife where punishments and rewards await us.[21] On his deathbed Hume joked with Adam Smith about wanting to delay his death till he had completed the revisions he was making to his works, including *EPM,* works intended to "open the eyes of the public." He wished, he said, that he could live long enough to see if they would hasten the downfall of "superstition," but knew that that would not happen for "these many hundred years." Hume's case against religion is not only its superstition, but also its socially divisive force and incitement to violence, when its devotees and enthusiasts go to war for their faith. It is not just that the "monkish" virtues/vices sour the lives of the monks, but also that they "harden the heart" and lead to persecution and religious wars. Even when the heart of the religious believer is not hardened, it may be corrupted by the prospect of divinely ordained reward for virtue, or deranged by fear of punishment for vice.

Despite our disagreements about religion, and our varying cultures, we are supposed to be able to come to agreement on what mental traits we should welcome in each other, at least once our reason has been assisted by reading enough history. The point of view from which we are to discern true moral merit is one that looks beyond self-interest, but not beyond the good of humankind. Hume's moral judge does not, like Shaftesbury's admirer of moral beauty, look beyond human communities to the wider "systems" in which they are included, eventually to the whole cosmos, but limits herself to the good of the human species. (She will, however, look with a cold eye on those who do not "give gentle usage" to other sentient beings, without rights though they may be.) It is therefore appropriate that Hume renames the attitude that is needed for discerning virtues "the sentiment of humanity." Its viewpoint is no God's-eye view, no "view from nowhere," but an earthly perspective, that of a representative of "the party of humankind." Hume's version of mor-

20. J. B. Schneewind, ed., introduction to *Hume: Enquiry Concerning the Principles of Morals* (Hackett, 1983), 1–9; Isabel Rivers, *Reason, Grace and Sentiment: A Study of the Language of Religion and Ethics in England, 1660–1780* (Cambridge, 1991–2000), vol. 2, ch. 4; Gaskin, 369.

21. Gerhard Streminger, *David Hume: Sein Leben und sein Werk* (Ferdinand Schoeningh, 1994), 357.

als is unashamedly humanist, and those who want a more "ecological" and less "speciesist" version would do well to turn to Shaftesbury, rather than Hume, for inspiration.

What is the relation of Hume's "sentiment of humanity" to two of the main virtues it discerns, the virtues of impartiality and benevolence? Do we have to possess the main Humean virtues in order to recognize them as such?[22] Hume's terminology is a bit sloppy, and has changed. In *Treatise,* Book 3, "humanity" was the name of a particular virtue, associated with the attempt to relieve human misery, so was close to compassion and pity. It was not the same as sympathy, which can be felt for any passion, not just for suffering. Like benevolence, of which it was one form, it was more a motive than a sentiment. In *EPM,* "humanity" has become a sympathy-based sentiment, "fellow-feeling," and, in its extensive form, generates the point of view from which moral merit is discerned.[23] Benevolence the virtue is a tendency to have "good" *intentions,* to try to *do good* to others, and to relieve their suffering. It may have quite a limited object, say, one person whose welfare can be improved by the benevolent person's action. Indeed, Hume says that it is best if the focus of our affections and well-meaning actions be limited; otherwise they might "be dissipated and lost for want of a proper limited object" (E 229, note). The sentiment of humanity is sympathetic concern for all human persons, and need not lead to any intentions or action, except the expression of its findings. To reach them, it has to "correct" the "inequalities" of natural sympathy and natural benevolence by "reflection" (ibid.), and it is impartiality that does the correction. Still, some benevolence, in addition to impartiality and extensive sympathy, seems a prerequisite. "A creature absolutely malicious and spiteful," just as much as a hopelessly partial person, or one without any fellow-feeling, will be constitutionally unfitted to take up this moral point of view, so there may be what we could call a virtuous circle in recognition of the components of true merit.

Hume's moral point of view, despite the formal similarities noted above to Rousseau's law-generating general will, is not that of a would-be world legislator, pretending to issue binding and enforced laws, nor

22. See Taylor, 43–62.

23. See Kate Abramson, "Sympathy and the Project of Hume's Second *Enquiry,*" *Archiv fur Geschichte der Philosophie* 83, 1 (2001): 45–78, for a discussion of the relation of sympathy to the sentiment of humanity.

even that of a person forming a policy for her own life, but rather that of a reflective surveyor of human character who, through the breadth of her sympathies, her humanity (Adam Smith says humanity is a woman's sentiment),[24] and her impartiality, admires beneficent human traits, and dislikes those whose "tendency is pernicious to society." The mood of its expressed findings is optative, not imperative, and they will be only indirectly action-guiding. Hume cites, but does not commit himself to, the view of some "modern enquirers," perhaps including himself in *Treatise*, Book 3, Part 1, Section 1, that "the end of all moral speculations" is to "engage us" to embrace virtue and avoid vice (E 172). His "speculative" inquiry (177–178) does not find that our possession of the sentiment of humanity need make very much difference to the way we actually behave. Sometimes strong private passions may "yield the dominion of our breasts to those social and public principles" which, although "somewhat small and delicate," are "cherished by society and conversation" (275–276); at other times the moral sentiments are lulled into lethargy. But even if our "generous sentiments" be "ever so weak . . . insufficient to move a hand or finger of our body, they must still direct the determinations of our mind, and where everything else is equal, produce a cool preference of what is useful and serviceable to mankind, above what is pernicious and dangerous" (273). The sentiment of humanity reliably enables us to "discern" virtues, to have a cool and expressed preference for them, perhaps to love those who possess them, but not to come to acquire those we lack. It may give us some sort of "rule of right," but the only pressure it can exert to get conformity to this rule is through its own expressed findings, in "company, in the pulpit, on the theatre, in the schools" (229). Should a person not care about being judged a bigot, a fool, a tyrant, a hypocrite, a busybody, or a knave, then Hume's version of morality is powerless, unless magistrates, or the tyrant's victims, take action to limit the harm done by persons with the undesirable character traits. Hume's answer to the "sensible knave," to which I now turn, makes it very clear how little coercive force he takes his gentle nonvengeful morality to have.

In the second part of the "Conclusion," after his account of the viewpoint from which virtues are discerned, Hume takes up the question that Shaftesbury had turned to in the second book of his *Inquiry*, that of the

24. Smith, 190.

interested obligation to virtue. This is a rather pressing question for moralists who disdain appeal to divine sanctions to underwrite moral obligations. Is there enough incentive for a Humean to show virtue, given the likelihood, recognized by Shaftesbury in his *Sensus Communis,* "that knaves are advanced above us, and the vilest of men preferred before the honestest?"[25] Shaftesbury discusses the bid for happiness of the "accomplished knave," his willingness to sacrifice "a character with himself and others" for the sake of tempting "plums," and Hume takes up this discussion in the second part of his "Conclusion." For him, as for Shaftesbury, to establish the presence of an "obligation" is to establish that the obligated person risks some cost if the obligation is not met. Obligations had barely figured in *EPM,* except where justice was concerned. There were "obligations" not to cheat and steal, nor to break promises, since we withdraw trust from those known to be offenders, and magistrates may punish some of them. So it is appropriate that it is obligations to this sort of convention-governed conduct that Hume's knave is seen to be neglecting. But such obligations will not restrict a clever knave, who is confident he can get away with his knavery. Hume allows that judicious dishonesty may serve a "sensible knave" better than honesty. As Shaftesbury says, honesty is a "sober mistress," despised by those who are intent at all costs on worldly success. If one has the knave's preference for "toys and gewgaws" over "consciousness of integrity," then one's interest may indeed lie in taking advantage of the loopholes in the law and the gullibility of one's fellows, and so making additions to one's fortune without "causing any considerable breach in the social union and confederacy" (E 282). Hume's unanswerable knave is "sensible," and so sensitive to his own dependence on the social union, and he may have some virtues along with his profitable vice of dishonesty. (Hume, as his summaries of monarchs' characters in his *History* make clear, is no believer in the unity of the virtues.) The knave sacrifices "invaluable enjoyment of a character, with himself at least" to his ill-gotten luxury. But if luxury matters more to him than such supposedly higher pleasure, then there is no "satisfactory and convincing answer" that can be given him (283). Everything depends on his preferences and his tastes in pleasures. Just as there is no arguing with

25. Anthony Ashley Cooper, Third Earl of Shaftesbury, *Characteristics of Men, Manners, Opinions, Times,* edited by Lawrence E. Klein (Cambridge, 1999), vol. 1, 60–64.

Diogenes, who opts for his "beastly" offensive pleasures, or with Pascal, who prefers his spiritual satisfactions to ordinary innocent ones, so there is no arguing with the knave who forgoes "enjoyment of a character" for the sake of monetary gain. Hume dutifully says the knave is "the greater dupe," but allows that he cannot convince the knave of that. It is a standoff. Hume hopes that few are tough enough, or clever enough, to live as successful and happy knaves, but he does not pretend that his version of ethics offers a way to turn knaves honest. (Nor does it promise compensation in kind to the knaves' victims. So does the interested obligation to honesty exist only for those of us who are not cut out to be accomplished knaves? Hume leaves this question as unanswered as the knave's challenge.)

Why did the knave's challenge not arise in the *Treatise?* The sensible knaves, along with the conspiracy-breaking women, and the self-denying Christians attended by theologians disguised as philosophers, were significant absentees from *Treatise,* Book 3, however close the women got to getting a hearing in the section on chastity and modesty, and however sly the satire of inefficacious hellfire moralists in the Book 1 section with the disarming title "Of the effects of other relations, and other habits." We were warned, in *Treatise,* Book 3, Part 2, Section 2, that in developed societies the interested obligation to justice can become "remote," and not so readily perceived. Some extra artifices of politicians and educators may be needed to "inculcate the principles of probity," and get each person to "fix an inviolable law to himself, never, by any temptation, to violate those principles, which are essential to a man of probity and honour" (T 501). Hume's knave has slipped through these educational and political safeguards, as some inevitably do. He cares little for probity, although he likely does care more about honor and reputation. Hume, in the *Treatise,* left it to educators and politicians to show warmth in the cause of virtue, while he concentrated on doing the "anatomy" of our moral sense, but, in the very last paragraph, he did a little "painting" of the happy man of virtue, who will not sacrifice "peace and inward satisfaction" for any "advantage of fortune" (620). This was an advance notice of his reply to the knave in *EPM.* Despite his earlier claim that his inquiry into merit is speculative, rather than practical, he seems, in its conclusion, to be making an effort to "represent virtue in all her genuine and engaging charms" (E 279). The analysis of panegyrics of virtuous people slips into a panegyric of virtue. The answer to the knave begins in candid calculation of interest, but ends in rather unconvincing edifying rhetoric. Hume performs better as skeptic than as painter, preacher, or rhapsodist, and it is not clear that it will be with his help that "truths, which are pernicious to society, if any such there be, will yield to errors that are salutary and advantageous" (ibid.). He is more open in *EPM* than in the *Treatise* about the godlessness of his moral philosophy, and about its generally Epicurean character, and his concessions to the knave should be seen in this light. He has no hellfire to threaten the knave with, or even a rigorously inquisitorial human police, only the possibility of self-disgust, and the need for secrecy and psychic isolation. Shaftesbury wrote that his only reply to the man who asks why he should not be "nasty" (dirty) when alone and in the dark is "because you have a nose."[26] Should the man claim to have no sense of smell, then the conversation has to cease, and the company of that man be avoided, just as one would try to keep clear of the man whose only reason for being honest is fear of the gibbet, or of hellfire.

It is only with respect to "the interested obligation" to justice, not with respect to virtue in general, that Hume allows that virtue may prove costly to the virtuous, especially if they become prey to accomplished knaves. The other Humean virtues, as David Gauthier puts it, "do not curb self-interest but rather instruct it in the means necessary to the greatest happiness of sociable and sympathetic creatures."[27] Hume says that the morality he has endorsed "talks not of useless austerities and rigours, suffering and self-denial. She declares that her sole purpose is to make her votaries and all mankind, during every instant of their existence, if possible cheerful and happy; nor does she ever willingly part with any pleasure but in hopes of ample compensation in some other period of their lives. The sole trouble which she demands is that of just calculation, and a steady preference for the greater happiness" (E 279). (It was *Treatise*, Book 3, not *EPM*, that Bentham said made the scales fall from his eyes, but this passage seems a clearer anticipation of his hedonic calculus than anything in the *Treatise*.) Hume's version of morality is neither austere nor rigorous, and has no inquisitorial function. "Who would live amidst perpetual . . . scolding, and mutual reproaches?" (267). Dugald Stewart, in a book intended for students at

---

26. Ibid., 58.
27. David Gauthier, "Three Against Justice," in *Moral Dealing* (Cornell, 1990), 41.

Edinburgh University in the decades after Hume's death, criticized Shaftesbury for neglecting "conscience" and its authority.[28] In Hume's ethics too, as Balfour, Kant, and even T. H. Huxley complained, its stern and scolding voice is replaced by an agreeable "dance measure."[29] Hume takes up Shaftesbury's question of the appropriate dress for "the moral dame" to wear. Penitential robes, and even sober gowns, are discarded in favor of more attractive dress.

Part of Hume's case for saying that virtue should bring happiness, without any divine intervention, is that we can cultivate a taste for the pleasures of surveying our own "inward beauty and moral grace" (E 276). Should we fail to do this, fail to have a "continual and earnest pursuit of a character, a name, a reputation in the world," a "constant habit of surveying ourselves as it were, in reflection," perhaps because we have retired from society into "solitary and uncultivated nature," where Hume thinks we risk falling into moral "lethargy," then his case for virtue may fail (ibid.). Some may find the prospect of this constant moral self-inspection distasteful, and prefer "the common beauties of nature," even enjoyed in antisocial solitude, to the narcissistic delights of "peaceful reflection on one's own conduct." It is therefore appropriate that Hume puts some emphasis on the need for moral education, and encouragement of this cultivation of character. The moral sentiments are to be given expression in schools, as well as in literature, from the pulpit, and on the stage. (And he himself supported the production of the controversial play *Douglas,* a moral tale about a woman's virtuous suicide, and may even have acted in it, so he did his public bit for the version of morality he endorsed. A wit, John Maclaurin, later Lord Dreghorn, summed up Hume's ethics thus: "that suicide is a duty we owe ourselves; adultery a duty we owe to our neighbour; that the tragedy of *Douglas* is the best play ever was written.")[30]

Is there a social need to monitor the incidence, not merely of knaves, fools, dismal delirious monks, and hare-brained enthusiasts, but also of those with a distaste for the self-inspection that Hume seems to be counting on to make us care about our own merit? The only pressure to

28. Dugald Stewart, *Outlines of Moral Philosophy, for the Use of Students at Edinburgh University* (Archibald Constable, 1818), 151.

29. T. H. Huxley, *Hume: With Helps to the Study of Berkeley, Essays* (D. Appleton, 1894), 239.

30. Earnest Campbell Mossner, *The Life of David Hume* (Clarendon, 1980), 367.

conform to Humean morality comes from pride in good character, from concern lest we appear "odious" in the eyes of others, and in our own eyes. Where the Christian has to please an all-seeing God, Hume's moral person has to please fellow-persons, and bear her own survey. But the threat of inability to bear one's own survey will not work if one can manage to avoid self-survey. Others' less avoidable reactions seem essential, if Hume's version of morality is to work.

Hume says his version of morality displays "the force of many sympathies" (E 276). Sympathy was first brought in, in the *Treatise,* to account for "the love of fame," and was found to be particularly influential, indeed a necessary prompt, "when we judge of our own worth and character." "The minds of men are mirrors to one another" (T 365), and the magic of Hume's morality is all done with these mirrors. Should we lack "a care for preserving a character with ourselves," or should we not "find it necessary to prop our tottering judgement on the correspondent approbation of mankind," then even the gentle force of the Humean sympathy-dependent morality, which the likes of Balfour and Kames found much too gentle, may be lost. Hume made lack of self-sufficiency a condition for the perceived need for cooperation on which one important virtue, justice, rests, but it is more than lack of self-sufficiency, but rather positive sociability, a concern to be acceptable to others, and to have them prompt and confirm our self-assessments, that is needed if his version of morality itself is to be of more than speculative interest to us. In *EPM,* Hume is not, as he was in the *Treatise,* putting forward a theory of human nature, the mechanics of sympathy, and the sources of human motivation, and then confirming that theory by looking at how our moral natures work. He is, however, sticking with his earlier conclusions about human nature, about the average person's sociability, capacity for sympathy, consequent tendency to self-survey, and need for confirmation of the self-assessments that are made. Morality is not, in his view, an "artifice of politicians," as it was for Mandeville, and certainly is not sired by flattery, but it is "begot upon pride," and it needs both midwifery and nurturing from others' candid appraisals of our merit.

The reliance on a form of pride, pride in one's "inward beauty and moral grace," as moral incentive, can be taken as another slap by Hume at the moral psychology of the Christians, for whom humility, not pride, is the mainspring of righteousness. Just as Hume relied on self-interest to curb itself, for justice to be a possibility for us, so he relies on a new direction to self-conceit, and the desire to be admired, for morality as a whole to be a possibility for us. Although the "selfish hypothesis" is rejected, and fellow-feeling emphasized, "partiality in our own favour" is accepted as innate. But it is the original of virtue, not of sin. Just as "there is no passion . . . capable of controlling the interested affection but the very affection itself, by an alteration of its direction" (T 492), so the thing to be done with self-conceit is not just veil it decently, but direct it on "character." Hume had spoken enigmatically, in the *Treatise,* of vanity as "a social passion and a bond of union among men" (491). Now we see just how it can be that, since it is vanity's redirection that enables us to care enough about our own characters.

In *EPM's* "Conclusion," Hume speaks the same Newtonian language as in the *Treatise's* "Of the origin of justice and property," both of the "force" and of the "direction" of passions on which morality might be thought based. Self-interest had the needed force, and once regulated, the right direction, to control the love of personal gain, and motivate initial conformity to cooperative schemes. But it does not have the right direction to explain the whole of morality, neither to explain all that we praise in others, nor to explain why we are pleased ourselves to be possessors of the recognized virtues. "Would you have your character coveted, admired, followed; rather than hated, despised, avoided? Can anyone seriously deliberate in the case?" (E 280). The sympathy-based "sentiment of humanity" has the right direction to explain all the mental qualities that we praise, however weak its intrinsic force as a motivator. Fortunately, it has a stronger ally: "Another spring of our constitution, that brings a great addition of force to moral sentiment, is the love of fame; which rules, with such uncontrolled authority, in all generous minds" (276). Moral self-conceit, and concern for "character with others," explains why we want to measure up to shared moral standards.

## What Pleased the Author

Hume has, in *EPM,* completed his account of how vanity can become a bond of social union, can replace fear of divine anger as the engine that drives human morality. Mandeville had spoken of "millions endeavoring to supply each other's lust and vanity." Hume shows us how two not very attractive passions, lust for gain and self-conceit, can replace dehumanizing fear of hell as moral incentive. With the appropriate redirection, and a little guidance from the "sentiment of humanity," they can become the guardians of a functioning morality, indeed of "the most perfect morality with which we are acquainted" (E 276). The Christian vices of greed and pride have, in Hume's hands, become the driving forces of a perfect, and almost perfectly nonpunitive, morality. The inversion of Christian morality is complete.

It is a measure of how well Hume's campaign for a secular and humane morality succeeded that many of the readers of *EPM* now find it uncontroversial, even "bland."[31] But to most of his contemporaries—to Balfour, to Beattie, to Reid—it was, both in its secular and Epicurean matter and in its playful manner, a dangerous threat, and one they felt obliged to try to counter. It takes some historical imagination to see what in *EPM* offended, and what Hume was so pleased with. Leslie Stephen judged the latter to be the demonstration that the good was the useful, and definitely not because of divine rewards and punishment.[32] This utilitarian inversion would be offensive to the religious, and surely at least part of what pleased Hume was precisely what offended, namely, *EPM*'s challenge to his own religious and puritan culture. A restrictive culture often produces its own subversives. Hume, descendent of Covenanters, devoted son of a pious mother, friend till the end of moderate clergymen in Edinburgh, teases his Christian contemporaries in this work, and invites them to let their "natural sentiments" prevail over their "delirious and dismal" religious proclivities. These humane sentiments, he says, "form, in a manner, the *party* of humankind against vice and disorder" (E 275). It has to be seen still as a "party," opposed by other parties, in particular by the grimmer sentiments played on by the hellfire moralists.

Still, it was not just as anti-Christian manifesto that Hume had reason to be pleased with this book. His *Natural History of Religion* easily outdoes it on that score. *EPM* makes several substantive adjustments to *Treatise,* Book 3's version of moral good and evil, while keeping unchanged the essentials of the account of the point of view from which they are discerned. "The circumstances of justice" are revised, and attention is belatedly given to the question of whom it is that justice protects. Some concessions are made to rationalists, and some hasty arguments

31. M. A. Box, *The Suasive Art of David Hume* (Princeton, 1990), 225.
32. Stephen, vol. 2, 92.

against them are removed, preparing the way for Hume's final judgment, in the first appendix of his *History of England,* that virtue is "nothing but a more enlarged and more cultivated reason" (H 1.App.1.179). In *EPM,* the main opponent is identified as the theological moralist, whether rationalist or not, who treats "all morals as on a like footing with civil laws, guarded by the sanctions of reward and punishment" (E 322). The emphasis on "mankind" as the only judge of human morality is louder and clearer, and the authoritative moral sentiment is appropriately renamed "the sentiment of humanity." These are important adjustments. And of course *EPM* has literary as well as philosophical finesse. It suits its manner to its matter by displaying some of the virtues it recognizes— wit, wisdom, politeness, decency. It avoids "pompous declamations," but its polite contributions to reflections on morality are scarcely "insipid."

When *EPM* appeared in 1751, James Wodrow, moderate Presbyterian son of the Calvinist preacher Robert Wodrow, read it eagerly to see what the "great infidel" had produced this time, then reported with some disappointment that it contained nothing new, but was about "Hutcheson's disinterested scheme." It was, however, "mighty fine polished, beautiful & entertaining, & which is odd, nothing at all Sceptical."[33] Wodrow cannot have been a very perceptive, or even a very careful, reader. Entertaining and mighty finely polished *EPM* certainly is, and plenty others have found it Hutchesonian. But nothing new? And without a trace of skepticism? The "civil" Balfour, and even the "silly" Beattie, saw and complained of the new antireligious emphasis, and the skepticism.

For *EPM*'s ambitious structure, Hume may be indebted, not so much to the benign but humorless Hutcheson, as to the eloquent and humor-loving Shaftesbury. He imbedded his "Inquiry into Virtue or Merit" in a longer, more methodologically exploratory and skeptical work, his three-volume *Characteristics of Men, Manners, Opinions, Times.* In the first volume we find, in *Sensus Communis,* a discussion of various types of knaves and their not-altogether-to-be-dismissed chances of happiness, and then, following the somewhat didactic *Inquiry* in the second volume, Shaftesbury places a dialogue, *The Moralists,* which, like Hume's "whimsical" one, has a skeptic as one participant, curbing the

33. My information about this unpublished letter from December 1751, in Dr. William's Library, London, comes from M. A. Stewart.

main (theist) speaker's rhapsodies in praise of virtue. Then, in the third volume, in the *Miscellanies,* Shaftesbury continues to comment on and to some extent distance himself from the "positive" and "dogmatic" claims of his own *Inquiry.* Hume too has much more to say after the official conclusion of his inquiry into merit. His dialogue queries whether we in fact find that agreement on which morality is supposed to be based.[34] Palamedes points out that we do not all agree on the rule of right for regulating sexual relations, or for regulating the killing of human beings. Nor, as the "I" of "A Dialogue" acknowledges, does Pascal agree that friendship, wit, and eloquence are always valued, even by those disagreeing on tyrannicide, homosexuality, infanticide, and abortion. The metaphor of differing customs flowing, like the Rhine and the Rhone, in differing directions from the same mountain does little to alter the fact of moral disagreements, and disagreements about which of them are more important. Hume's whimsy, in the dialogue, is as teasing as his pretense, in the work it follows, that his catalogue of virtues will be acceptable to all his readers. (He does not expect Scythian scalp-collectors or Topinamboue cannibals to be reading him, but he does expect some communicant Christians.)

Both Shaftesbury's and Hume's skeptical wrappings for their more positive inquiries into morals leave the reader in healthy doubt as to just what is going on, and in both cases, this is surely intentional. Hume had at one point conceded the "uncertainty" and "natural obscurity" of merit (E 193) and had referred along the way to some very ugly human traits that have been admired, even by respected historians. In his official "Conclusion," after his relative warmth in the cause of his version of virtue, he drops a hint. Were he right about what we admire in each other, and why, he muses, then there would not be the disputes there undoubtedly are about morals. His conclusions would, "long ere now, have been received by the unanimous suffrage and consent of mankind" (278). In *EPM,* Hume gives us the case for a shared sentiment of humanity that can give us an agreed list of virtues. In various dropped hints and in "A dialogue," he balances that with the contrary case. His inquiry is left open and inconclusive. As "a true skeptic," and one who is reputed to have taken skepticism to be a "sturdy virtue" (even if it did not get

---

34. See E. Mazza, "Cannibals in 'A Dialogue' (In Search of a Standard of Morals)," in *"Instruction and Amusement": Le ragioni dell'illuminismo britannicco,* edited by Emilio Mazza and Emanuele Ronchetti (Il Polygrato, 2005), 45–66.

named in *EPM*'s catalogue), he has reason to be proud of his performance in this teasing work. Could he even be one of those disingenuous moralists, apparently censured in *EPM*'s first sentence, who have "a desire of showing wit and ingenuity, superior to the rest of mankind"?

The next pronouncements Hume went on to make about morals, after *EPM* (if we leave aside the considerable moral content of his history of the Stuarts), were in his *Four Dissertations*, six years later. His *Natural History of Religion* continues and intensifies his attacks on Christianity, adding ridicule to his calmer diagnosis of the doctrines of popular religion as "sick men's dreams." Intolerant mutually warring monotheists, those who imitate their vengeful god, and those who "make and then eat their god," are added to the rogues' gallery begun in *EPM*. If *EPM* shows "extensive genius," it is the *Natural History* that shows more "intrepid courage." In the accompanying dissertation, *Of the Standard of Taste*, Hume, more explicitly than in *EPM*, keeps his near promise at the end of *EHU* to make the fixing of a standard of beauty the object of his reasoning and inquiry. And he begins by warning us that such agreement about moral beauty as we may think we find is more verbal than substantive. Even when we appear to agree on a list of virtues, we may not mean quite the same by, say, "courage," or "prudence" (Es 228). He also says there that, although in judging works of literature we should make allowance for the author's culture and religion, we are, rightly, always jealous of our own moral standards (247). And whose taste in morals is an expert taste? Hume instances Bunyan as an inferior author, compared with Addison (231), despite the great popularity of *Pilgrim's Progress* in his own culture, so the tastes of the people are not counting for much. The secular, humane, enlightened, and peace-loving morality that Hume had delineated in *EPM*, and was so jealous of, is, as he well knew, not to everyone's taste, not even to every historian's taste.

## Final Note

Should we confirm Hume's own assessment of his "performance" in *EPM*? As he allowed, he was not the best person to judge it. But to what judges, then, should we turn? To his contemporary readers in Britain, who, more than most of us today, were in a position to have some preference between Suetonius and Tacitus, or know what Fabius and Scipio achieved by their differing military styles? They, however, were more likely than most of us are to be prejudiced by some "false religion." To his enlightened French admirers and translators? To any cultural heirs of the elegant Shaftesbury? Hume hoped that his works would be judged by "posterity." But a suitably educated and in other ways well-qualified readership may not yet be available to confirm, or disconfirm, his verdict on *EPM*. Few of his commentators have followed his request to let it, not the *Treatise,* be taken to give his "sentiments and principles" in ethics. (As far as I am aware, only Henry Sidgwick, C. D. Broad, and more recently Frederick Rosen, have complied.) Of those who have looked at both, most twentieth-century commentators (such as Laird, Greig, Noxon, and Mackie)[35] prefer the less diplomatic and less polished *Treatise.*

This Hume reader, who appreciates the intricacies and boldness of the *Treatise,* and certainly prefers it to *EHU,* which ends in a book-burning mood very different from the whimsical dialogue with which *EPM* ends, admires *EPM's* intellectual acuteness, especially on "justice," welcomes its clear-eyed working out of the implications of determinism, its "humane and beneficent" version of a gentle morality, and its refusal to look for any secular substitutes for hellfire as moral inducement. (The contrast with Adam Smith here is great. Even when Smith, in later editions of his *Theory of Moral Sentiments,* plays down the terrifying prospect of the "Great Judge," he still waxes edifyingly eloquent about the horrors of remorse.) Also admirable are *EPM's* literary craft, its demonstration of some of the virtues it discusses, its Shaftesburian and Theophrastian resonances, its lightness of touch, its playful wit, and its teasing doubleness of message. But are these what its author hoped we would admire? Who is to know? "I fall back into diffidence and scepticism."

35. Laird, op. cit.; J. Y. T. Greig, *David Hume* (Oxford, 1931; reprint, Garland, 1983); James Noxon, *Hume's Philosophical Development: A Study of His Methods* (Clarendon, 1932); J. L. Mackie, *Hume's Moral Theory* (Routledge and Kegan Paul, 1980).

# Conclusion

Hume began his account of justice with loan repayment, and I began there too. Then I looked at his treatment of the passion which the rules of justice regulate, and moved on to consider the relation of justice to equity. In Chapter 4 I surveyed Hume's enlargement of the narrow notion of justice he began with in the *Treatise*. That initial account saw it to comprise both honesty in matter of property and fidelity to promises. These two different parts of Hume's justice are more clearly differentiated in his *Enquiry Concerning the Principles of Morals (EPM)* than in the *Treatise*. Had Hume in either place listed all the parts of justice, of distributive and criminal justice as well as property and promise, the overassimilation of promise to property, discussed in Chapter 5, would have been less likely to take place, as the natural constraints of equity would have been more evident, and so also the double sense of honesty, as both respect for property and avoidance of lying, and of truth as including both truth to another and truth-speaking would become more evident, so that being true to one's word could draw on elements in both of these.

Truth comes from troth, and both concern trust. Hume sees the rules of justice as enabling even strangers to trust each other on some important matters. We should be able to trust all others, in solemn contexts, to speak the truth to us, and be able to trust those who have given us their word to keep it. For justice and equity govern both what we owe to everyone else, and are owed by everyone else, that is, respect for property, and truth-telling, and also what we owe only to special others, those to whom we have given our word. In *EPM* Hume scathingly asks if the reason we should be true to our word could be that we have given our word to be true to our word. But he himself had suggested something close to that in the *Treatise,* when he described the convention giving rise to promises as an agreement of all with all to be true to our word (T 522). What binds in a promise is the express agreement made with another person, not any general agreement of all with all. Such general agreements are what lie behind the legal *enforcement* of promises, behind contract law, the law on duress, and promissory estoppel, but only the agreement on the meaning of the word "promise" lies behind the force of "I promise. . . ." As Hume says in *EPM,* the virtues of honesty, fidelity, and truth have complicated sources. They do promote the interests of society, and that also of the person who displays them. But they also are only fair to the others whose property rights we respect, to whom we tell the truth, not lies, and to whom we keep the promises we have made. Among their complicated sources are equity and fairness, as well as justice. And so there may be an element of altruism, of concern for the one whom one has led to depend on one, in keeping a promise, so Jiwei Ci may be right to query whether all of justice is as lacking in altruism as Hume took it to be.[1] Just imagine if Hume had begun with promises, and raised his puzzle about motive for that case. Suppose it were the promise to pay the surgeon who tends one when one is injured, and maybe overcharges for his services. That makes him a bit like the vicious moneylender, but there is no way that Hume's puzzle, designed to show that artifice is involved, could get going in this case. If one promised a certain payment, in return for one's injuries being treated by the expert, then both concern for one's own reputation and concern for equity, for fairness to the surgeon, would provide sufficient motive for payment, and both are quite approvable motives. If we take a promise that did not involve payment, such as a promise to bring help to an injured person, to go off and find a surgeon, then the motive for doing what one promised seems quite clearly a proper concern for the one who is relying on one. If one assured another that one will bring help, then of course one should do just that. No artifice seems needed to generate this obligation, merely common decency. Nor is the public interest much involved, as it would be if the question was whether a promise made under duress, say, to grossly overpay the surgeon, should be held to bind. On such matters as degree of allowable duress, and whether a quid pro quo is needed before

---

1. See Chapter 5, "The Janus Face of Hume's Justice," for a discussion of Jiwei Ci's views.

a promise binds, some artifice and variability from community to community in the rules decreeing the details of promissory obligations will be found. But the main obligation, to do what one voluntarily assured another one would do, seems as natural as the obligation of a parent to care for a child. If Hume is right, this latter also, for a father, depends on the artificial virtue of chastity in the mother. But even if the child has been bought from its biological parents, as was claimed about the Douglas heir, the ones who took it on as their child still have a duty of care. As with children, so also with those who rely on promises: they should be able to count on those who encourage them to rely on them, and to trust them. Promissory estoppel, in the law, is a matter of equity. It is deemed unfair that a person should be encouraged to rely, to his detriment, on another doing what she said she would do, and then fails to do. The law on duress is also a matter of equity. It is deemed unfair that a promise extracted from one under duress should bind one.

Hume knows that equity and justice go together, but, as I argued in Chapter 5, he underplayed natural equity, and overplayed social artifice, when he first discussed promises. The inequity of disregard for others' property rights lies in making an exception of oneself, in exempting oneself from constraints one wants others to keep, while that of breaking promises is that of taking on an exceptional obligation, encouraging another to rely on one's discharge of it, and giving an assurance that one will, then disappointing this individual warranted expectation. The two cases are different, and different vices are displayed in them. By treating promises as conformity to the rules of promising, as honesty in conformity to the rules of property, Hume underplayed the naturalness of doing what we said we would do, and overplayed the elements of artifice in promise, made it just a useful commercial device, a form of transfer by consent. But, as the gunpowder plotters showed, its use is broader, its power to bind less dependent on society-wide cooperation and coordination. Both society-wide cooperation and cooperation with chosen others are vital to human life, but different virtues are shown in them. As Michael Thompson has recently argued, keeping our promises is as much a part of our human form of life as blossoming in spring is for cherry trees.[2] Partition of property, and the rule of law, may also be natural to us, but there is more to learn about the local "game" in their case,

---

2. Michael Thompson, *Life and Action: Elementary Structures of Practice and Practical Thought* (Harvard, 2008), ch. 11.

more socially varying artifice. Hume put them together in his concept of justice, and so supported the Hobbesian tradition that "what all men have agreed to, no man can call unjust," despite his carefully distancing himself from it in his essay "Of the original contract." In the social contract account of obedience to local law, conformity to local rules is assimilated too closely to keeping agreements, while Hume made the reverse assimilation. He was quite clear that the reason we obey our governors and conform to local rules of property is not that we have promised or covenanted to, that promissory obligations are quite different. "To obey the civil magistrate is requisite to preserve order and concord in society. To perform promises is necessary to beget mutual trust and confidence in the common offices of life. The ends, as well as the means, are perfectly distinct" (T 544). But to call both the property rules which magistrates enforce and the promises they leave it to plaintiffs to enforce the parts of justice, taken as artifice or social practice, was to assimilate rule obedience too closely to keeping promises, to forge a link that helped inspire Rawls, Scanlon, and others to see some hypothetical agreement behind conformity to law. Thompson's book is the first important challenge to this recent orthodoxy. But maybe his targets should have included Hume.

In his "Of providence and a future state," Hume has Epicurus ask those who believe a provident God to be the cause of the world, *"Are there marks of a distributive justice in this world?"* (E 141, Hume's italics). He did see justice as a matter of fair distribution, of goods and of burdens and benefits.[3] His account of how property is distributed, by human societies, had accepted inequality as something that was inevitable, even if we began with equal holdings, given different industry and enterprise in improving one's holding. It would take rigorous inquisition and severe jurisdiction, he says in *EPM,* to prevent it, but he knows that some redistributive tax policies had been tried, and were not so obviously tyrannical. (Tax policies, however, did provoke both the American and the French revolutions.) Justice as Hume comes to understand it does include distributive justice and fair taxation.

Was there something a little too cautious and jealous about Hume's first account of justice? What was cautious was to refrain, in the *Treatise,*

---

3. Tito Magri, in "Hume's Justice," forthcoming in the *Cambridge Companion to Hume's Treatise,* says "Hume's theory of justice has no distributive concerns." This may be correct about his concerns in the *Treatise,* but not beyond that.

from including more than he needed to in what he took justice to cover, to show its "artificiality," while leaving open the possibility of enlarging the concept. What he needed to do, to counter the view of Hutcheson,[4] was show that justice was not a branch of benevolence, and that it did require local convention to determine its precise rules. Property was an obvious place to start, to show this. He knew his view might appear to be like that of Hobbes, and by speaking of justice as "artificial" he invited this assimilation. But he was also jealous of what was really new in his account, and was a correction of Hobbes, and that was his inclusion of covenants and promises in the scope of social artifice. I think his account of what counts as a promise is a great achievement, and made Hume a glorious innovator in social philosophy, but he could have allowed that, just as parents would have invented proto-property rights for their children, within the family, so some sort of serious assurance between friends or family members would be a natural precursor to formally giving one's word. Contract may be mainly a commercial device for exchange of future goods and labor, but promise is less purely property-concerned. What is so clever about Hume's account of promise is that it builds in its own enforcement in a way that property rules cannot, in that the promise-breaker instantly loses trust, and his status as in good standing in a group who communicate with one another, whereas the sneak thief may get away scot-free. (Now where did that phrase come from?) There are, and can be, no sneak promise-breakers. Hume brings out these features of promise, but does not see that they really do make promises not merely a special case of "transfer by consent," as he presents them. His jealousy of the special features of his theory of justice, especially in relation to Hobbes and Hutcheson, may explain the overassimilation of fidelity to promises to keeping the rules of property and its transfer by consent. He was less concerned to distinguish his views from the Natural Law tradition; indeed, he presents what he says as a reinterpretation of the "laws of nature," and cites Grotius on pacts in a footnote to *EPM*.

Hume was a splendid innovator in social philosophy, and his corrections of both Hutcheson and Hobbes are made in the course of a well-developed account of how schemes of cooperation were adopted, in se-

4. That this was one main aim of Hume's is persuasively argued by James Harris, in "Hume's Peculiar Definition of Justice," in a forthcoming volume about Hume's *Treatise* edited by Marina Frasca-Spada and P. J. E. Kail (Oxford).

quence, by our wise ancestors. The sequential account was conjectural, and is left out by him in *EPM*. When he read Adam Ferguson's *Essay on Civil Society*, in 1767, he must have wondered if his *Treatise* had started a fashion in natural histories of society.[5] Ferguson had taken more care to match the schemes of cooperation he describes with the way of life of the group—pastoral, agricultural, or commercial—while Hume may have been too fixated on the landowning and commercial society of his day, and on the institutions it needed, so his sequence of artifices—first property, including property in land, then transfer by consent, then promise and contract, and only after them, government—does lack anthropological verisimilitude. I think he was wise to move away from that sequence, despite the clever way he had made each new stage solve a problem which developed at the previous stage, by a kind of Hegelian dialectic. He was wise to switch from conjectural to actual social history, and it is a pity he did not give us a revised theory of justice, after writing his *History of England*. But we must not be too greedy—he left us much to think about, and left it for us to speculate on what he might have said, after the *History*, about what justice includes, and about what parts of it might have been the first to develop in primitive societies, what parts are later accretions, and in particular what its core is, in a civilized society, and one which is part of an international community of nations.

Hume, when reproved by his friend Gilbert Elliot for thinking of retiring in France, said he was certainly not an Englishman, as Elliot had called him, but a Scot living in Paris, and a citizen of the world (L 1.47). The theory of justice we now need has to be a cosmopolitan one, as well as one that does justice to local rules of justice and standards of equity, be they those of Scotland, France, or New Zealand. The court at The Hague, as well as our local courts, now administer justice. Hume was cautious about the "laws of nations," which were not well observed in his day. He saw them as mainly a matter of observing boundaries, keeping treaties and the law of the seas, and abstaining from poisoned arms. The latter are still of vital concern. Hume thought these obligations "of

5. See David Raynor, "Why Did David Hume Dislike Adam Ferguson's *An Essay on Civil Society?*" in *Adam Ferguson: Philosophy, Politics and Society*, edited by Eugene Health and Vincenzo Merolle (Pickering and Chatto, 2009), 45–72, 179–188. Raynor suggests that Hume may have thought religion should have been brought in, by Ferguson, but he himself had left it out in his own conjectural history of society. Raynor more plausibly suggests that the Stoicism of Ferguson, and his failure to ground ethics on an accurate account of human nature, also contributed to Hume's unfavorable opinion of Ferguson's *Essay*.

princes" to one another were, like husbands' obligations to be chaste, honored more in the breach than in strict obedience. Now that we have moved away from a double standard for husbands and wives, we might also move to regarding the constraints of international law as just as incumbent on us as conformity to local law. Caution about change and reform is always a virtue for Hume, and jealousy of what is ours can be a vice, if, like travel on the high seas, it is best enjoyed if shared with all. Standards of justice and equity are of this sort, impossible if not shared with our own group, working better if shared with all groups.

Now that climate change threatens the prospects of all societies, the need for international cooperation is greater than ever before. Hume thought that the rules of justice cease to apply in cases of extreme need and famine. He gave us no lifeboat ethics, but once the sea levels rise, and food and drinkable water become very scarce, the only sort of ethics there will be any scope for will be lifeboat ethics, or the laws of war, as our descendants fight for self-preservation. "Suppose a society to fall into such want of all common necessities, that the utmost frugality and industry cannot preserve the greatest number from perishing, and the whole from extreme misery; it will readily, I believe, be admitted that the strict laws of justice are suspended, in such pressing emergence [emergency], and give place to the stronger motives of necessity and self preservation" (E 186). Justice, Hume had thought, once invented by our wise ancestors, would extend to all times and places (T 620), since although not an optimist, he did not foresee the grim future that our descendents face. Justice as Hume understands it may be a luxury that our descendents will not have, any more than they will have the means to survive. The circumstances of justice as Hume understood them, in that grim emergency, will have ceased to hold, and it is unlikely that we will invent any new social artifice to enable us, and most other species with us, to go gracefully out of existence. Will future people curse us as they drown, or die in firestorms or in destructive gales, or of radiation after nuclear wars for control of what habitable land remains; will they curse us for destroying the material circumstances of justice? Or is there still time to avert the catastrophe? I have argued elsewhere[6] that we do have obligations to future people, not to leave the earth less habitable

---

6. In "The Rights of Past and Future Persons" and "For the Sake of Future Generations," in *Reflections on How We Live: Essays on Ethics* (Oxford, 2010).

than we found it, that future people may be the victims of our greed and lack of foresight. Even if the material circumstance of justice, moderate scarcity, is destroyed by human overconsumption of resources, and by our carbon footprints, the demands of equity and humanity may still be heard by our descendants, leading them, while they deplore what we did, not to judge us too harshly, since for so long we did not realize what we were doing. And even now we do not want to know uncomfortable truths. Hume's other circumstance of justice, besides moderate scarcity, was moderate selfishness, or "confin'd generosity." Our selfishness has been more than moderate. Generosity can still be shown, in grim emergencies, and we have to hope for some generosity from future people, when they consider how we failed them, if indeed they give us a thought, as they struggle to survive. The circumstances of the justice we have known would, by extreme global warming, be changed from moderate to extreme scarcity, from limited generosity to ruthless desperation, challenging people to find new ways to cooperate, perhaps accepting lotteries to select which few survive.[7] We would then have to look back to Noah for inspiration on how to cope. Those of my generation are the lucky ones, who did inherit both a not yet spoiled earth (though some deserts may be due to human deforestation and overgrazing) and fine institutions and understandings of justice. Hume's is one of the wisest. It is wise not only in what he takes justice to consist in and to require, but also in his understanding of the precarious underpinnings of the cautious jealous virtue.

7. This was suggested by Tim Mulgan, in his public lecture on "Ethics for a Broken World" at the University of Otago, August 25, 2009. But worldwide lotteries are unlikely, and any country with the composure to conduct and carry out survival lotteries will, like all habitable countries, be besieged by desperate refugees, so will have to become a fortress to keep them out. There may be no ethics for a really broken world, only the skill of ark-building, and wisdom in selecting who and what is to go on board. The past gives us little guidance in how to cope with catastrophe. Hume tells how in times of plagues, such as leprosy, non-Christians, both Muslims and Jews, in England were blamed for "poisoning the wells" (H 2.14.181), and some saintly people would risk infection by disposing of the corpses of bubonic plague victims. At least if future people die by drowning, the fish will take care of the disposal problem.

# Index